Here's what associates have to say about Michael Mark, the man and the engineer:

"God said: Let there be light," and Michael Mark was born. He's a living testament to "where there's a will, there's a way." —Richard Walls

Once you get to know and understand this self-propelled person, you will not forget him. —Lee Ann Partridge

Having attended the same school as Mike, I know of his grassroots upbringing and his dedication to his family and career—and, above all, his ability to laugh at anything. —Rob Reid

After meeting Michael for the first time, I was quick to name him, and have always referred to him as, "The Rock 'n' Roll Engineer."
—Andy Malyk

Generally, people, clients, and business associates expect a level-headed, pragmatic, and cautious approach to everything we accountants do and say. My only exception is Mike. If I ever was practical or pragmatic with him, I know what he would say about that, and his words would certainly embarrass a truck driver. Mike's approach to business, life, and people in their little sandcastles is refreshing. —Nelson Collins

As a business friend, I appreciate the fact that Mike is honest and upfront when dealing with salespeople. His eccentric personality is the reason for his success—and, of course, the fact that he is also a shrewd businessman.
—Dieter Schmidt

Mike's story is like the David & Goliath of the engineering world: a very small company taking on the corporate world with all the red tape and curve balls thrown at him. —Rick Levesque

Having had the opportunity to deal with Michael a couple of times, I can tell you his bark is worse than his bite. He's the type of guy who loves life but works hard and earns everything he gets. And once a deal is done, the deal is done, no matter how acrimonious the negotiations were.
—Sean Crawford

Mike's way of doing things is simple: if you're right, you're right; and if you've got to fight to prove you're right, then FIGHT! Many weaker men have quit because that's the easy thing to do. Mike has never done the easy thing or taken the easy way out. —Joe Lockhart

Crazy Mike . . . has never let us down. He's hard-working, generous, loyal to his friends, and always holds true to his commitments.
—Paula Grant

What I like best about Mike is that any time you visit him at his office, you can be sure he'll brighten up your day by the time you leave—kinda like: Life is great. Don't worry, be happy. —Gilles Morin

Seeing the first 44 years deserves a book, the next 44 should be a barn-burner! —Bob Lagimodiere

WORKING CLASS

Engineer

FROM MISFIT TO
Millionaire

Michael J. Mark, BSc (EE)

Winnipeg, Canada

Cover design by Art Bookbindery.

Library and Archives Canada Cataloguing in Publication

Mark, Michael J., 1962-
  Working class engineer: from misfit to millionaire /
  Michael J. Mark.

ISBN 978-0-9738401-0-0

1. Mark, Michael J., 1962-. 2. Engineers--Canada--Biography.
3. Determination (Personality trait). 4. Success. I. Title.

TK140.M37A3 2007   620.0092   C2007-902773-3

For my three sons,
ALEX, BRENDAN, and CONNOR
(the ABCs of my life)

With appreciation to:

Ozzy (John Michael) Osbourne

I have always been a fan of your music. During my struggles through university, it provided the inspiration I needed to obtain that elusive engineering degree.

"Bark at the Moon," brother!

Lemmy (Ian) Kilmister

Reading your biography, *White Line Fever,* provided the spark I needed to finish writing this manuscript after many dormant years.

"Another Perfect Day."

Contents

Acknowledgments

Believe it or not, there were people who stood beside me, took an interest in my story, and helped me get it into book form. My thanks go out to:

Laurie, my wife, for reading over the manuscript without buggering around with the text too much. Thanks, Laurie, you're the best.

Marjorie Anderson, editor, for believing my story was important, and for bossing me into connecting random parts.

Trish Loewen, copyeditor, who initially pointed me in the right direction and ultimately provided the finishing touch.

Character cannot be developed in ease and quiet. Only through experience of trial and suffering can the soul be strengthened, ambition inspired, and success achieved.

—Helen Keller

Introduction

In the fall of 2000, I was at rock bottom. My dad had died, I had just gotten my engineering license back after an unjustified two-month suspension, and my marriage was strained to the max. (My wife, Laurie, seemed to hate me—and for good reason.) I needed an outlet or I'd have exploded or landed in Selkirk Mental Hospital. Despite the proverbial engineer's handicap—you know, "doesn't read, can't write"—I started on this writing project, alone in the basement. After the kids were in bed, I'd take my laptop down to my "Ham Shack" and pound away nonstop for hours and hours, with ham-radio static in the background.

First, I needed to write about all the bullshit that had happened to me—as a student in university, as an entry-level engineer in low-paying jobs, and as an entrepreneur trying to make a go of it in my own business. In particular, I felt I'd been royally screwed by the engineering licensing body, and writing about that was my attempt to expose the unscrupulous tactics of an old boys' club that seems to punish and persecute those who aren't in its inner circle. Not enough has been written about that kind of crap. Maybe because it's just too risky to put in print what is usually recognized and talked about in professional circles.

I wrote for close to two years and then stopped writing for over two years. Writer's block, possibly, or maybe because it took that long to empty my tank of misery. Then I started again on May 21, 2005, and for some strange reason I was able to finish the book in two fourteen-hour days—upstairs in the sun during the daylight hours. (Kinda symbolic, isn't it?) I don't know what made me finish after the long break. It might have been that I realized my story is about more than the misery I went through—it's also about the family I grew up in, where I am now, and how bloody fortunate I feel. I run a successful business, make enough money to do anything I want, and have three great kids and a wife who doesn't hate me anymore. (*Right, Laurie?*) I've also gained a lot of respect for myself and my ability to survive, no matter what.

Now I want people to read my book and be inspired to NEVER give up. If I can go through so much BS in my life and become successful, then others can do it too—it just requires determination, a never-say-die attitude, and, unfortunately, a few battle scars along the way.

This book was written from the heart and from memory. Only a few items were researched so I could get dates correct. I have no apologies for the foul language I use because at times that's the only way I can clearly express myself so that you, the reader, will "get it." (There are freedom of speech laws in North America, aren't there?) I've changed the names of most of the characters, mainly for my own protection from the evils of society, but—I can promise this—I have physical proof of every fact I have written in this book.

What started as a form of healing has become "a testament to gutsy survival and an unstoppable determination to succeed." (A friend of mine used those terms after reading the manuscript—impressive, aren't they?) For me, this book is even more than that: it's also a narrative of my life to date for my children to read later in their lives. If I die tomorrow, there will be a record—a record of my words, not just the thousands of engineering letters and drawings signed and sealed by me.

So, sit down, strap yourself in, crank up the tunes, and start reading. What follows is the roller coaster ride of my life—so far!

Chapter 1

Exit Night, Enter Mike

I landed in this world on June 30, 1962, at the Grace Hospital in Winnipeg, Manitoba, Canada, at around 10:30 p.m.—just an hour and a half prior to my parents' first anniversary. According to my father, he asked the doctors if they could delay the delivery until 12:01 a.m., in order, I suppose, to make that day a double-whammy celebration. But, true to my nature, I arrived when *I* was ready to take on the world. My parents named me Michael John. I was their first-born and must have inspired them 'cause they went on to have four more children.

My sister Susan was born in 1963, followed by my sister Alison in 1964. My brother Robert came along in 1967, and my third sister, Heather, was born in 1968. After that, the Marks' baby-making machine was officially turned off!

My parents, John and Stephanie, both came from working-class families where they had to get their hands beat-up and bruised, or at least dirty, just to scrape by. My mom had one sister, Carrie, ten years older—who is now, by the way, my godmother. When my mother was born, her family lived in Winnipeg's North End, at 1006 Aberdeen Avenue, in a 400-square-foot house built in 1907. It had only three minuscule rooms, and the four family members shared the only bedroom. (Cozy living, eh?) The family then moved to 1025 Alfred Street, a 650-square-foot, single-story house built in 1914. This was no "movin' up" in the 'burbs: even though the house had two bedrooms, they were so small the beds took up more than half the space.

My mother's parents, Peter and Mary Paradowski, both worked at Keewatin Box Factory in St. Boniface. Mary also worked as a cleaning lady at Eaton's department store downtown, on Portage Avenue. My mom's parents didn't own a car though Mary's parents did. My mom tells me that, even though her parents made minimal wages, she and her sister never considered themselves poor. One of the reasons must have been that they never went hungry. Apparently, their vegetable garden took up every inch of the backyard, and they would work hours on end to preserve what they grew—tomatoes, carrots, beets, and so on—for winter consumption.

My mom's family does have some history that adds a bit of prestige. Tokarz Park, a public park located in the Garden City area of Winnipeg, is situated on farmland originally owned by my mother's grandparents, the Tokarzes. The dedication ceremony honoring them took place on June 25, 1998, and my family and I, as well as both my parents, attended.

My father grew up in the Fort Rouge area of Winnipeg with his two sisters. He never talked about his childhood, or actually about anything from his past. He didn't keep many possessions from his past either, which still really bothers me. I know from my mom that his father, Joseph Klaponski, died from kidney failure when my dad was about twelve months old. Dad's mother, Carolyn, remarried shortly after, to Joe Maruszczak. Because of prejudices that existed in the '50s against, for one, Eastern European immigrants—remember the "dirty DP" slur?— my father legally changed his last name from Klaponski to Mark in 1958 when he was twenty-five years old. Mark was a nice short version of Maruszczak (being the first three letters and the last letter). Dad's mother and stepfather unofficially adopted the last name of Mark as well, because it was easy to spell.

My father's family lived at 120 Scott Street in an 1,800-square-foot, four-bedroom house built in 1887. According to Granny, it was originally a five-story house built for a wealthy family but it was subsequently chopped down to two stories because of a failing foundation. (I'd like to have seen that!) The home has an unusual tilt to the front, which I discovered when I was a youngster playing with marbles in the kitchen. The unfinished attic would have made a cool pad for me, but I only found out about it after I graduated from university, and by that time it was too late. Grandpa Mark (as I knew him) worked for the Canadian National Railway while Granny stayed home, except for occasionally cleaning other people's homes, including, I believe, the home of Sterling Lyon, one of the former premiers of Manitoba. (She used to receive hand-signed Christmas cards from him, which is how I figured that one out.)

My father reminded me of Elvis. He was a tall, handsome man with dark black hair who was always happy (just like Elvis used to be before drugs and booze got the best of him). My dad attended Gordon Bell High School, and was an all-star athlete in track and field, and football.

My father's parents dreamed he would become a lawyer. He was accepted into the faculty of arts at the University of Manitoba, but academia was not his thing and he dropped out after two years. He had no regrets—at least none that I know of—about not having a university degree. He probably wasn't keen on studying because he just wanted to get on with life. But times and attitudes change. My parents sure wanted all their children to attend university, and four of us did get university degrees—some with more sweat and tears than others.

My mother was a slender, attractive brunette. She attended Isaac Newton School where she completed Grade 11. Grade 12 didn't matter much for females back in the 1950s—or so my mom says. She was pretty, popular, and a cheerleader to boot, so I guess she and everyone else figured she'd be able to snag a husband without finishing high school. Most students held part-time jobs through high school in the 1950s. My mom followed suit and worked at Eaton's on Saturdays. (The store wasn't open during the evenings in those days.)

My parents met on a blind date. One of my father's friends worked at Eaton's and knew a coworker whose friend (my mother) needed a date. My mom would have preferred the real Elvis, but since he was not available, my father was a good substitute. Apparently, Dad liked Mom right from the start. (Good thing too, or where would I be?)

After high school, and up until I was born, my mother worked as a keypunch operator at the Canadian Wheat Board. (Not to be too dated, I also used punch cards in 1981 and '82 while I was attending the University of Manitoba. So we *both* used the old IBM computers and card-readers!) After I was born, my mother became a full-time homemaker, pretty much like the TV portrait of the perfect mom, except that she was bossy (*sorry, Mom, but that's the truth*), a definite clean-freak, and a perfectionist. The house was so clean you could literally eat off the floor. She did everything efficiently and well: breakfast on the table, beds made before 9 a.m., never any dirty dishes in sight, never any laundry stacked up, and the bathrooms were always spotless. You know, a *Leave It To Beaver* kind of mom.

My father worked from Monday through Saturday at three jobs: for the City of Winnipeg Parks and Recreation department as a community club director; for the Canadian Pacific Railway as a brakeman; and for his own small sporting goods business—all at the same time. He spent a lot of the time on the road doing sales calls for his small business. Sometimes we wouldn't see him for two weeks at a time, especially when he would do his Winnipeg to British Columbia trip. Mom was always worried when he was on these trips, especially during those brutally cold winters back in the '60s and '70s. One time he almost died while traveling in the B.C. mountains. During a blizzard he hit some black ice and his car slid toward the edge of the mountain. He said he thought for sure he was going over, and just closed his eyes and prayed. By a stroke of bloody luck—or by some kind of divine intervention—when he opened his eyes, the car was back on the highway. My father had amazing reflexes. He was driving a large Chrysler New Yorker at the time, so maybe a combination of both his quickness and the sturdiness of the car directed him into the safe zone.

Basically, my father was the breadwinner and my mother the homemaker. She did all the housework and my father did absolutely none. I don't ever remember my dad doing anything around the house or in the yard. From the time I was nine years old, I shoveled the driveway and cut the grass. Before that, my parents hired a contractor to cut the grass in the summers, and paid neighborhood kids to shovel the driveway after blizzards in the winters. It was my mom, not my dad, who would shovel the driveway with us if the local kids were too busy shoveling out other neighbors' drives.

They were good parents for the most part. They gave us kids everything they could—and not just material possessions. They also provided us with a good moral foundation—to work hard, be honest, never steal, and be nice to everyone. They treated all our friends like their own children, and in more than one case they practically raised some of the neighborhood kids. Their door was always open. That must have left a lasting impression on me because my wife Laurie and I are like that with all our children's friends. (And according to my kids, their friends classify our home as "the best"!)

After her kids were in school full-time, my mom started to do the accounting for my father's business. She would still stay home at lunchtime to make meals for us, which was the best thing a kid could ask for. I never had to stay at school for lunch, and I felt sorry for the kids who did. One winter day, just before school lunch break, I stuck my tongue on the metal monkey bars. When I pulled it away, the top layer of my tongue was left behind. It hurt like *hell*! When I arrived home in tears, my mom made me some hot soup. Imagine going back to a school desk to eat a cold salami sandwich after that ordeal.

When my dad was diagnosed with diabetes in 1981 at the age of forty-eight, things became more difficult for him, and for all of us. He changed because of physical and mental stress—a lack of energy and a whole shitload of worries. As well, the recession of 1981 hit and interest rates skyrocketed to 24 percent. It must have seemed to him that the world was against him, and he became moody, testy, and distant. Some days he wouldn't get out of bed till noon. Diabetes sure fucks a person up in ways that nobody really understands. An extra factor in my dad's case was that whenever his doctors told him to exercise and eat better, he just ignored them. He never really complained, though, even when my sister Heather had to jab him in the arm with an insulin shot every morning.

My mother took care of him until his death in 2000, which really was not fair to her. It wore her out, but she never complained. She also took in her mother for four years before Grandma was admitted to a nursing home. Mom even babysat Laurie's and my first child during this stressful time. She never gave up on or quit anything or anybody. According to my wife Laurie, I am the male clone of my mother, and it drives her CRAZY.

— ¤ —

When I was born, my parents owned a rooming house at 92 Balmoral Street in downtown Winnipeg. They lived on the main floor, which was basically a 500-square-foot, self-contained suite with a full bathroom, and a small kitchen addition on the back. The other nine units were single rooms spread out on the main, second, and third levels, with a shared washroom on each floor. There was a single showerhead installed in the middle of the basement where, like it or not, the other tenants would have to shower, without a speck of privacy. Hey, this was the '60s, the tail end of the baby boom generation. You know—peace, love, sex, and all that jazz.

In 1964 my father built a new home at 518 Laidlaw Boulevard in Tuxedo, the new, wealthy area of Winnipeg. Back in those days, land was available and cheap. Homes were also relatively inexpensive, property taxes and income taxes were low, and labor was cheap too. And with an income of over $50,000* a year in 1964 (remember my father held three jobs at the time), a new 2,100-square-foot house with a 6 ¼ percent mortgage was almost free!

The house was located directly across from Laidlaw School, which was a definite advantage to me and my siblings. We could walk to school, and our yard was often the place to be, after school, for our buddies. In 1973, my father had a concrete swimming pool installed in the backyard. That was the beginning of my athletic obsessions. I ice-skated

---

* [Note: All monetary figures within the text are stated in Canadian values except where indicated.—Ed.]

on the pool in the winter and skateboarded in it in the spring. A lot of great times took place in our backyard. On the whole, we were one happy *Brady Bunch* family.

Except . . . the bathroom was a real sore spot in our family. It caused more infighting than any other issue—ever. The real trick about living with six other people in a house with only one bathtub is to get up early in the morning. The reasons are obvious: (1) You have hot water. (2) You don't have to use a filthy bathtub. (3) You have a clean towel. (4) You don't have sore fists from banging on the door to get one of your siblings to come out! It didn't help that we had no shower that worked properly. The plumbers who installed the bathroom fixtures did such a shitty job that the water leaked through the wall below the showerhead. *So why wasn't it fixed?* Good question!

Five kids, two parents, and four bedrooms make an interesting living situation. If you're doing the math, then you come up two bedrooms short. Susan and Alison shared a room, and Robert and I shared one for a while—until I moved him into the basement when he was nine years old. This maneuver was actually amazingly easy. One day I asked him if he wanted his own "pad" and he said, "Sure." So I cleared out a space near a window in our finished basement. When I showed him his new bedroom, he liked it, so the deal was done. We both moved his stuff in, and his favorite part was when I gave him a ride on his mattress down the two sets of stairs. I was happy as hell because I finally had some privacy. After all, I was fourteen years old, and the majority of my friends had their own bedrooms. I NEEDED my own pad.

To this day all my siblings say it's entirely my fault for the way Robert turned out. He's essentially estranged from the family now. My wife thinks it's my parents' fault because they should have booted *me* into the basement instead. (I'm glad they didn't. It might have ruined me forever.) My friend Alan lived in his parents' basement and he'd only completed Grade 10 by the time he was eighteen. A lesson here: DO NOT ALLOW KIDS TO LIVE IN THE BASEMENT! IT CAN BE HAZARDOUS TO THEIR PROPER DEVELOPMENT.

I was never close to my brother Robert; the five-year age separation between us was just too great, I guess. That's too bad for both of us. (My three sons were each born two years apart and they play well with one another, and have lots of friends. I like to remind them how lucky they are.) I'm still close with my youngest sister Heather, and during my teen years my eldest sister Susan and I were buddies. We traveled together to and from university for about four years, and sometimes went together to the roller rink to hang out with our friends. I played the protective-older-brother role and let it be known that none of my friends could date any of my sisters, even though each of my buddies had a favorite Mark sister. Heather did some modeling for Eaton's in the '80s and she was probably the #1 pick among my friends. I made sure she married a doctor. (True. She married Neil Harte, MD. And Neil shares the same birthday as Ozzy Osbourne, so he's okay in my books.)

Chapter 2

Into the Great Wide Open

Developing asthma as a child probably affected my early friend-finding experiences—or lack of them. For my first five years of life, I was always sick, and in and out of hospitals. According to my mother, I almost died a few times. When I was older, I missed a lot of school because of the asthma, and this was reflected on my report cards. (No excuses, just the facts.) We also lived in a new subdivision, and in those early days there weren't many small children. I don't remember playing with friends much before I started school. My sisters Susan and Alison were so close to me in age that we just played with each other.

Of course, once I started school I made friends, and we played at each other's homes after school. In 1968 I met my first close friend, Steve Dubois, when he was walking down the street with his father. We remain friends to this day. My other longtime friends, James Inco and Lloyd Feigelman, were with me in kindergarten and the first few grades.

I started working on Saturdays when I was nine, which meant I couldn't play much on the weekends with the few friends I did have. Still, I found it easier to have friends in grade school than later, in high school. Up until Grade 9, almost everyone in school was a friend to everyone else. Then most of my grade-school friends went to St. Paul's, a private high school for boys, while I chose to go to Tuxedo-Shaftesbury High, a public school. Attending some stuffy private school where you had to wear a Sunday suit all the time wasn't for me. I knew that one day I would have to wear that polyester crap when I got a real job, and I couldn't figure out the point of wearing a suit to school, especially when I was only fourteen.

— ♮ —

For almost fifteen years our family would go to my father's parents' house every Sunday for dinner. Granny would make her famous fried chicken, or we'd pick up the Kentucky Fried variety or order in pizza. Sometimes she would make Polish specialties like perogies, cabbage rolls, and kielbasa (sausage). We would arrive in the early afternoon to visit, and most of the time other relatives—cousins, aunts, and uncles —would be there as well. Dinner was usually served early so we all could watch The *Wonderful World of Disney* at 6 p.m.—a BIG favorite in our family at that time.

Another great memory is driving home down Wellington Crescent, especially during the holiday season when most of the mansions along the way were lit up with Christmas lights.

One time before leaving my grandparents' house, instead of turning off the black-and-white TV, I turned down the brightness and volume. I thought this would be a great joke to play on Granny and Gramps. The next morning, their TV blew up—it had overheated and the glass shattered. *No big deal,* I thought. *That TV was on its last legs anyways.* Regardless, I was blamed, and I never heard the end of that for many years to come. Since it was too costly to repair, my dad bought my granny a smaller color TV. But she just couldn't part with that old black-and-white TV, and used it as a stand for the new one. She even placed a lace doily on it to protect the wood finish. (I know that my granny loved me the most, and she wouldn't have kept it just to remind me of my crazy hijinks.) Later, when the color TV broke, for some strange reason she kept it too—atop her new, larger color TV. Maybe that's why I've kept every single piece of paper from my university days. I'll just blame that on being too much like Granny!

No one knows why Granny loved me the most out of all the grand-kids (this is a fact!), but I do know that she spent countless hours watching over me when I was sick as an infant. She also spent many nights with me at the hospital when I had pneumonia. Best of all, her pampering didn't stop when I became an adult. My wife remembers us being at Granny's home one time and yelling at me when I drank milk out of the container. Granny interjected and said, "Leave him alone; it's okay." Now, is that favoritism or what!

From the time I was born, we celebrated Christmas both at our family home and at my dad's parents' home. Christmas Eve would be at our place with our extended family—aunts, uncles, cousins, and both sets of grandparents. Mom would prepare a turkey feast. It was my job to light the logs in the fireplace. (Remember, my dad did noth-ing at home.) We would have dinner, and after the cleanup was done, all of us would open presents. An aunt or uncle or my dad—this was one thing he didn't mind doing—would act as Santa Claus and hand out the gifts. After the gifts were opened, my sister Susan and I would play Christmas songs on the piano in the family room, and everyone would sing—or try to sing. (Believe me, we were no Osmond family.) I never let a sound escape my mouth; I just concentrated on the key-board, even though my playing was no great shakes either. I took piano lessons in my younger years until both my piano teachers quit on me. Embarrassing to be fired by my teachers, but hell, if they'd given me better music to play, maybe I wouldn't have lost interest—and might have become a rock star instead of an engineer!

On Christmas Day, we'd open our smaller gifts from Santa, and then go over to my grandparents' home for Christmas dinner. (My mother continues to give me and my wife "Santa" presents even now. I guess no matter how old I am, I will always be my mother's baby.) Dinner would be served early so we could watch whatever Christmas special was on TV. I would normally get sick on the Pot of Gold choco-lates, especially since there were no fewer than five boxes open at one time. Eventually, half of each box had chocolates that were mangled or had the tops pushed in because, after the good ones were gone, the kids would poke the others to see what kind of filling they had—or would take a bite and then put them back. (Surely every kid remembers that!) In my opinion, most of the chocolates were crap anyway, and we'd end up throwing out box after box of half-eaten chocolates.

— ¤ —

I've always been competitive and I love to kick butt, which helped me in sports in my early years. Whether it was floor hockey, ice hockey, intramural school sports, skateboarding, or swimming, even if I was not the most talented player, I would always give my all. From the age of nine to fourteen, I was a competitive swimmer with the Cardinal Swim Club at the Pan-Am Pool. I started this swimming program in hopes it would cure my asthma. I'd swim Monday through Friday, a two-hour program that consisted of half-hour workouts in the small gym adjacent to the men's change room, with the balance of the time spent doing laps in the pool. My mom would usually drive me there and pick me up. After I was eleven, I took the bus to and from the pool. This was easy in the spring and fall, but the winters were another story—there was no time to dry off properly before catching the bus, and I normally froze on the way home.

The swimming was good, both physically and mentally. It did cure my asthma, and the competitive nature of the swim meets developed my focus and discipline, and prepared me well for the grind in life to come. The discipline was to go to the pool every day no matter how boring the training was, to persevere and not quit. The mental part, or focus, was gained in the preparation I had to do for weekend swim meets. In 1975, I won a swimming trophy for Best 11- to 12-year-old Swimmer in the Manitoba A Finals. Competitive swimming at the Pan-Am Pool stopped when school let out for the summer, so I disciplined myself to train in the swimming pool in our backyard. I wanted to keep in the best physical condition year-round—besides, I was hyper and needed to work off that nervous energy in some way. With the off-season training at home, I gained some competitive advantage.

One day in the spring, I missed the bus home from swimming practice by about one second. The driver saw me running but didn't stop. I was so pissed off—*Fuck him, he ain't getting my dime*—that I walked the three miles home. That was one example of my stubborn determination at a young age. (Should I thank that bus driver for my later success?)

My mother came to watch nearly every one of my swim meets. My father came to . . . well, maybe one or two. He came to only one of my house league hockey games. At the time I figured he was busy with work or just too tired to come and watch my extra-curricular activities. (I sucked at hockey anyway.)

I quit swimming when I was fourteen or fifteen. I was just plain bored after five years of doing laps. Plus, girls, CB radio, and skateboarding took precedence. (Exit laps; enter bruises, scrapes, chicks, and tricks!)

Chapter 3

Caution: Kid At Work

When my father stopped working with the CPR and City of Winnipeg, he expanded his home business and started Markwinn, a wholesale sporting goods business that sold to schools and retail sports stores. He also made custom-ordered club jackets for sports teams. His place of business, located on McPhillips Street in the west end of Winnipeg, was a steel building with no insulation and a concrete floor. It was always frigid in there, especially in the winters of the '70s, which were a lot closer to the frikkin' ice age. He purchased the 2,000-square-foot building from a brewing company for about $10,000 in a fire sale. That was a gift.

I began working for my father in 1971, when I was nine years old. He insisted that I work for him, but didn't ask the same of my siblings. (*Where was Granny when I needed her?*) I never understood why I had to work there every Saturday throughout the year, especially since the store wasn't even open to the public on weekends. But every so often Joe Public would walk in, wondering what kind of store it was, and (fortunately) would leave without robbing or strangling me. My father never seemed to worry; he'd be off socializing with his buddies, smug and secure because there was only a bit of small change in the till anyway.

Driving with my dad to work in his four-door Chrysler New Yorker, which was built like a tank, was an adventure—sometimes nearly a deadly one. One morning he took a corner too fast and I fell out of the car! His reflexes were so good that he caught my arm just before I was about to hit the ground. It was my fault, I guess, and my dad let me know that. The doors on the old New Yorkers were heavy and hard to maneuver, and I hadn't closed the door all the way. And then, of course, cars in those days didn't have safety latches like they do now. I remember another time riding with my dad down Notre Dame when just across from TanJay, we were t-boned by a car and I took the hit. The driver had gone right through a stop sign and hit our passenger's side door. Turns out that heavy Chrysler door that had almost caused my death one day, then saved my life on another. (Is that ironic, or what?)

I guess I hadn't learned enough about the hazards of working for a parent because I started working full-time in the summers for my dad's business. My duties didn't require a lot of brain energy. I'd fill orders, pack boxes, type things like invoices, shipping labels and packing slips, and load the trucks. A step above that was answering the phone, calling trucking firms for pickups, and going with my father to the bus depot for deliveries. I'd also do janitorial work and sweep the parking lot and warehouse. I was just a regular Molly Maid, or jack-of-all-trades; take your pick.

The working conditions were the pits too. The building had no air conditioning and was as stuffy as hell inside. A tough way to learn, but I learned. Later, when I worked eighteen hours a day for about seven years straight at my engineering firm, it was no big deal. That's just the price to be paid for success. I don't know if my dad was deliberately trying to teach me a lesson, but I was getting the picture that there was no free meal ticket for me.

To keep myself from going crazy from boredom during those summers, I took a radio to work and also brought a small black-and-white TV so I could watch the few channels I could pick up with a built-in antenna. Being plugged into what was happening in the outer world paid off 'cause I got my chance to hear history being made, on the Saturday Elvis Presley ("the King") died. I had the radio on and remember clearly the stations playing Elvis songs all day long. I wasn't affected much because I thought his music sucked anyway, but it's possible that my mom mourned for her idol. (At that time I never took much notice of things beyond my own self-obsessed interests.)

Playtime was at a premium during those days. When Dad and I got home at the end of the workday, I'd eat dinner as fast as I could so I could meet with my friends and hang out with them for a while. These were the summer holidays, what was supposed to be the "glory days" of my youth, and I had to make the most of them before the sun went down.

During the week, Dad normally picked up lunch for me or we went out to eat, so that was okay. Lunches on Saturdays, though, were a problem. My mom never made lunch for me, probably because Dad would always promise to feed me. But then he would go out socializing with his buddies all day and leave me by myself. Since he didn't leave me a key for locking up, I could never go for lunch. I would scrounge around for food and hope for the best, which sometimes turned out to be Lipton's Cup-a-Soup or some other crap I needed to add water to. Boy, times sure change—I couldn't imagine leaving my kids alone at the age of nine, even in our own home.

After a year or two of this bullshit, I gave my dad an ultimatum: my sister Sue had to go to the shop with me, or I wouldn't go anymore. So he conned her into working with me on Saturdays. Then at least I'd get lunch. Sue and I would scrounge in the till for a couple of bucks and one of us would go to get some burgers—usually at Truckers Lunch on the corner of McPhillips and Pacific. It was a little greasy-spoon luncheonette owned by a Chinese man and his wife. He made the BEST cheeseburgers ever! He and his wife ran the restaurant and were always there when one of us came for our burgers. I never saw him without a cig in his mouth. This was around the time I hounded my mother to quit smoking—and she did. Spurred on by the success of my first conversion, I took him on and told him that he was killing himself. Back then, it sure took a lot of balls to tell anyone to butt out—and I was only eleven or twelve at the time. Unfortunately, a few years later he died from lung cancer. Tragic. But his legacy lives on. I can still imagine the taste of those burgers thirty years later. The restaurant is now called the Titanic. Go figure.

The only other place we could grab a bite was one of the first Mr. Submarine sandwich shops in Winnipeg, in an old gas station a block away. I liked their cheese subs without tomatoes—they were damn good. Sue or I would occasionally buy some bottled Pepsi at Snowberry Grocery, a small corner store located in an old apartment complex at the corner of McPhillips and Notre Dame. We'd rummage around our dad's shop for bottles, and hunt for others in the grass along the way to the store. Back then you could get a nickel for a bottle, so our available cash would increase according to the number of bottles we'd find.

—¤—

I worked summers for my dad from age nine until I was twelve. The year I turned thirteen, I had my first summer job outside of my father's shop. It was for one of his Jewish buddies, Joe Schacter, who ran a firm called Jay Dee Products, located on the 7th floor of the Codville Building, at 43 Westbrook in downtown Winnipeg. Each day I would catch the bus at about 6:45 a.m. at the corner of Laidlaw and Grant, get off at the Eaton's Building downtown, and walk a few blocks to work. I arrived at 8 a.m., and left at 4 p.m. to head back to the Eaton's Building and catch the bus home. I kept to the same routine every day, like someone on a chain gang—and remember, I was just a kid. (By the way, the downtown Eaton's store was a place that held many memories for Winnipeggers; even so, it was torn down to make way for a new arena—business wins over tradition, I guess. I went down to the site when the store was being demolished and collected a few bricks from the old building, for nostalgia's sake.)

Jay Dee Products was a screen-print and embroidery business. My job was to put T-shirts on a drying rack after they were printed, or to put them on a conveyor belt so they could go through a drying oven. (The type of ink used determined the type of drying process.) It was a typical Winnipeg sweatshop. Only the managers had air conditioners in their office windows; everyone else would swelter and sweat. It's no wonder all the factory workers were skinny, myself included. The building was kitty-corner to Portage and Main, the windiest location in Canada. At lunchtime, I would grab my cheese sandwich and orange juice and sit atop the fire escape to enjoy the view of the river and to feel the warm breeze blowing through my hair. A peaceful time—until that lousy bell would sound "back to work."

One bright spot was that I bonded with many of the employees. Since this was just after the '60s, a couple of hippies were my coworkers: long hair, long beards, tie-dyed shirts with drug logos, lots of rings—you get the picture. My wage was two dollars per hour. It was a far cry from the twenty-five cents a day my dad paid me. *Holy shit, I could make millions!* (When I was eleven, my dad actually gave me a raise to seventy-five cents per day. He kept telling me, "I don't charge you for lunch . . .")

I managed to survive at Jay Dee for the summers of 1975 and '76, plus I worked there during the Christmas break. Now I know why I had so few friends at school.

—⌑—

My nose for business led me into a few money-making ventures of my own. While I was in Grade 8 at Laidlaw School, I started up a little business selling floor-hockey sticks. The ones the school gave us to play with were junk—the shafts would bend out of shape. My father sold good floor-hockey sticks with really rigid shafts and straight blades. If a player had one of those, he could score all the goals! I placed ads with prices on the bulletin boards and sold a couple dozen. I also started selling ice-hockey sticks and pucks and tape. Bobby Hull, who was then playing professional hockey for the Winnipeg Jets, lived behind us on Bower Boulevard. His sons, Bobby Jr., Blake, and Brett, attended Laidlaw School. Blake was in my class. I had a little store set up in a corner in my parents' basement, and one time Brett Hull came over and bought some hockey tape and pucks. Maybe if it wasn't for Mike Mark selling him that hockey stuff, the Golden Brett may not have made it into the NHL, earning upwards of US$6 million a year! (Little joke there.)

During the summer of 1977, I saw another chance to make a buck. Jay Dee didn't have a summer job for me, so I created one for myself. I set up my own silkscreen printing business in the back of my dad's warehouse. I knew how to print T-shirts and I knew where to order the equipment, so thanks to my dad who paid for the screens, drying rack, ink, and art supplies (a thousand-dollar investment), I was in business!

I was still so frikkin' short that I had to build myself an eighteen-inch platform so I could reach the printing table. My friend Wesley and I built the drying rack one Saturday, and my father paid him with a new hockey stick. Now you know why I'm semi-retired in my forties—because I learned how to be cheap from the best: my dad.

Dad purchased tens of thousands of shirts from Brazil and sold them with Canada, Winnipeg, and Manitoba logos on them, mostly done in red ink. I did the artwork, which back then was simple. I just bought a Letraset (a pre-printed font set with individual letters and numbers that can be transferred to paper for artwork), an X-acto knife, and lacquer film. I burnt the film onto the screen, peeled back the plastic, and *voilà*, an original MM design appeared.

Dad also bought a transfer machine that would, with heat and pressure, affix a pre-made ink transfer to a shirt. That sped up the operation when we printed each shirt because the transfer was an instant-dry application. We could handle rush orders by having another shop print the transfers and then we'd put them on shirts at our shop, and out they'd go to the Eaton's store for sale. (Another reason I'm sentimental about that place.)

Dad paid me a dollar per dozen printed T-shirts. Each summer I printed about 1,000 dozen, which meant $1,000 for me. Not bad for a fifteen-year-old. My sister Susan helped me during busy times, placing the shirts on the drying rack and folding them after the ink dried. I paid her a paltry ten cents per dozen. (Told you I had learned to be cheap!) When I went to university in 1980, I was totally amazed to see so many students wearing the T-shirts I had printed years earlier. My first taste of business glory (ha ha).

In 1978, Joe Schacter decided to hire me back at Jay Dee Products for the summer, so I worked at the sweatshop during the week, and on weekends I did my own printing at my dad's shop. I did the same in

1979—but by then, at least I could drive to Jay Dee instead of taking the bus.

That first glorious business of mine came to an end in 1980. My dad sold all the printing equipment to Jay Dee. I know for sure he was proud of my business accomplishments—and, of course, I made him a lot of money too. (I didn't fare so badly either.) I also worked at an Esso gas station part-time in 1980. (More on that later . . .)

— ♯ —

By the time I was sixteen, I felt I was a frikkin' working machine. My father had *made* me work for him and there was just no arguing the point. I guess he insisted I work at such a young age because his stepfather had made him do the same. Maybe it was the old way of doing things. I've read scads of biographies of successful people (my favorites are listed at the back of this book), and often the person started work at a very young age, usually selling or delivering newspapers. I guess performing slave labor early on is the price we "success stories" have to pay for greatness!

Even though I felt hard done by as the only one of us siblings dragged off to work, I did learn, at an early age, to interact with my father's customers and with the public—great experiences for developing communication skills and business savvy that can't be learned from textbooks. I know engineers who have absolutely no social skills, and others without a clue about business. At the "Mark School of Business" I got experience in both areas. I learned to understand markups and profit margins by reading my dad's business magazines. I also studied the wholesale and retail price catalogs from Cooper and CCM, so when I went with Dad to places like Canadian Tire, I knew exactly how much profit the companies were making on various hockey items.

But there was a personal cost to having my young nose to the grindstone so much back then—I often missed out in connecting with other kids. Sure, I had a few friends at school—James, Lloyd, and Steve.

Oh yes, and a neighborhood friend, Richie Broder, whose father was a general surgeon. (According to his son, Dr. Broder could perform an appendectomy in six minutes flat.) But during those years of child labor, I never really had much time for them or for other people my own age. I couldn't bond with them because I was always at work, or sleeping because I was so damned tired. I clearly remember one Sunday afternoon, watching some of my classmates playing football in the schoolyard across the street—and not one of them came over to invite me to play. Even throughout high school at Tuxedo-Shaftesbury I felt like an outsider, despite having lived in the area since 1965. Each and every summer from the time I was nine, I'd had a full-time summer job.

Of course, I did have some minor acquaintances in school. Since all my siblings attended Laidlaw School and we lived so close by, everyone knew who the Mark kids were. I had an extra bit of attention because I excelled at gym and was the fittest in the class from swimming. But I haven't seen these people in decades. (I do see some of their parents from time to time and they all are taken aback on how successful I've become. I've actually designed projects for a few of them, and their comments on my work are always positive.)

Early patterns stay, though. To this day I don't make friends easily. I keep my distance until I feel a person is genuine. Currently, in my engineering practice, I don't take on new clients unless they're referred by a trusted client and I know which contractor will be performing the work. If those conditions are not met, I just refuse the work. Period! I've been screwed around enough in the past. If I knew back then what I know now, I would never have taken on some of those clients, or the work. Ain't that the irony of life?

Generally though, as I look back on my young working years, I know that the various experiences, good and bad, were beneficial to me in the long run. I worked in sweatshops with decent people who, because of unfortunate life situations or lack of education, were making the same two dollars an hour wage I was. These were people with families, even pregnant women in their twenties and thirties, all working for the paltry wages that were the norm at that time. I saw all this when I was just a kid. So now I always treat every person as an equal. Many engineers think they're better than the job-site workers, and treat them like shit. I work with a lot of contractors and they tell me stories about snobby engineers—and their screw-ups—all the time. I believe that success is not just what a person has gained in education, position, and power; it is determined more by attitude—the realization that all people should be respected for what they do and who they are.

Chapter 4

The Shortest SK8 Board Career in History

When I was fifteen, I got into skateboarding. My bank account was growing, twenty-five cents at a time, and I could afford the best board that money could buy. My friend Steve and I went to visit the newest skateboard shop, on St. Mary's Road in St. Vital, and each of us dropped $120 on a custom board—Santa Cruz fibreglass deck, Tracker trucks, and Kryptonic wheels. We had the coolest ride in town.

My parents had drained their concrete swimming pool because it needed a paint job, so bingo! I had a skate park in my own backyard. With Paul Henderson hockey helmets, CCM elbow pads, cheap knee-pads and work gloves, Steve and I went totally crazy struttin' our stuff in the empty pool. It was a blast, and soon the whole neighborhood was either watching or joining in. Steve was a decent skateboarder but I really rocked on that board! We spent hours practising. Some of my school friends who tried it sucked so BAD it was amazing they didn't wind up in the hospital. They thought it would be easy, and didn't bother wearing helmets. I've never in my life heard so many heads cracking. (Concrete is not the most forgiving material.)

I also skateboarded at a few other locations with some of the local Tuxedo skateboarders who were a grade ahead of me. They thought they were the best in the world, but that was only in their own minds. They spent more time smoking weed than skateboarding. I hate drugs

25

so I never touched the stuff, saving all my brain power for mastering finesse with the board.

Steve was (and still is) a classic daredevil. Together we'd try anything. One day when we were looking for a challenge beyond pool-skating, the low-sloped shingled roof of Laidlaw School looked incredibly inviting, just like a mini skate park. So we grabbed my parents' ladder and, skateboards in hand, we climbed onto the roof. We cruised and flipped like maniacs on top of that building. What a rush! We attracted some attention too. I can still recall the stunned looks on people's faces when they looked up and saw us. They were totally perplexed as to what was going on, especially when a skateboard would come flying off the roof after one of us had bailed before falling off the edge. Now that I think back on it, we were morons. Never since have I seen kids skateboarding on a roof. Most have more sense than we did in those days. Luckily, our parents never caught wind of this insane antic.

After the pool was painted—courtesy of my siblings and me—Steve and I lost our skate park. There was no way we wanted to give up this new-found coolness, so we came up with an idea: we'd build a skateboard ramp! In 1978 there was a housing boom in the new part of Tuxedo: hundreds of large homes were under construction on the south side of Grant Avenue, a block away from my house—and scrap lumber was just what we needed.

One Sunday we grabbed the old steel red wagon I'd used as a kid and crossed Grant on a hunt for our ramp lumber. We loaded that sucker full of old four-by-eight plywood sheets, two-by-fours, and any other leftover lumber we thought we might need. On the way back to my house, we stopped by Steve's to grab a pail of nails. We had no real plan, but—inventive geniuses that we were—by the end of the day we had an eight-foot-high ramp. We christened her Rad Ramp (short for Radical Ramp), and spray-painted the name in large black letters right across the back.

What an engineering feat! We had built a ramp with a concave bend, and vertical top section, with no plans, and no construction savvy. We were on the road to greatness! Steve and his family had just moved into a brand-new custom-designed home in New Tuxedo, and his parents wouldn't allow him to store the ramp there, so it stayed in the side yard at my place. For the rest of the summer of '78, I rode that sucker day and night, like an obsessed creature.

My tendency to make a hundred percent use of everything led me to the next bit of construction. With the leftover lumber, I built a take-off ramp. It was really crude, just a few two-by-fours and a small piece of plywood. With a rip down the driveway, I could jump about four feet in the air and land at a distance of around fifteen feet. I would jump over any old stuff we had lying around. Too bad my buddy James Inco didn't end up with any decent clear pics of me airborne off that ramp. I do have a few on a proof sheet he made for me, and with my new scanner I've enlarged them to a decent size without too much loss of resolution. Thank God for technology! And I mean it.

Some of the tricks I'd do were amazing—handstands on the moving board, jumps over four or five stacked skateboards, and then there was the feat of having all but one wheel off the top of the Rad ramp and still making a perfect landing. I'd drag the Rad ramp onto the driveway at lunch hour, and kids from Laidlaw School would be pop-eyed as they watched me perform. James took some amazing black-and-white photos of me trick-boarding, which he developed and printed in his own darkroom. (That kid had everything!) I have five of his eight-by-tens framed and hanging on my basement wall. Some of those photos are in this book.

I recently found out that I have a bona fide skateboard fan here in Winnipeg. (Yes, more than twenty-five years after my short-lived fame!) This new—actually only—fan, Darren, is currently researching the history of skateboarding in the 'Peg for a website he's creating. He stumbled upon the skateboard pics on my website and told me he was blown away. Being in the spotlight—kinda—spurred me on to go hunting for home movies taken back then. So far I've found only a few minutes of film footage taken of my brother and me in the empty pool in 1980, but the quality is so bad you'd think it was from the Charlie Chaplin era. (Check it out at www.winnipegskateparks.com.) Maybe with the new digital technology, someone can repair the damage. If that were to happen, I'd love to see that footage on the big screen.

— ¤ —

Skateboarding served a double purpose for me. It was a challenge—and I love challenges of any kind—and it was also a great way to burn off a truckload of my nervous energy. (Don't forget I was tremendously hyper as a child.) I didn't skateboard for anyone but me, though. I wasn't a show-off, and still to this day what I do is for me, not to impress the neighbors. Of course, I did like to demonstrate my talents to whoever would give me the time—I was damn good at the sport and I wanted others to see that. Looking back at the professional photographs in the one skateboard magazine I owned in those days (still have it!), I guess I wanted to be able to do the same tricks the California kids were doing—you know, to be hip with the times!

That skateboarding summer of '78 was the BEST. Too bad it had to end. But you know how it is when you're good at something: some asshole wants to take it away from you. Some shitheads in my area must have been jealous, maybe because they just didn't have the talent that I had, and they managed to steal my pride and joy—my skateboard—from my garage. I did buy another one, the same brand as my first cherished board (Santa Cruz), but I didn't use it as much because it didn't have the flex my first one had.

In the fall that year, I wanted to leave the Rad Ramp beside the north end of the house where there was nothing but mud, but my dad would have none of that. So Steve and I took it apart and moved it to the field at Laidlaw School—and it disappeared. Either some miserable kids or the maintenance staff took it. Whatever happened, I was without my ramp, and it felt like a part of my soul was missing. My dad had basically stunted my skateboard career, and I was pissed off at him.

Shortly after, James conned me into selling my second skateboard to a local skate park. (He must have been jealous of my talent on the board and wanted to see my career over and done with.) Luckily for me, the people at the park only purchased the wheels and the trucks and left me with the Santa Cruz deck. I'm also damn lucky that, by some force of nature, I kept that skateboard deck close to me for twenty-four years, no matter where I roamed. It sat in my parents' basement; at my condo; in the basement of my first house at 639 Centennial; in storage at my workplace at 1046 St. Mary's Road; and, for a time, in a corner of the storage room of my current home. It's a little beat-up now from being thrown around, but it's a solid remnant from a youthful, innocent time when I had freedom and a sense of accomplishment.

I always had the dream of eventually owning exact models of the two skateboards I rode in the late '70s, but I knew it would be impossible to source the parts because the manufacturers had discontinued them. Thanks to the advent of eBay, the online auction site with its thousands of sellers, my dream became a reality. I've been able to purchase the remaining parts for my second skateboard, as well as—get this—the exact model of the first skateboard I'd used to zip around in my parents' pool. (Too bad it cost me five times the price of the original one in 1978.)

I'm really proud of the talents I developed as a skateboarder during that short time period in my teens. With some coaching and encouragement, I believe I could have been a world-class skatepunk. Maybe I was years ahead of my time, or maybe I was living in the wrong country. Back then, skateboarding was thought of mostly as a fad, but I knew differently—and I was right. It took some time for it to be taken seriously as a sport. In 2005, Canada Post issued a commemorative stamp when skateboarding became a recognized youth sport in Canada. Because of this new wave of popularity, there have been numerous skateboard movies produced from 2002 to 2005 but, according to the movie critics, they just don't cut it.

Apparently, people still idolize some trick-boarders from the '70s. Mind you, a lot of them wound up in jail and are still riding on the small fame they had thirty years ago. Sad, isn't it? Even though I do wish I had some recognition from my skateboarding days, I'm glad I'm not behind bars, pining for days of lost glory. In reality, the engineering degree I worked so hard to get has provided me with more personal satisfaction than I could have imagined back when I was careening off rooftops on my Santa Cruz skateboard. Still, it's cool that I'm finally getting what I wanted deep down: a complimentary comment about my skateboarding talents—even if it's from a stranger. Some things money can't buy, and one of those things, my friend, is real, raw talent.

Chapter 5

Growing Pains 101

In September 1978 I got my driver's license on my first try. My friend Steve got his license a few months earlier, after taking a whack of driving lessons. Since my mother idolized Steve, she thought it would be a good idea if I took driving lessons too. So I took a few and, in fact, they *did* make me a good driver. (I've never totalled a car yet!) Not long ago, I found out why Steve had to take driving lessons. Apparently, he was driving with one of his parents when he crashed the family car into their garage wall. (I've never asked him if it's true. Had it been me, it would have been a lifetime secret.) No big loss about the car though, because Steve's parents owned a few Honda car dealerships in Winnipeg. Actually, theirs was one of the first Honda dealerships in Canada and it made them millionaires over and over.

Cruising for chicks was the coolest thing to do back then. The two of us would cruise all night in a new Honda from the dealership—for about a dollar's worth of gas—talking to any cute girls we'd see. It was a blast. Steve was (and still is) a good-looking, blond-haired stud, so the matter of confidence was a non-issue. When you're young, all that counts is if the opposite sex is attractive.

We usually headed out to one of the middle-class residential areas where the girls were rumored to be hot. Windsor Park was one of those areas. The streets there were laid out like an incomprehensible maze—and, guaranteed, we'd get lost. Our usual strategy was to drive around slowly until we saw a couple of nice-looking girls walking down the street, and then pull up near them and just start talking. (We'd get a better reaction whenever I was driving my parents' 1978 Camaro Z28 because it was considered a cool muscle car.) We eventually got a few phone numbers and became friends with a couple of the girls.

Though none of the girls we met from cruising in Windsor Park ever became steady girlfriends, I do remember having a crush on one: Marcia, a really cute, slender blonde with blue eyes and braces. She had a friend, Melanie, who was also good-looking, but nothing like Marcia. Steve and I hung out with them for months but—it's hard to believe now—never got beyond first base. In fact, I was forever in the no-go zone with Marcia. I did eventually get a kiss, but that was it. Better than nothing, I suppose. (She idolized her older brother and maybe I was just not good enough.) Wish I had a picture of that babe. She was a heartbreaker!

We were having good clean fun, but occasionally we ran into some attitude. I suppose Steve and I did think we were king shits—or maybe cool shits. But there was a bias against us that would have been out there, regardless. "Rich Tuxedo kids" is how other kids, cops, and people in general, perceived those of us who lived in Tuxedo in those days. Case in point coming up . . .

One evening, while out cruising in the Z28, I turned the wrong way onto a one-way street. With my good luck, a cop was watching my every move. Within two seconds of realizing my error, I pulled into a parking lot, but I guess the cop felt he had to give a ticket to this rich punk in a brand-new car. What a piss-off—and my parents weren't too impressed either. I had to go to driver-safety classes as penance. But as life has shown me, there's always a chance of finding gold in the pile of crap a person gets himself into. By some happy coincidence, one of my high school classmates, Rick Kuffel, was in that safety class too, so we carpooled, and became good friends. (Rick was the son of the dean of engineering at the University of Manitoba. When we both graduated from engineering, his father signed our degrees. Rick went on to get his masters in engineering.)

The fall of 1978, the year I went into Grade 11, was effectively the end of an era for my large group of buddies. Steve was shipped out to the Selkirk School for Boys, a boarding school thirty miles north of Winnipeg, and Lloyd and James were already attending St. Paul's, a private Catholic high school. (Lloyd is Jewish and yet he attended a Catholic school. Call me crazy, but isn't that kinda weird?) A huge void immediately appeared in my life. With no pals at Tuxedo-Shaftesbury, I pretty much was on my own.

That also meant a change in my cruising habits. James, the one friend who'd kept up with my interests, was not yet sixteen and didn't have a driver's license. I had the use of the family's new 1978 Camaro Z28, so I became the designated driver. James and I drove around like a couple of long-distance truckers—you get the point. I put on six thousand miles in two months. My dad must have felt like killing me because of the wear and tear on the car, and the cost of the fuel we used, which he paid for. James didn't put in a nickel of gas in the Camaro, even though his parents were millionaires. I figure he paid me back in other ways though. He got me into shortwave radio, and subsequently amateur radio, which in turn led to my earning a degree in electrical engineering. And he did take those awesome skateboard pictures of me the previous summer, so I figure we're pretty much even.

It was at that time that my father insisted I take a job at a car wash at 101 Salter in Winnipeg's North End. He wanted me to stop cruising, I guess. I worked every Saturday from 8 a.m. until 5 p.m., washing cars and pumping gas. I was not too thrilled, but as the eldest child, I had no choice. I had to carry on my father's work ethic to set a good example for my siblings, although it did seem to me that my father was quite lax with the four of them. (That always pissed me off because I was a good hard-working kid anyway. I didn't particularly need his boot-camp work training.)

My dad drove me to my first day of work at the car wash in his brand-new 1978 Cadillac. So right off the bat I was seen as the rich kid and, for the most part, was resented for that. Here I was, living in the wealthiest area of Winnipeg, and working in the poorest. Winnipeg's North End was one of the first developed areas of the city and many

European immigrants settled there. Most started off with nothing, like my grandparents did, and built small homes on a shoestring budget. Many of the families were from the blue-collar working class. I have nothing but respect for anyone who makes an honest living, no matter what the job, and even at an early age I thought it unfair that the blue collars hated the white collars. (Kinda like a turf war.)

Winnipeg wasn't the only place where that antagonism between cultures occurred. I'd spent a week visiting relatives in Chicago with my parents a few years earlier. I knew the deal with the blue collars in that city too, and knew what their living conditions were like. While riding the train there, my cousin Wally told me not to say a word to anybody from one of those areas or they would kill me—even though I was only twelve years old.

The car wash and gas bar were owned by the Mohawk Company, which had purchased the place from Esso. It was a drive-through, not unlike the place in the 1976 movie, *Car Wash*. In fact, I thought that working at a gas bar/car wash would be just like what was depicted in the movie. I was pretty much bang on. The place was full of characters (and I was the rich dad's kid). There were full-time guys, lots of jokers, and normally tons of laughs. A bloody movie could have been shot each and every Saturday I worked there!

I met two guys my age that first day in October '78—Todd Warren and Alan Norris-Elye. They were from River Heights and attended Kelvin High School, the same place rock star Neil Young spent some time in class. Todd's brother Blaine, who was one year older, also worked there with a few of his buddies. So the group was essentially made up of a few guys from the South End, a few from the North End, and a couple of old-timers.

Todd, Alan, and I became fast friends. Since I had no real friends at school then, meeting those guys came at the right time. They were easy-going and both loved cars and chicks, maybe not in that order. They didn't have snobby Tuxedo attitudes either, which was the norm in my high school. Most kids in Tuxedo never had summer jobs and seemed spoiled to me, especially the girls. Lots of them drove brand-new expensive cars and wore the best clothes. That never impressed me 'cause I don't equate material possessions with the worth of a person. And besides, I had no time for attitude; I was just too busy working my fingers to the bone.

My first duty at the car wash was working the gas pumps, which was the worst fucking job in the world. Back then, the temperature every day in the winter was at least −20°F, and we would all freeze our asses off. On Saturdays we would put about four hundred cars through the wash, plus fill them up with gas. Boy, those were the days: five dollars could get you a full tank of gas—and a free wash too. You can't even get a full-service car wash for under fifteen dollars today. And with the price of gas now, you almost have to *push* the car to the car wash. (Okay, a little extreme maybe, but one day soon, fossil-fuel-propelled vehicles may end up being used as huge paperweights.)

My friendship with Todd and Alan went beyond work. They liked to go to the Saints South Roller Rink on Clarence Avenue in Fort Garry on Friday and Saturday nights to pick up chicks, and one day they invited me to go with them. I was reluctant because I thought roller skating was kind of gay. (Back then, when we used the term "gay," it meant corny, uncool, or lame.) Todd convinced me that the place was full of girls. As it turned out, he was a hundred percent correct. All the kids at the rink were young like we were, and most of them were girls. A deejay in a booth played the latest rage in music and the rink was lit up with a disco ball and light show. There was also a small area with video games, a canteen, and tables and chairs—all that a teen (or a tween) could ask for.

Alan was tall and skinny with long blond hair, so he got most of the attention. He'd sail around the rink, the strobe lights bouncing off his long mane, with the most gorgeous of the roller chicks clinging to each arm. Todd and I had more of the clean-cut look, so we had to do quite a few laps by ourselves before we managed to get some girls to hold on to us. The music at that time was a mix of disco and rock— kind of a confusing time in music history, if you ask me. We'd do a few turns around the rink to the sound of Supertramp or Led Zeppelin;

then the next minute some lame disco song would be played. (Related news flash: I just heard Ozzy singing his rendition of "Staying Alive" and it took me back to those days.)

I did luck out at the roller rink and meet a girl I liked a lot. Her name was Linda and we dated until the fall of 1979. She was thirteen at the time and I was sixteen. Everyone bugged me about robbing the cradle. Linda and I got along really well, and we went to movies, to the roller rink, and to lovers' lane in Headingley. For the most part it was an innocent adolescent relationship, no sex involved. (I was too young and never cared about it back then.) I was attracted to her because she was slender, had long, thick blonde locks, and great teeth. Plus she was an academic, got straight As, and was a bookworm. (Just like my wife Laurie is. I guess I go for the brainy type!) Linda's mom was in her forties and divorced, and had a live-in boyfriend who was twenty-five years old. He didn't like me much—must have thought I was some rich punk with a new car. Oh well, you can't please everyone.

Linda was the only girl I dated from the rink. The other girls I hung out with there were just friends. My two sisters Susan and Alison and their girlfriends went with us to the rink sometimes. It was good clean fun, no booze or drugs. That shit is just a waste of time. And there were lots of adventures without it.

One evening, shortly after Linda and I met, I went over to a house where she was babysitting. We played with the kids until they went to bed. After that, we watched a Paul McCartney & Wings concert on TV and had our first kiss. Being dumb, I never scouted out an escape route from the house in case the parents came home early. Of course, they did. The home didn't have a back door and there was no back lane, so I was screwed. I had to dart out the front door, and they saw me running through the snow to my car parked nearby. Linda got shit for that, but, hey, we still dated for six months after that embarrassing event.

In February '79, my father traded in the Z28 for a brand-new 1979, fully loaded, gold Pontiac Trans Am. That was the car I was driving one summer's evening when Linda and I went to lovers' lane in Headingley, a little spot at the edge of the Assiniboine River. It was a hot, muggy night, and while we necked in the Trans Am, I left the air conditioning and the radio on. Two hours later, when we had to leave to meet Linda's curfew, the car wouldn't start. The bloody battery was dead. I'm never one to panic (unless one of my boys needs stitches), and seeing it was Steve who first told me about lovers' lane, Linda and I walked across the highway to a house to call him. There were no cellphones back in 1979, and I was damn lucky to find someone who let me use his home phone—and to actually get Steve at home! He came in a Honda (of course), maneuvered the small car to the front of the Trans Am, and boosted it until it started. Steve was my savior: we actually met Linda's curfew! (Her mom would have killed me, otherwise.)

That first relationship was great. I really did love Linda, but at the end of that summer she blew me off when she saw me out with other girls. I had just turned seventeen and didn't plan on marrying any-time soon, so I guess I wanted to play around a bit. Our breakup was a blow to the ego but I deserved it. That was the beginning of a down-ward spiral for me.

A year later Linda and her mother moved to Toronto and I never spoke with her again. I did, however, persuade two of my friends to call her for me, just to make sure she was doing okay. She actually wrote a letter to one of them. I sent her one of my original eight-by-ten black-and-white skateboard pictures and another color pic of me standing beside the Trans Am. I wouldn't be surprised if she threw them in the garbage.

I've heard from mutual friends that Linda ended up dating more jerks until she finally figured out which was the best one to settle down with. (My wife says that I was the best jerk *she* ever dated!) I did date girls after Linda and before I met Laurie, but I never loved any of them. It took me eight years of dating before I found another girl who really meant something to me again—and I ended up marrying her.

I still have a picture of Linda, plus all the stuff she gave me. Ever since my father made me get rid of the skateboard ramp Steve and I built, I've had a hard time getting rid of anything I've collected. I have over twenty-five boxes filled with stuff from my past. My 1994

Mustang GT has been sitting in my front yard for seven years now. I just can't part with it.

— ¤ —

Back to the cruel world of work . . . The memories of those bitterly cold days at the car wash I'll take with me to my grave. Working at the entrance, where the cars were chained and sprayed down and vacuumed, was brutal because the entrance doors never closed. When some four-wheeled toilet—dirty, rusty-old-piece-of-shit car that hadn't been washed in years—would pull in, my job was to bend over and hook the drive chain to what I hoped was a solid part of the chassis (or the bumper would be pulled off), then remove the mats, spray them down, and vacuum the interior. With two guys spraying, everyone got soaked. Eight hours, four hundred cars, –20°F outside, wet hair, wet clothes—I must have been nuts. We were all nuts.

After work I'd go to my Granny's house, which was on the way home, to warm up. My jeans would be frozen solid from the knees down. Granny had a huge heating floor-vent that I'd run to as soon as I got there. It would take about fifteen minutes to thaw out, and then I'd head home and have a hot bath. After that, I'd call Todd and we'd go to the rink. Later, we'd grab a burger at Juniors and go home, or else I'd just hang out with Linda.

During that time I was not only perfecting my romancing skills (yeah, right), I was also learning how to handle myself without the watchful eyes and guiding hands of my parents. When a person turns the magic age of sixteen, life seems to change dramatically. While I was working at the silk-screening factory, almost everyone treated me like a kid. They liked to take me under their wings to show me the ropes, and I had no problems with that. But at sixteen, I was on my own and had to fight my own battles.

One winter day, I was pumping gas with a North Ender named Donny. He didn't like the fact that I often drove a new 1979 Pontiac Trans Am, and he kept telling me how sucked-out he thought the car was in comparison to the old muscle cars from the '60s. Donny was a tall beanpole who looked like the drummer from the rock band, The Police. He and his older brother used to let the air out of my tires by jamming a matchstick into the valve stem. I can barely remember the exact details, but Donny must have cracked some insult about my father. At first, I brushed it off and walked away to work in the drying area of the wash. After a while he followed me there, looking for trouble. We were side by side, drying off a car, when he made another wise-crack. Something like, "Your dad's just a fatso driving a fat Caddy." That was it. Just like in the 1983 movie *A Christmas Story* when Ralphie blew his cork and beat the crap out of bully Scott Farkas, I grabbed that motherfucker by the hood of his jacket, pulled it over his eyes, and punched the living daylights out of him. I then threw him under the rolling car. He was lucky someone grabbed him or he would have wound up in the hospital.

Our boss Gene, who had been my dad's friend for many years, was totally freaked out by what happened and shouted at me to leave. Hell, it wasn't my fault; I just finally reacted to the abuse from that beanpole shithead, but I left anyway. Crazy thing was that on that day, I had caught a ride from Todd to work, so I had no wheels, and no money for a bus or a pay phone—and, once again (this being "Winterpeg"), it was bloody cold outside. I was frozen and incredibly wired: the adrenalin in my system was still pumping like crazy. I managed to walk to my dad's shop where his delivery van was parked. By some fluke, I had the van keys in my pocket, so I drove myself home.

I've never forgotten that day. I'd never fought with anyone before, and I was stunned at my own courage. After all, this guy was a foot taller than I was. But I guess I spooked him. More important was the fact that I'd finally stood up for myself—and for my father. Before that, I would have just taken that shit and let the abuse continue, but this time it was different. If I'd had to, I would have gone down fighting!

The following Saturday I told my parents that I was thinking about quitting the car wash job. (I had to make my case before I faced their trial by fire . . . you know, *Why the hell did you quit a perfectly fine job?*)

It was likely that Donny was going to kick the shit out of me, but I decided I'd go back to work one more day, no matter what the consequences. As a backup, I recruited about five River Heights guys who would go to bat for me if it came down to some ugly fighting. They agreed to drive to the work site and hover around there the next morning.

On that Saturday morning in February 1979, I was nervous as hell when I picked up Todd at his home and went to the wash. But—get this—on walking into the place I was greeted by everyone as a hero, like Rocky. It was crazy. All the guys said that after our fight Donny had been bleeding everywhere and almost had to get stitches. Lesson learned: draw blood when you're sixteen and you become a hero. No need for my backup muscle friends.

I don't look for praise (unless it's for skateboarding!) but I do expect to be treated fairly. That's how I've always lived my life, so to be greeted that way was almost embarrassing. From that day forward, though, everyone at the wash respected that "rich kid from Tuxedo." And I even pumped gas with Donny later on.

I sometimes wonder where I get my overdose of stubbornness. I can see it every day of my working life, and it was there in my university days too. The slogan "Winners never quit and quitters never win" makes sense to me. I learned that at the car wash, and it has stayed with me ever since. Good thing, too, in this dog-eat-dog business world. If someone tries to abuse me, I fight back—and eventually I win.

I haven't seen Todd or Alan since the late 1980s, and I wonder if Alan is still living in his parents' basement. One day a couple of years ago, I saw his father working in their yard while I was on my bike, but for some reason I didn't bother to say hi.

— ¤ —

The summer of '79 was a good one. I worked weekdays at Jay Dee Products printing shirts, and sometimes worked at the car wash on Saturdays. Then Todd got a summer job and took Saturdays off. After that, I kept my weekends free so we could hang out together. Alan quit the wash and had also "dropped out" of school, so to speak. His parents had let him use their Toyota Celica and, instead of going to school, he'd spent 1978 and '79 driving friends around. He told me he used his lunch money for gas. I've never figured out how his father missed seeing his son's report cards for two whole years.

Our family went to California for a holiday in the fall of 1979, and by the time we got back I had acne in the worst possible way. Much later, after reading medical journals, I learned that it was from my overuse of brewer's yeast and vitamin B complex. I took the shit so I could have a healthy head of hair but I overdosed and it came out of my system that way. (I did have a healthy head of hair, though.) I started to see a dermatologist and was put on drugs and cream. It took about two years to clear up the acne, and I had to see the doctor for annual follow-ups for the next fourteen years.

That skin condition put my social life on a fast downhill slide—not to mention my grades; they sucked too. I can't believe that I was accepted into engineering with those shitty grades. That was the only lucky thing that happened to me in the years around that time. I am grateful to that supreme power above, and to the University of Manitoba, for giving me a chance—actually two chances.

— ¤ —

During the winter of 1980, I made a commitment to myself that I would not work for the entire summer prior to entering university, because I felt I needed—and deserved—a summer off. The reality was, however, that I also needed about five thousand dollars for first-year engineering. So, in January, I applied for a part-time job at the Esso car wash/gas bar near Polo Park Shopping Centre, about a five-minute drive from home. I got the job: pumping gas and running the car wash. It had a new fully automatic wash that required no human hands, so at least it was a step up from the last place I worked.

I worked every Saturday and Sunday at that joint, as well as some weekday evenings. There was one incentive there: a thirty-cent commission to whoever sold a wax with a car wash. They would calculate this in the control panel at the counter where we keyed in the wax option prior to the car entering the wash. I must have been a born salesman because I set all sorts of records for Saturday wax sales.

For the first two or three months, I had my mother drive me to work because, at that time, I was driving a 1980 Trans Am Indy pace car—the hottest car of 1980—and I didn't want to have to put up with coworkers' jealousy of "the rich kid." My father had purchased the car from McNaught Pontiac and intended it to be my mom's car, but she never drove it. To add to my "cover," whenever anyone asked where I lived, I told them River Heights. Tuxedo at that time was still classified as the snobby area, and I just didn't want to have to put up with the jibes that came my way from people who automatically assumed I was a snotty rich kid. I know that there were a lot of people from my area who did play the snob game, but not everyone—and certainly not me. I think people are people. If you work hard, you deserve a nice place to live; plain and simple. My father worked three jobs to afford to live in Tuxedo and to give his five children every opportunity. He did the best he could, and I think he succeeded for all of us.

After a while, my mom got tired of driving me, so I had to drive myself to work in the Trans Am. I parked it in the shopping center lot across the street where I could keep an eye on it. One day, at the end of my shift, a young guy I was working with saw me walk to the car. The cat was out of the bag. All of a sudden, the manager gave me a new job: digging out the 100-foot-long, 5-foot-deep trench that ran the length of the wash. That trench collected all the mud, salt, garbage, and other debris from the cars, and terminated in a single-compartment sediment pit by the sanitary sewer. Its design was a plan for disaster—if the trench was not shoveled properly, the pit would fill up with debris and block the drain to the sewer. (I know now that it should have been a three-compartment sediment pit.)

That duty became the worst part of my job. I didn't mind hosing out the car wash and lubricating all the bearings, but the weekly trench-shoveling was backbreaking. The "dig" would take about two hours. I would be by myself after shutdown at 9:30 p.m., shovel in hand, loading debris into a wheelbarrow and dumping it behind the building. It was freezing-cold outside and I'd be wet, tired, chilled, and sick of the putrid smell—I can still smell it now. I got spooked a few times when in amongst the sand was a dead rat. One cold winter night, I had finishing cleaning out the trench and was soaked to the bone. I didn't want to get the interior of the Trans Am dirty, so I took off all my clothes and drove home in my underwear. It was obvious to me that the eight-dollar-an-hour managers wanted the kid to quit. But as you already know, I never quit anything, unless it's the only option.

Since I knew something was up, I tallied my earnings and was relieved to discover I had enough for my first-year university tuition and books. Still, I wasn't going to quit; the buggers were going to have to make the first move. Sure enough, in early June I was called into work and fired. The reason was so trivial that I can't even remember what it was. I do remember telling those guys that they had to pay me for the time it took me to come in to work that day or I would file a complaint to the Labour Board. I picked up a check two hours later. That Esso station was torn down recently to make way for a new Mark's Work Wearhouse. (Some small satisfaction: the gas bar is gone but I'm still here.)

— ¤ —

I graduated from high school that June (1980) with no fanfare. I didn't attend the convocation or go to any of the dances, and I didn't show up for the class picture. Maybe if the chicks in the school hadn't been so stuck-up and had given a guy a chance, I might have been more involved. But they were mostly Tuxedo princesses—and, of course, too good for me.

In my yearbook picture, I'm sitting on the rear spoiler of the Trans Am. Most photos had comments beside the students' names written by their friends, but the space by my name was blank. Probably the way I wanted it. Maybe I should have written my own: *Michael Mark . . . no comment and fuck ya all.* (By the way, I looked really good in that picture!)

Even at the high school reunion I attended with Laurie in 1994, I made sure we split before the class of '80 group photo was taken. I saw the class standing on a riser and I thought to myself, *I don't even know any of these people. Fuck this.* At the dinner, the people at our table had spent the hours bragging about how great they were and how much money they made . . . *blah blah blah.* And no one planned a 25th reunion for 2005—and who the hell cares?

I didn't give a rat's ass about a useless high-school diploma—and still don't. It gets you into university and that's about all. I never picked up my diploma. (My sister Susan picked it up in September while I was at university.) It's sitting in the bottom of one of my many storage totes and I've never displayed it. No sour grapes here; it was just a non-issue for me.

I don't want to leave the impression that I was some sort of outcast either. Really, I was used to being alone because of working so much from the time I was young. And that tendency to sit on the sidelines away from the crowd is still with me. I'm on the phone all day at work. Some days I have to deal with morons, telephone solicitors, and the clowns who come in to sell me shit I don't need. After I finish each day at the office and arrive home, I just want to be left alone to enjoy time with my family. I need the peace and quiet for my soul. Occassionally, I'll go into the office on Saturdays to catch up, but what I really like the most is the alone-time there. I have nobody yelling at me to turn down my Motorhead CD. (And yes, Ozzy still rocks!)

Chapter 6

University Daze

When you're young, things can turn 180 degrees in a flash. The summer of 1979 had been great—I'd had a super girlfriend, a couple of great buds, and I was at the height of my "coolness." I felt on top of the world, and anticipated that the upcoming summer of 1980 would be as good as the summer before. No such luck. It would be the worst to date!

That spring of 1980 was the hottest on record (the record in my life, at least) and we were able to open our backyard pool in April. Prior to paint-the-pool day—which, for some obsessive reason, our dad insisted we do every year—my brother Robert and I managed to skateboard in it. We filmed each other with our dad's old Bell & Howell movie camera. My performance was a bit rusty compared to the summer of '78 when I was in my skateboarding prime, but I have to say, it was still pretty rad.

The heat wave continued, and I spent the last days of Grade 12 daydreaming about swimming. I stuck to my plan to take July and August off. I had been working every summer since I was nine years old and that had really affected my ability to make friends, let alone hang out or go cruising with anyone.

On June 30, 1980, the last day of high school, I turned eighteen. It was pretty much an uneventful day. There was a small family birthday party for me, and that was about it.

—¤—

That scorcher of a summer turned out to be boring, friend-wise. Todd was working at a gas bar on Pembina Highway and Alan was sleeping his life away at his parents' home. Richie, who had attended as many activities in school as I did (zero!), never got a job and was at home all summer too, so we became closer friends. Our activities were a bit lame though. We didn't cruise for chicks because my confidence was at an all-time low. (I was still recovering from the facial acne.) I did laps in the pool each day and rode my 12-speed bike to Kildonan Park and back (about 20 miles) almost every day. I was in great physical shape, but unfit mentally. I probably had a bit of depression.

I know one thing for sure: I didn't work a day that summer—not exactly what my slave-driving father wanted from his oldest son. Every day, Dad would burst into my room, his fists clenched, and yell, "Wake up, you bum, and get a job!" I guess he just didn't get it. I was my own person, and had decided that I wanted to do just what I wanted to do, despite his dictating. Maybe his parents had treated him like shit and he didn't know better than to try that on me. I'm not sure. I wish I'd had more conversations with him. But he never told his children anything about his childhood, except for the fact that he had worked practically from the time he was out of the cradle. It's too bad that I'll never really know what growing up was like for him.

With this book, my three boys will know almost everything about my youth and my adulthood—maybe more than they ever wanted to! I'd like them to know about and learn from my life; also to appreciate what they have and not take it all for granted. I've sacrificed my blood and guts in the many battles in my life, and I'd like them to avoid some of the crap I've had to wade through.

— ¤ —

From the time I was in Grade 11, I'd wanted to become an electrical engineer. I've always been fascinated by electronics, especially radio. Seems to me that everyone sees radios and televisions as just boxes with wires and parts, but me, I'd always wanted to know "how and why" they worked. (Think about it: an invisible signal of waves below the ionosphere that can reach across a country—or the world—and be received as audio via a speaker, or as an image via a cathode ray tube. Pretty amazing, don't you think?)

I was accepted into first-year engineering—not such a big deal because all anyone needed at that time was a C average, which (miraculously) I had obtained. Still, the moment I got accepted, I knew without hesitation that there really was a divine being hovering somewhere out there in the clouds. I was a lost soul at the time, feeling that the world was against me, and this stroke of luck—or fate—convinced me that maybe, just maybe, I'd eventually have a job other than as a gas jockey. (Still, if I *had* become a career gas jockey, I know I would have been the best damn gas pumper ever!)

With this one small boost to my self-esteem, I started to feel cocky again, and assumed that university would be a breeze, like high school. After all, it doesn't take much to drag in a few Cs. Unbeknownst to me, I started what was to be one of the biggest battles of my life.

—¤—

The day before I started university, I drove to the campus and cruised around to find out where the engineering building was and where to park. (I didn't want to be late on the first day.) That proved to be a total waste of time; I got lost the next day anyway.

James Inco was also accepted into first-year engineering and asked me if I wanted to catch a ride with him that first day. We set off in his 1979 Datsun 280Z sports coupe at 8 a.m. It was raining like hell out, windy, and so cloudy it looked like night. It was just like ol' Will Shakespeare wrote about, with the "dark and stormy" weather being an indication that tragedy is coming. We got lost after parking the car, and of course we were late for the first 8:30 a.m. class.

Luckily, the lecture hadn't started. But we had to sit on the lecture room stairs because the goof who'd reserved the room couldn't count. Anyway, the first thing the prof at the podium said was, "Look to your left and then look to your right, because only one out of three of you will graduate from the engineering program." *Holy shit, what a way to start university!* I swore to myself that I was going to be that one out of three to walk out of there with an engineering degree, no matter what it took.

At the end of that first class, some senior engineering students gathered all two hundred of us and marched us to the dean's office to meet him and the president of the university. This was a stupid waste of time for me because the dean, Dr. Edmund Kuffel, was my buddy Rick's dad, and we'd met at his home. (By the way, Rick currently owns a firm in town that does real-time digital simulation for high-voltage power generation. I saw him at a Wendy's restaurant a few years back and he hasn't changed a bit. I don't keep track of former university classmates, but when I see them, I always make a point of saying hello.)

At the end of the first day, I was overwhelmed. I felt like an insignificant ant in that place, and knew I could be crushed, without warning, at any second. The whole campus, in general, was a real shock to my system. It was huge, with tons of buildings and a sea of strangers. I was one of 25,000 students, considerably more than the two hundred at high school. I did meet a few people who were in all my classes, but James and I were in only one class together and eventually grew apart. Not enough together-time, I guess.

That first term was really brutal. I had six courses: Math, Drafting, Calculus, Chemistry, Technical Writing, and Physics. I had no bloody clue how to study. I had never bothered cracking the books in high school (didn't have to, 'cause passing was good enough for me then) and, of course, no one at the university gave a rat's ass if I attended class, or studied, or not. There wasn't much motivation at home either. Both my parents had only high-school educations, so they were no help in guiding me during my stay at the Ivory Towers.

My days at university consisted of going to class and breaks for lunch. With over forty-two credit hours for the year, including labs, there was just no time to fool around. Each day wore on: pure drudgery from 8:30 a.m. until 5:30 p.m. That's what brings about the dropout rate, I suppose: *If ya can't take the heat in the kitchen, just get the hell out!* I really hated going to university in the dark in the morning and leaving in the dark after the day was done. As if that wasn't depressing enough, I had headaches every day, and the coursework was bloody heavy— enough to make almost anyone want to call it quits.

That first term, I got a pass mark in three courses, a D grade in two others, and an F in the sixth. In first year, a D is considered a failure, so I had to repeat three courses the next term. If I'd had another D in first term, I would have been kicked out. I barely squeaked by in the ones I did pass, and probably didn't deserve the B that I got in Drafting. (My grades on the drafting assignments were low and I thought for sure I'd failed the exam. The instructor must have made an adding error while tabulating my final grade, but I sure the hell didn't bother to check that out—I took the mark and ran!)

I remember writing one exam in the decrepit old Bison East Gym. The place had a thirty-foot-high ceiling and was basically a huge echo chamber filled with dense, sweat-filled air. Being December, it was cold as ice. And we were all treated like potential criminals. During that three-hour exam I needed to take a leak so my bladder wouldn't burst. I put up my hand for permission, and was *escorted* to the washroom! The guy practically held my hand while I did my business.

When the marks came in the mail just before Christmas, I was blown away by my poor grades—as well as surprised as hell at getting a B in Drafting, the only course I thought I *had* failed. My parents were as taken aback as I was because I'd never failed a course before. None of us knew the dedication and effort it took just to obtain passing grades in university courses. This was the first of many letdowns that would plague me over the next twenty years.

Pissed off as I was at myself for the pathetic grades, I managed to drag my ass back to the university after Christmas break. I had to repeat the three failed courses and take three new ones, so then I was behind and knew I could never finish the four-year program in the allocated time. I did better in the second term, but I was still down some courses and took them at the spring intersession. It meant losing two months of summer employment but I paid the price because I wanted to catch up. You see, I wasn't lazy—just stupid as a log. But I was tough and knew what I had to do—be like the grinder on the hockey team. You know, not the most talented player, but the one who works more than twice as hard as the gifted ones and gets the job done all the same.

During intersession, I managed to pass two of the courses but failed Electrical Physics. Actually, it felt more like the professor had failed *me*. This guy was a goof and couldn't teach his way out of a paper bag. All he did was stand up in front of the class and regurgitate the same stuff he had been teaching for decades. No wonder I failed. I should have dropped out of the course, but my stubborn attitude kicked in and I refused to quit. What I needed was at least a 2.0 GPA (grade point average), but thanks to this prof's ineptitude (and my inability to learn on my own, I suppose I should add), my GPA was 1.99 out of a possible 4.0, which meant that because of 1/100 of a grade point, I would be on academic probation in year two. A total bummer.

Being gutsy is one thing, but I was banging my head against the same brick wall over and over again. A step back would have made more sense. If I had withdrawn, I could have done so without penalties. But no one told me that and I didn't do much investigating of the ins and outs of the bloody university system, so when I failed Electrical Physics, I was screwed. And, of course, now my back was up against a wall with no room to spare: if my GPA went below 2.0 at the end of second year, I would be automatically suspended from the faculty of engineering.

My summer plans were affected too. Because I had to take courses in the spring session, I missed the boat on the good summer jobs. Most employers wanted student workers to start at the beginning of May. The only job I could land was working at McNaught Pontiac, the dealership where my father had purchased his Caddies and Trans Ams. One day I took the Trans Am in for warranty work and asked the service advisor if there were any job openings for the summer. With a stroke of luck, I landed a car jockey position: moving cars in and out of the rear storage lot to the service bays. I was a good driver so the job was no problem—until I drove the Trans Am to work and stirred up attitude from the other car jockeys there. (Same shit, different pile.)

The other four jockeys were mainly young and uneducated, and this work was their full-time employment. The pay was $3.05 per hour—a kick in the teeth for me after making six bucks an hour at the Polo Park Esso a year and a half earlier. These guys started to hate me because they knew I wasn't stuck there like they were, and also because I didn't join them in smoking, drinking, doing drugs, or having lunch in the filthy, unsanitary shack that served as a staff hangout. (You'll get the idea when you see the picture of the shack in the photo pages.) They would tease me about everything, and basically acted just plain ignorant. One guy sold his car to buy a Fender guitar; then he rode his bicycle to work, and told everyone he was going to be the new guitarist for Led Zeppelin. I did my own thing, minded my own business, and went to Granny's for lunch every day—her house was only a three-minute drive from work. Maybe it was my retreating to Granny's that really pissed them off.

I managed to stick with the work through most of the summer, but one day I'd had enough of those losers. It was like the car-wash scenario—I blew up after one too many insults from those career nobodies, and just up and walked out. I had the money I needed for the next year of university anyway, so I felt my job was done.

I wonder where those four guys are today. Alive? Who knows, and who really cares. It was my first experience with full-time nobodies—guys, with families, earning $3.05 an hour, and with ignorant attitudes, and mean streaks to boot. People have to earn a living, I know, but when they make the workplace miserable for others, I have no respect for them. Attitude in life is half the battle. The rest is doable. (Being good-looking and having great teeth doesn't hurt either!)

In later years, I had a moment of sweet irony, proving the point that no experience goes wasted. In 2002, I designed the electrical systems for McNaught's new 50,000-square-foot car dealership in Winnipeg. I met the owner just before the project was completed and he complimented me on the great job. It has been many years since the grand opening and I haven't heard another peep from anyone at McNaught's, which means a job well done. (That's how it works in the construction biz—silence is golden.) Oh yeah, Madsen Electric did a great job of the installation, so they deserve credit as well.

Chapter 7

GPA of 1.99 and Sinking

In the fall of 1981, I entered my second year of engineering. My dad bought two Pontiac Acadians that year: one for my mom, and one for me and my sister Susan to share for traveling to the university. (The Trans Am was now doing winter-storage duty.) Susan had been accepted into first-year science and we tried to arrange our schedules to co-ordinate the times we started classes and headed back home.

No car is complete for me without a souped-up sound system; therefore, my first order of business with our Acadian was to install a cheap Radio Shack cassette deck under the dash and a pair of fifteen-dollar speakers on top of the rear seats. The whole system was what I'd now consider total crap, but back then it kept my favorite tunes from Ted Nugent, Ozzy Osbourne, Saga, Rush, Alan Parsons Project, and local bands Orphan, Streetheart, and Harlequin, blasting in my ears as we drove to the university.

I will now formally apologize to Susan for making her listen to that stuff at full volume. She still tells the story about how many times I played cuts from Nugent's *Cat Scratch Fever* and APP's *I Robot*. I was such an ass because I never let her play any of her music. (I guess I'm still an ass—when my wife and I are in the car, my music still dominates.)

Music and sibling-bonding aside, second year turned out to be a bigger bust than first.

The second year of engineering is the year students choose a specialty. Electrical, as I was told by many students, is the hardest engineering discipline. Stupidly, I took a full load of six courses the first term, including a few first-year courses I'd missed the year before. Again my grades were pathetic, but I was allowed to finish out the year. Even stupider, I took another full load the second term. Though I put my head down and worked like a maniac, when you're in classes from 8:30 a.m. until 5:30 p.m., you end up brain-dead and burned-out. There was just too much cramming needed for the gazillion assignments, projects, and tests—information overload for me. I didn't skip lessons or labs and was never late for class, but I was sinking. It's easy now to see that I should have taken fewer courses so I could focus more on less material.

My GPA at the end of that year was below 1.99 and *boot!* I was kicked out of engineering.

My punt from the faculty of engineering was pretty embarrassing. I also had the guilt of knowing I had really let my parents down. That motivated me to have the guts to appeal to the Board of Governors and appear before a committee of ten tight-lipped, disapproving academics to plead my pathetic case. (I never know when to give up!)

I was nervous as shit before the meeting. (What can a person say when his grades show it all, clear as day? No amount of bullshit is going to help.) When I entered the room, these old guys (everyone looks old when you're a kid) were looking at my transcript of marks, and I could tell from the scowls on their faces that I was toast. I think the meeting lasted about two minutes. It's tough to remember what they said because it was like living a bad dream. "You're stupid, dumb, lazy . . . did we remember to say stupid?" Okay, maybe not quite, but that's how I played things for years in my recurring dreams about that meeting.

Not surprisingly, a letter arrived in the mail shortly thereafter, denying my appeal.

I had to dig myself out of the shit hole I'd fallen into. There was no way I was going to stay in the loser position for long. I took my remaining first-year course, Thermodynamics, at intersession. I actually started to read the textbook and listen closely to what was going on in class. I even gave up some chick-cruisin' time for studying. And what d'ya know—I passed. Then I had my second lucky break. Thermodynamics was a Mechanical Engineering subject. The professor knew I had been enrolled in Electrical Engineering and must have taken pity on me (or thought, "What the hell, he won't be in any of my classes anyway"), so I squeaked by with a C. The good news was that I had finally finished all my first-year courses. (*Thank you, Mr. Professor.*)

The university's advisors informed me that in a year's time I could reapply for engineering, but first had to meet with the same board and plead my case for reinstatement. They also told me that I should enroll in the faculty of science and take courses that could be transferred back to engineering in case I managed to be reinstated. Finally, some guiding light in the academic jungle!

Not to lose any more valuable time, I applied to the faculty of science, was accepted, and took courses that were worth full credit toward an engineering degree. But this time I was smart: I took half the number of courses per term as required in engineering so I could train myself to study properly. (The way I figure it, the heavy course load in engineering is for a rapid weeding-out of the non-academic types.) The faculty of science seemed more laid-back and more suited to me anyway.

Because I was out of the engineering loop, I was by myself again, pretty much without any friends on campus, which, looking back, was probably a blessing—there was no one to interfere with my studies. I was still buddies with my neighbor Richie, but he was busy studying to get into medicine. (Richie didn't make it into medicine; he became a dentist instead, a better choice if you're living in Manitoba and want to make big bucks. Medical doctors in Manitoba are generally underpaid, and unless you specialize or work lots of hours, the wages are not that great. My brother-in-law Neil, an emergency room doctor, moved to New York, and at the time of this writing has been there for ten years. A familiar case of a Winnipeg-trained doctor leaving for greener pastures.)

During the summer of 1982, I took a job as an installer at a burglar alarm company, for about four dollars an hour. It was a great job because I got to visit homes in Winnipeg and meet a lot of interesting people. The job didn't last long, however, because about a month into it, a chance to earn more bucks lured me away. One of my dad's friends landed me a job at Labatt Breweries working in the bottling plant. This job paid $5.75 per hour, which was a good wage back then. I was movin' up!

The shifts of this new job were varied because the plant never shut down. My normal days were from 7 a.m. till 3 p.m. but on occasion I would work the afternoon shift from 3 p.m. till midnight. Only once during the summer did I work the midnight shift. I guess they liked me!

One afternoon I was put to work with an ex-con. The shift ended at midnight and I was worried this guy was going to ask me for a ride home. It seemed like his criminal mind would not shut off. He told me about his crimes: armed robbery, assault, and a few petty crimes, and then showed me all his tattoos. I called the boss the next day and told him I was scared for my life. As it turned out, that same day they had already fired this guy, so I was safe. Apparently he had lied on his job application, and when Labatt's personnel somehow found out about his past, he was outta there. I had worked with an ex-con before and it seemed to me that these guys thought society owed them a living and felt hard done by because employers looked down on them for having criminal records. My tank of sympathy runs dry for guys who commit crimes.

There was some fun to be had that summer too. I'd introduced my car wash buddy, Alan, to Richie, seeing that neither of them worked. They'd become friends, so after the afternoon shift at Labatt's I'd drive over to Richie's house and all three of us would watch movies or play video games together. I bet you're thinking about the first video game, Pong. We did play Pong, but Richie also had the new Mattel Intellivision, which was a fairly state-of-the-art video game that included baseball, basketball, and hockey. First- and second-generation video games were introduced when I was young; with the explosion of these games today, I feel I was a pioneer as a gamer. (Not too much different from my skateboarding experience.)

I also had a couple of non-serious girlfriends during that time. Near the end of the summer, Alan and Richie met some chicks in River

Heights and called me over. Turned out that one of them liked me. Her name was Lisa. Her father was a professor at the University of Manitoba and her mother was a music teacher. Because I took a half course-load, I had lots of free time, so I again took up reading music and playing the piano. I could learn at my own pace, and I actually enjoyed myself without the iron fist of a piano teacher down my throat. I also needed to impress the committee the following year when I pleaded my case to be reinstated into engineering, so I thought I could tell them about my musical efforts. Lisa at the time was taking voice lessons, so this was definitely the musical phase of my life.

One day while visiting Lisa, I played a few tunes on their baby grand, and her old man thought it was his daughter playing so well. When he found out it was her boyfriend—me—he was freaked out. I had a good ear and played most of the songs by heart (no sheet music), which also made a lasting impression. I'd also put my own spin on the songs just to spice 'em up a bit: change the rhythm and add a few bars—I guess they call that ad lib in music circles. Too bad for me that I never joined a rock band; maybe I could have made it as a superstar rocker.

After a few months back at university in the faculty of science, I found myself spending all my time studying. Since I didn't want any outside interference, Lisa and I split up. Plus she was an energy grabber with her depressing attitude, and I needed all my good energy to make it back into engineering. She eventually started dating an ex-engineering buddy of mine, and I'd always wondered if he was the one she married. Well, small world—her two children are now in the same school as my kids are. Turns out she married and divorced my ex-engineering buddy and then remarried. I found this out after I purchased a 1992 University of Manitoba Alumni Directory on eBay for ten dollars. Nobody can hide from me for too long!

My new regimen was to attend all classes and then, every Friday night, pack up my stuff and spend the weekend in the spare bedroom at Granny's house. I'd spend the entire Saturday and Sunday studying—other than the time I took off to have dinner with her and

Gramps and to watch a few first-generation music videos on CBC. Sometimes I'd ride my bike instead of driving over to Granny's, but it was a bitch carrying all my books and paraphernalia. I remember riding home down Wellington Crescent one Sunday night when the autumn temperature had dipped to sub-zero—I almost froze my balls off. The ride is five miles and normally quite scenic, but that evening, it was a nightmare.

During the fall term of 1982, with only a half schedule in the faculty of science, I had some spare time, so I started to shovel driveways for the alarm company I'd previously worked for. They were so fucking cheap that I had to *manually* shovel the driveways. We had a snow-blower at home but I had no way of transporting the thing, and the company wouldn't help out. And of course, that winter was a bitch: cold, with mountains of snow. I would work all day, twelve or thirteen hours, shoveling—by myself. Most of the driveways were in Tuxedo, so at least I could have lunch at home.

— ¤ —

Aside from endless work, I also got into one of my passions that winter. While visiting the Engineering library one day, I picked up a *QST* magazine, published for amateur radio (or, the slang term, ham-radio) operators. I'd taken licensing courses for ham radio back in 1978 and '79 but had lost interest. It was now time for me to study the material, learn Morse code again, and write the exam. I had the time, the passion, and this would aid in my journey back into the faculty of engineering. A guy has to think of all the angles.

I learned the code and the theory, and wrote the amateur radio exam on April 21, 1983. I passed with flying colors. I then had my call sign, VE4AMC, which is basically a ticket to operate on certain bands. I'd saved enough money from snow shoveling to buy my first rig, a used Yaesu FT-101E that cost $500. I set up some antennas and was on the air. For the first six months I was able to operate only the Morse code, but after that period I applied to use "phone," which is ham-speak for voice. (After 1984 I never used the code key again. I always believe in using the latest technology and Morse code, as useful as it once was, is old technology.)

My old buddy James came over just after I'd put up some antennas. It was a few years since I'd last spoken with him, but the new hobby brought us together again. I lent James my study guide and the Morse code tapes so he could study for his ham license.

The summer of 1983 was upon me and I applied to be reinstated into the engineering faculty. I had to meet again with a bunch of ivory-tower types at the university and plead my case as to why I should be allowed to continue studying toward an engineering degree. This time they seemed more receptive toward me and were interested in finding out how I had improved myself the past year. I was at ease and had a good feeling during the meeting, which almost made up for the nightmarish experience the previous time.

Basically I told them that I'd learned to read music, had earned my amateur radio license, and had obtained a 3.0 GPA in the faculty of science. I guess they believed me because, two weeks later, I received a letter kicking me back in! (In November 2003, I bumped into Glen Morris, the professor who wrote the reinstatement letter. I shook his hand and thanked him again—twenty years later. Then a few days later, I sent him a handwritten thank-you note and enclosed a copy of his letter from 1983. I never forget the people who have given me a helping hand in life, and I hope for the same from the people I have helped.)

That same summer I worked at Nygard International, the Winnipeg firm previously known as TanJay. This was a garment manufacturing operation owned by local tycoon and playboy Peter Nygard. He had a few children from his various relationships, and named his company spin-offs after his daughters.

I was hired to update the local factory's electrical and mechanical drawings. I had no previous experience with building systems, but with the hands-on approach, I managed to teach myself during my tenure.

Hard work will usually pay off in spades later on in life. Designing that stuff at Nygard is what made my career. There, I learned about working my ass off, especially from Peter and upper management. Maybe this is where I gained my motivation to be self-employed, fearless, and determined to make it in business, no matter how long or hard I had to work. Peter, in a way, became a role model. His success was no less than phenomenal. He has the largest house in the world in the Bahamas, eight Excalibur custom cars, and at least six homes across the continent, not to mention a gazillion factories. This guy practically owns everything. One of the things I also learned from him was that, for all his hard work and risk, there were many people who were jealous of his hard-won success. This prepared me for what I encountered many years later. (I like to keep track of Peter Nygard's success. In the spring of 2005, he purchased several historic buildings in Winnipeg's Exchange District with plans of investing upwards of $80 million in the redevelopment of these buildings. Now, that's giving back to the city where it all started for him, and I admire that!)

Chapter 8

Back in the Saddle Again

In September 1983, I went back into Electrical Engineering with a determination to do whatever it took to leave that place with an engineering degree. My resolve had nothing to do with making big bucks. Once I started the program I had to finish it. And once a degree is obtained, it's a ticket that no one can take away from you. I like that.

Back in the university saddle again, I finally found an extracurricular activity on campus that was right up my alley. I joined the University of Manitoba Amateur Radio Club, which had a nice "office" on the 5th floor of University Centre. There were hardly any members, so I had my own on-campus office, complete with a ham-radio station, phone, coffeemaker, desk, and pretty much my own private washroom.

In the mornings I would drop off my books, jacket, and lunch in the club before attending classes. During breaks, I'd visit the club to have lunch, operate the radios, and study. This was a real cool setup, and the only cost was a $10-a-year membership.

I managed to obtain a 2.62 GPA that year. It would have been higher except I failed Engineering Economics the first term. The teacher was an employee of Manitoba Hydro and rumor had it that he taught the course for free, which might have accounted for his lack of interest and zip. Whatever the reason, almost everything he said went in one ear and out the other. The next term I took the same course but with a civil engineering professor, and earned an A. Go figure. The Hydro guy is probably still making $50,000 per year and I'm semi-retired in my forties. (*So, Mr. Useless Teacher, who should have failed that course?*) No hard feelings though, seeing that was twenty years ago. I saw this guy in an Office Depot parking lot recently but I didn't approach him—the bad memories still lingered.

Ham radio was now a big part of my life, and was about to get even bigger. James had written and passed the amateur radio exam and was in the faculty of science, and I talked him into joining the U of M Ham Radio Club. In the spring of 1984 he needed some radio gear, so we both bought about five thousand dollars' worth of ham radios and accessories from a Canadian dealer. I helped James set up antennas and *voilá*, he was on the air. This was a great feeling for me—as I mentioned earlier, James got me into shortwave and CB radio in the '70s and now we were both hams. (James had been kicked out of engineering but had come back to the University to obtain a BSc. He never did re-apply to engineering.)

— ¤ —

In the summer of 1984 I managed to find gainful summer employment with the federal government and to connect with another role model. The Department of Indian Affairs and Northern Development was probably the worst federal department to work for because of the bad blood with the Canadian Indians and their reported wasteful spending of taxpayers' dollars, but the person I worked for made up for that.

My boss was Doug Layton, an engineer. I liked him right off the bat because he was a bit different: he actually got things done. He didn't have the typical civil-servant attitude that my father's opinions had caused me to expect, which was to "wait for coffee breaks, and retirement." Doug was a hard worker, and he liked me because I was as well. When he gave me a task, I would complete it in less than half the time of previous summer students, so maybe I impressed him. During that time he also quit smoking and started to chew nicotine gum. I gave him tremendous credit for that. And it made it easier for me to work with him because, as you know, I can't tolerate smokers.

The best part of this job was that I got to see most of the province of Manitoba, and was paid to do this! My job was to visit Manitoba's Indian reservations and confirm the capital assets on each site (which was mostly real property). I got to drive around the province, visit almost every town, meet every chief, and learn about the Aboriginal way of life. I examined all the buildings on the reserves I visited, including houses. I felt sorry for these people for the most part, especially the children. There were many new schools and band offices, but the housing was what always got me down. I lived in Tuxedo, the rich area, and I was learning about the other side of life. That just reinforced my belief that we should never take what we have for granted. That simple lesson has never left me.

— ♮ —

July 11, 1984, was a day I'll always remember. I had just returned from traveling to Brokenhead Indian Reserve and had parked the government truck in the parkade on Smith Street. I grabbed my Nikon camera and the paperwork I had taken with me and headed down Portage Avenue to my dad's rooming house at 92 Balmoral where I had parked my car. (I walked to and from work each day from Balmoral Street. It took about twenty minutes, was good exercise, and allowed me to think about the things happening in my life, and my future in general. Besides, a downtown parking space would have cost me $60 a month. I'm not cheap, just frugal!)

Anyway, that day, while walking to my car, I spotted a crowd of people at the corner of Portage Avenue and Donald Street. I pushed my way through the throng and saw the horror of a young boy covered in a liquid. He was totally motionless and in shock. A police officer was offering him a blanket. I immediately snapped two photos of the boy and the officer. Then, with two frames left in the camera, I snapped photos of his mother and sister.

I knew right away that the photos were important, even though I felt uneasy when taking them. I was capturing a moment of terror, confusion, pain, and the unknown. Recording a tragedy is something a person doesn't want to do on purpose, but some inner sense told me to record the event.

I asked the bystanders what had happened and was told that the sewer had exploded. I'd heard of sewer covers popping off their mounts, but never exploding. I was still confused as to what had really caused this accident, but I knew it would be of interest to a lot of people. I then ran like mad to the *Winnipeg Free Press* newspaper office, which was just down the street. The people in the newsroom directed me to the news director on the night shift. He said they would develop the photos, and if they were good, print them in the morning edition of the paper.

As it turned out, I was the only person to have an actual photographic record of the incident.

The next morning while walking to work, I passed by a newspaper stand. To my astonishment, one of my photos was on the front page of the paper. I hadn't been sure of the quality of any of the photos, but the shot they chose of the boy was clear enough to give me shivers up my spine.

The accompanying article, written by Doug Speirs, Bob Cox, and Don Retson, explained that an underground transformer had exploded. The boy, Ian Bland, had been covered in extremely hot transformer oil. After reading the article I immediately knew that his injuries were serious, really serious. I think he had burns to about 80 percent of his body. I prayed, probably along with every person in Winnipeg, that he would recover.

About a week later, Ian, who was only twelve years old, succumbed to his injuries. More than twenty years later, I still think about him on occasion. What a tragic loss of life. His death was difficult for me to deal with back then—and my friend James was no help. He said I took the photos for the money. The *Free Press* did pay me a hundred dollars for the use of the negatives, but I definitely did not take the shots for that reason. I just happened to be on the scene with a camera, and automatically recorded the horror I saw. Those pictures became part of Winnipeg history: they were printed again in December, in a special section of the newspaper that featured memorable images from 1984.

Two years later, a reporter from CBC Television who was writing a television documentary about the incident called me and asked for permission to use my photographs. I met with her and gave the CBC permission to use the negatives for any purpose. I know that those photos helped the family win compensation from the City of Winnipeg and Winnipeg Hydro, because I received a letter from the Bland family, via the CBC, thanking me. I was glad that I could help the family in a time of need. But what that event impressed upon me the most was the fact that life is really precious, and should not be taken lightly and wasted.

Winnipeggers will remember the incident always. I was at a meeting with a local developer in May 2005 going over my designs for the electrical and mechanical systems of a new hotel near the airport. As we were discussing the location of the transformer, the project manager stated he did not want the transformer located where it could blow up and kill someone like that boy who died in downtown Winnipeg.

Chapter 9

GPA Rising

The summer of '84 ended and my third year of Electrical Engineering started. I knew I still had to prove myself, and strive for a year without any Fs or Ds.

I jammed my schedule with ten courses (42 credit hours) of second-, third-, and fourth-year courses. I still needed one second-year course, Electric Fields, which was the most difficult course in that year; that's why I waited until I'd been back for a year before I attempted it. I managed to get all the class notes from Richard Epp, a guy I'd worked with the previous summer at Indian Affairs. I went to the first lecture, and it was so unbelievably boring that I missed every lecture that term, and instead studied off Richard's notes. I did attend the labs though, so I could get credit for the assignments. I managed a B, which was pretty amazing for attending only one lecture.

Finally, after all the sacrifice and hard studying, I was achieving great grades. The big payoff was showing my parents my transcript of marks, and telling my grandmother I was actually going to make it through Electrical Engineering and get the Iron Ring she always talked about. For many years Granny rented rooms to university students—mainly Chinese, for some reason—who had told her the story of the Iron Ring. (In fact, she told me the "Ring" story before I even knew it actually existed. Freaky.)

I've heard a couple of versions of the story of the Ring, but the one I remember the best is about an incident involving a bridge in Quebec sometime at the beginning of the century. Apparently, the engineers who designed it had screwed up and the defective structure collapsed, killing a bunch of workers. The Ring is supposed to have been taken from the debris of that fallen bridge. It's a physical reminder of the tragic cost of human error in engineering work. I looked up a quotation we were often told about in engineering classes. It's by Rudyard Kipling: "The Iron Ring is cold because the material is unforgiving when engineers make mistakes." (I sure agree there!) I couldn't wait to get my own ring and show it off to Granny.

I excelled in Control Systems and Digital Controls and obtained a B+ in both! I also obtained a B+ in Solid State Electronics, which was a continuation of the Physical Electronics course that I'd received a B+ for in the previous year. (Maybe I should have been a microchip designer.)

In October, I wrote my Advanced Amateur Radio exam and passed with flying colors. I could then operate with full amateur privileges. That meant I could use voice on all bands. James wrote his Digital Amateur Radio exam and also passed, so we were both flying high.

In November, the University's Ham Radio Club hosted two "hams" from Purdue University to operate the radio eqiupment for a contest. They were Electrical Engineering students with the call signs KX9G and KK9W. They operated twenty-four hours of Morse code on a Saturday and Sunday. The reason they came to Winnipeg was that during the prior year's contest, they had missed working a station from Manitoba. They'd made a pact that they would travel here to make sure that a station from Manitoba would be active for the 1984 American Radio Relay League (ARRL) Sweepstakes, a ham-radio contest basically for the purpose of contacting as many other ham-radio operators in North America as possible in a certain timeframe. They won first place for Manitoba and gave out hundreds of contacts for other hams in the contest. James and I visited the guys a few times but didn't enter the event ourselves. The Monday after the contest, we drove them to the airport in James's mom's Lincoln. Talk about first-class service! It was nice to spend some quality time with engineering students from another university who had a hobby in common. My network and contacts were growing.

— ¤ —

I put my nose to the grindstone for the next five months. The university year ended great—in fact, it was my best year ever. I passed every course and wound up with a 2.60 GPA, which is a B–. I finally figured out a good system: preparation prior to the term starting, and a strict study regimen. After years of struggling, this strategy was really paying off for me.

In June I got a summer job with the federal government again. This time it was with Energy, Mines and Resources. I was hired to inspect wood furnace installations. The government had an "off-oil" rebate program, which would give rebates to homeowners if they removed their old oil furnace and installed wood furnaces, or combination wood/electric furnaces.

I traveled all over Manitoba again, to about 120 homes across the province. By the end of that term, I was really sick of traveling to every hick town. Some of the people were doozies too. At one home I visited, the lady tried to get me drunk. But since I hate beer, I couldn't drink even half of the bottle she gave me. She talked my ear off and proceeded to get pretty bombed. I had to politely excuse myself before something sexual happened. I guess she was horny, living in the sticks where action was limited. I wouldn't consider having sex with a female unless I had previously known her . . . or met her through friends . . . or at a social function . . . or something! I wasn't the traveling American Gigolo, you know.

Most other visits were uneventful except for the time I met a potato farmer who owned three airplanes, five cars, and two hangars— and he still got the $500 rebate check from the federal government. So much for farmers complaining about how much money they don't have. He would have made J.R. Simplot proud. (Simplot is a billionaire involved in the agribusiness; his biography is entitled *A Billion the Hard Way*.)

—¤—

After that summer of 1985, I entered my final year of Electrical Engineering. Things were a little slow at first. I had lightened my course load to the final 28 credit hours required for graduating, so I had time to write a study guide for the Digital Amateur Radio license, which was published in ten installments in a Manitoba ham-radio magazine.

I wrote my Digital Amateur Radio exam in October and received a 90 percent. I then had all three classes of ham license in Canada. No more than a handful of hams can say that—only about two hundred digital licenses were ever issued by the Department of Communications. (I like that—being unique.)

With all these academic successes under my belt, I was hyped up with confidence and visions of conquering the world! There was one more hurdle though: a thesis had to be written as part of the fourth-year coursework. I was unlucky enough to be partnered up with another student named Danny. I had known Danny from regular engineering classes and we became friends as we had music as a common interest. Our thesis topic was a Musical Instrument Digital Interface (MIDI) guitar controller. This device was to convert a guitar note into a digital format that could then be transferred to another MIDI instrument and played back in an analog mode. We designed the hardware, and I wire-wrapped the electronics and wrote the thesis document while Danny wrote the software. The device didn't work; however, we were able to send a digital note to a MIDI synthesizer through the software.

Just prior to the presentation, I was doing some last-minute checking on the hardware, in the ham-radio clubroom. Danny was complaining that the hardware was not working correctly and placing all the blame on me. A few other hams were present, and Danny just wouldn't shut his fucking trap. My blood was boiling, but I had to keep my cool so we could complete the thesis. (Where's Jack the Ripper when you need him?) After Danny left, one of the hams said that if he'd been me, he would have punched the guy. But I'd heard of more than one student who didn't graduate because his thesis was never finished, and I knew I had to stay focused. I just took the bullshit—and the rest is history. We ended up with a C+, which was a big downer because most of my engineering friends got As. I never spoke another word to Danny after the presentation, not even at the graduation ceremony.

— ¤ —

In my final year, I hammered out three B+s, two C+s, and two Cs. The best year yet. No Fs or Ds, and my GPA was a 2.77.

Both my father and my mother attended my graduation ceremony on Thursday, May 29, 1986, in the sweat pit known as Bison East Gym. Man, that was the proudest moment in my life—and I knew that my parents were just as proud. Because of all my struggles through post-secondary academia, they must have thought the day would never come. Even though the pictures of my parents and me didn't turn out (because my mother brought a lousy pocket camera that never did work properly), the day is indelibly etched in my mind.

Chapter 10

Welcome to the Jungle

For me, the most important thing to do after graduating was to get a job. My work ethic (and common sense) dictated that—as well as a touch of gut-wrenching fear. I knew of university grads who couldn't get a job for years after being handed their diplomas.

I started scanning job postings months before I graduated. A few months prior to my successful exit from Electrical Engineering, I saw in the *Careers* section of the *Winnipeg Free Press* an advertisement for a sales engineer at a local branch of Honeywell Inc., a multi-national company that had a division selling temperature controls for commercial buildings. I cut out the advertisement and told my mother, "I'm going to get this job." (No word of a lie. I still have that newspaper clipping to this day.)

I did get the job. According to the receptionists at Honeywell, over a hundred résumés were received and six candidates (including me) were interviewed. After the interviews, Honeywell's head office interviewer asked the two female receptionists in the Winnipeg office which one she should hire. They said, "Hire Mike; he's the cutest." I'm not sure that was actually the reason I got hired, but having them tell me that pumped me up. My image of myself at the time I applied was as a young skateboard stud in a Sunday suit. I didn't anticipate that my career path would be determined by some chicks who thought I was cute, but maybe it was. I figure a person has to take whatever good fortune comes along. In April of 1986, I started off as an official Honeywell employee, full of plans to impress the hell out of the boss and to take on the world!

On my first day at work, I was given all these books on Honeywell's history, benefits packages, pensions, and stock-option purchase plans. There was no doubt in my mind that this would be a lifelong job and that I would be looked after by the firm until retirement. Wasn't it a prophet in the Bible—or Shakespeare, or some other dude—who claimed pride goes before the fall? Well, another fundamental lesson for Michael Mark was coming up.

After my first-day orientation, I was shown my workstation and given product catalogs. I put my head down and immediately started to work—my MO for every other job I've had since then. The job description was to provide quotations to mechanical contractors on temperature-control systems for buildings, as well as to write specifications for consulting engineers. I catch on to things quickly, so a few days later I was right in the thick of dealing with purchase orders because the projects I'd quoted had the lowest price.

My first encounter with work colleagues wasn't the greatest. My supervisor Gary, the branch manager, was someone I definitely was *not* impressed with. He was a man in the middle of an identity crisis. Although he was in his fifties and had been with Honeywell for over twenty-five years, he had the haircut of a sixteen-year-old surfer dude—dyed and feathered in the middle, just enough to cover a small bald spot. He called himself an engineer, but when I looked him up in the Manitoba Professional Engineers membership directory, his name was not there. He had a huge ego and always took credit for purchase orders on the larger projects, whether he had anything to do with them or not. He liked to brag about all the profit the branch was making and about how he schmoozed with the architects and engineers so that they would specify Honeywell. A genuine pain in the butt for me.

My coworker Gord, a thirty-something technologist, was a typical bullshitter, and had a heavy smoking and drinking habit. He was as much of a pain to work with as Gary because he gave me all his boring work, I guess so he could do other more interesting stuff. He had a hair problem too—a large bald spot on top and long strands in the back. Some older guys back then were just in love with those pathetic comb-over, bad-rug hairstyles. (Can you tell that hair has been an issue for me? When my hair started thinning, I just had it cut short. My wife tells me I look better now than I did with longer hair anyway.)

Smoking was allowed in offices in those days, and with my asthma, Gord's habit of puffing on one cigarette after another caused me a lot of agony. Finally, I installed a self-contained electronic air filter between our office partitions, which, I guess, pissed him off greatly, seeing it was right there before his nose every day.

I really dug in with my first job. I liked having a permanent office cubicle and a phone number and, especially, secretaries answering the phones. My main job was to do take-offs, which basically entailed looking at a set of mechanical HVAC (heating/ventilation/air conditioning) design drawings and specifications for a building, figuring out what temperature controls were required, and prior to the tender closing, providing the mechanical and ventilation contractors with a cost to supply and install the equipment.

Honeywell had a price book and specifically designed pricing sheets that the sales engineers would fill out when estimating the cost of material and labor, plus travel, for the job. Standard markups were added to cover head office and branch overhead. After potential jobs were identified, the minimum price was determined and we would phone in our bid. That consisted of obtaining a list of the mechanical contractors (subtrades) and, long before the tender closed, calling them with our price. We would try to shop the competitor's price. By contacting contractors loyal to Honeywell early on, if we were not low enough, there would be time to adjust our figures and call back with a better price. Our chief competitor was Johnson Controls Ltd. (JCL), and shopping their price was done like clockwork on almost a daily basis.

The firm's remuneration for a sales engineer was a base salary, with a commission on the gross price of the job (paid quarterly), as well as a commission payable on the net profit after the job was installed.

Honeywell had some phenomenal electricians and pneumatic installers, who, for the most part, installed each and every job well below the estimated cost for labor. It was these guys who made the salesman's commission check big. These were the silent employees I generally never saw, or even met, which is kind of sad. Field guys were seldom in the office, so the only way I could meet them was to visit the job site, a rare occurrence since my job was to sell, and nothing else.

My first introduction to corporate structure and management was through this job. Honeywell, even at branch level, was tightly structured. Salesmen had their jobs—to sell, sell, sell, *period*—and everyone else, from system-designers to secretaries, was slotted into tight silos of work. A stupid, inefficient system. Employees should be able to take on more responsibilities than just their allotted tasks. In my own office now, I can do every person's job; if someone is sick, I can fill in seamlessly. (Before I had any employees, I did everything myself anyway.)

I was pretty much a model employee, at least according to *my* books. I started work at 8:30 a.m., took a one-hour lunch break, and finished at 4:30 p.m. I wore a suit and tie every day, was well groomed, polite, and cooperative with the other employees. Because of my efficient work style, I rarely had to work overtime. I may have worked a bit extra on Saturdays, but I never worked evenings.

This first job was really just a job—that's all it meant to me. It was not a personality contest or anything of the kind. I did what I was told, never talked back to anyone, but I kept to myself, never revealing anything personal about my family or myself to anyone. I also went home for lunch every day. No casual mingling with the office personnel, except when I organized a hockey game for the branch in 1987 and stayed for a post-game celebration. In retrospect, I could have socialized a bit more with my fellow workers. Maybe I was just scared of saying or doing something stupid that would cause me to lose my first job.

After I was proficient in providing take-offs and my estimating was almost perfect, I started to provide estimates for 90 percent or more of all the projects out for tender, which ultimately proved to be deadly boring. The routine went like this: I would arrive at work in the morning, check the interdepartmental mail, and catch up on things from the previous day. Then I'd drive to Southam News Service, a firm that provided the leads for the projects. There, I'd check the plan board to see what plans were out for tender, would review the plans in-house, and do a take-off if the job was small, or book the plans for a day or night so a take-off would be performed at the office. Then I would return to work and review the mail, which included little three-by-five-inch kraft paper sheets with typed information about the job (i.e. job name, closing date, architect, electrical engineer, mechanical engineer, list of contractors), and if the job looked like it required temperature controls, check it out at Southam. The rest of the day consisted of doing the boring take-offs, and tendering out a job if there was one to close. As well, I would take, on average, fifty phone calls per day.

As you can see, estimating is boring, and if you don't get the PO (purchase order), then all your work is wasted. I hated that: wasting my time—and wasting my education. Fortunately, at Honeywell we would get POs for seven out of ten jobs quoted. The other main competitors combined—Johnson Controls, Powers, Barber-Coleman, and Trans-Alta—received only three out of ten. Honeywell was a force to be reckoned with in Winnipeg when I was there. (I'm not saying I was the sole reason, but I *was* working nonstop for them at the time.)

One thing I really did enjoy was speaking with and meeting the mechanical contractors, mostly friendly and hard-working people. I still know many of them today. Some of these guys would gladly provide the competitor's price to us prior to the tender-close of many jobs. This was a key component to Honeywell's winning most of the projects in Manitoba and NW Ontario. A tad unethical, you say? Nah, this is just how the business world works.

Thinking back, the best part of the job was looking at two thousand sets of blueprints a year, which meant that I got to see the plans produced by every consulting engineering firm in Winnipeg. I knew which firms produced great designs and drawings and which ones produced garbage. (No insults intended—these observations are based on fact.) Later, when I worked on hundreds of projects for Johnson Controls, at the end of each project I would visit the job sites and speak with the trades and owners, so I damn well knew which jobs were screwed-up. But I'm getting ahead of myself . . .

After I'd been at Honeywell for about six months, the branch manager set quarterly quotas, and if we obtained them we would get awards. These awards consisted of having our names mentioned in the Honeywell Canada monthly newsletter, as well as receiving a sticker for our "Honeywell plaque" stating the quarter and year. I still have my plaque with the two stickers I received for my hard work back then.

When I first started, I was supposed to attend the Honeywell training school for salesmen in Minneapolis. After months and months of delay, I figured I would never go. And I was right. The training budget came at branch level, and I guess Gary, the manager, wanted the money in the bank so year-end looked good. Consequently, I was never sent for any training or seminars with Honeywell. So I trained myself—to perform at a hundred percent.

Busting your guts for a company isn't enough if someone has it in for you. And, for a number of reasons, Gary resented me. Also remember: he was not the person who actually hired me; it was Rosemary from head office. During my first summer there, Gary saw that I drove a 1980 Pontiac Trans-Am Indy 500 pace car. Not to be outdone, he drove his 1982 Ferrari 308 GT to work. It was black with aftermarket wheels, tons of swirls in the paint, and a broken two-way radio antenna. I didn't think it looked so cool, and wondered why he would have that kind of car, considering Winnipeg's poor winter-driving conditions and brutal potholed roads. I figured it out later: I saw him at Grand Beach in a tank top and sandals, riding his windsurf board and trying to look like a young stud. He must have thought of me as a threat, or else he was trying to compete with the younger generation. For crying out loud, he was old enough to be my father.

After a year, by May 1987, I had met my sales quotas, but the economy was slowing down. That must have been the reason Gary started going through my long-distance phone bills. (Each telephone extension had a separate monthly summary.) He found out that one month I had ten dollars' worth of calls to my friend James in Toronto. He made me pay for these calls. (Not only was I never paid for overtime or for working on weekends, I couldn't even have ten bucks' worth of long-distance phone calls!)

The other factors may have been that Gord got sick of my air cleaner, or I pissed him and Gary off because I wouldn't attend their liquid lunches or light up a cigar with them. I still kept to myself. Whatever his reasons, Gary fired me.

I'll never forget that day in June when Gary called me to his office to inform me I would be laid off following the required two-weeks' termination notice. He told me that, due to an economic slowdown, the branch could not afford me. He also stated I should work my last two weeks as hard as I had been working throughout my tenure. He then said, "Toronto is booming and Winnipeg is not the place to stay if you're a young, educated person. I think you should move there and get a job." It was all BS. All the time I was thinking: *Are you nuts, you idiot? I'm going to get a job at Johnson Controls and ruin your life at Honeywell. Once I'm satisfied that I've paid you back, then I'll quit Johnson Controls.* I have no mercy when I think someone has screwed me around, and I never forget them. It may take a bit of time, but in the end they all pay—and most of the time I don't have to do anything for revenge; they just do it to themselves. How's that for a useful life-lesson!

I decided I would move all my stuff out of my cubicle after work that day. I retained the services of two of my friends to help out. When we arrived at the office early that evening, to my surprise the locks were changed. I managed to get the attention of one of the cleaning staff, who opened the doors. Just for fun, I tried my alarm code, but the buggers had also changed that. When we started to clean out my desk, I noticed Gary had also removed my Honeywell picture ID card. We moved all the stuff out in less than five minutes, including all of the Honeywell proprietary pricing books and product information binders. I knew this information would be helpful for Johnson Controls' head office when I got a job with them. (I had no doubt I would get a job there because they knew how good I was at Honeywell.)

I never did go back to work at Honeywell, and I don't think Gary ever tried to contact me to demand that I immediately return to work. But I wasn't finished with him yet. Gary had written a letter to me after my firing meeting, promising to pay me full commission for all my outstanding projects. Well, when I tried to collect, the office manager said that I was out of luck, that the contract I'd signed voided all my commissions payable at termination. This was a sum of about $5,000, a considerable amount when a person's salary is only $24,500 per year.

Not to allow Honeywell to get the best of me, I contacted the provincial Labour Board and explained my situation. I gave the caseworker the termination letter and the employment contract. He told me he had to read the contract a hundred times to fully understand its intent. It must have been drawn up by lawyers—by the insertion of one comma, it voided all payable commissions after termination.

The caseworker later told me that he managed to obtain information on how much Honeywell owed me—much to Gary's embarrassment, I assume. I am not sure how much power the Labour Board actually has, but I'm sure glad that the caseworker managed to get all the information required to assist me in my plight.

Gary called me sometime later and said he had a check waiting for me to pick up at the branch. I went down the next day with my father to get it. When Gary came to the reception area, he presented me with an envelope, and with a cocky smile on his face he said, "Here is all your money." I immediately opened it, and the check was only for around $2,000. I threw the check in his face and watched it fall to the ground. I told him "That's less that half of what you owe me." As my father and I left, Gary looked like a real loser in front of the receptionist and a client who was there.

The caseworker for the Labour Board later said that I should have taken the money and run, causing an immediate back-down on my part. He arranged for me to pick up the check again. This time the receptionist was the one who handed me the money. Lesson learned: if someone has money for you, even if it's less than expected, take it!

—¤—

I did apply for a job at Johnson Controls. They called me immediately for a job interview, and subsequently for a written technical exam, which I took in early fall 1987. I was called in by the branch manager, Dan, and informed that I would be hired to run the newly formed small-business unit. This was a pilot program created by Johnson Controls' head office so the firm would be more competitive on smaller projects. Now I could teach them what I had learned about sales at Honeywell!

The four months off prior to starting my new job—lounging around my parents' pool, for the most part—made me really hungry to start my plan to get back at Honeywell. I was well rested, full of vengeance, and nothing could stop me. Gary's number was up. This was my chance—but I couldn't let anyone at Johnson know of my secondary motive.

Chapter 11

Time's Up!

Full of enthusiasm, I started work at Johnson Controls. On my first day, November 12, 1987, I quoted two projects and received an order for one of them.

Things started out pretty smoothly. I was this unknown guy from Honeywell who had beaten out the Johnson Controls salesmen on most projects. The guys knew how to use me to their advantage and quickly started to ask me how Honeywell managed to get all the contracts and what its branch prices were for items. Also they quizzed me on who the contractors were that shopped prices during tender-times. I was more than happy to supply all that information.

I was a model employee, going in at 8 a.m. and finishing at 4:30 p.m. or later. Never late, always wearing a suit and tie, totally respectful of the branch manager and all the staff—that was me. The staff at JC was about one-third the size of Honeywell's and, thankfully, I fit in socially as most of the employees were around my age, twenty-six.

The orders started coming in steadily. I had to learn control-system design, which I was not taught at Honeywell. The learning was a little stressful but the staff system-designers were always helpful. Learning the model numbers and associated parts, such as damper linkages and relays, was kind of a pain. The pneumatic controls were tricky, as spring ranges on various devices had to be verified before ordering, and selecting control valves when hundreds of types were available was not what I call fun. But at least this time the work seemed interesting because I was doing the jobs of at least three people on a smaller scale and I could tap in to the other pigeon-holed employees for their expertise.

In this new position I retained my salesman status since I had already formed relationships with many mechanical contractors and was now well known in the construction industry in Manitoba. The other duties included the design and drafting of the control systems, some project management, as well as training of owners. This was pretty much like running my own microbusiness without the cost of overhead and financing. I didn't know it at the time but this opportunity was preparing me for eventually starting my own company.

— ¤ —

The Christmas holidays that year were uneventful for the most part. I think I spent most of my time playing scrub ice-hockey with some friends and operating the ham radio. The romance scene was non-existent at this time in my life.

Then, on January 1, 1988, I met my future wife. A female friend called me up and asked me to come over to a house party, but I was really not interested. Fate was actually the one calling, I guess, because some of the partiers called three times until I finally agreed to go, just so they would stop bugging me. I remember my sister Heather saying, *Mike get the phone; it's those stupid girls again.* (My phone number was unlisted at the time but they'd found my sister's number in the phone directory and called it.)

The girl whose house I visited was just a chick I'd had a summer fling with. I guess she thought we were dating, even though the last time I'd seen her was six months earlier. There were a bunch of people there, but one of the girls, Laurie, was kinda cute and had great hair. (Okay, there's the hair thing again. I just like nice hair, especially on girls.) I started to talk with her—actually I did most of the talking because she was shy and quiet. I have the gift of gab so I just asked questions, and when her reply was something I could relate to, I carried on the conversation.

I found out that she was working at Peter Nygard's clothing company, TanJay. Since I'd worked there the summer of 1983, we had some common ground. At one point, the hostess started getting close to me, huggy and stuff like that, but I inched away from her so Laurie would get the drift that I wasn't interested in this attention.

After watching a movie, we were all hungry so I suggested we should go out for pizza. We went to Papa George's restaurant on Osborne, and I picked up the tab for everyone. I had ulterior motives: I was trying to impress Laurie, who by this time had warmed up to me a bit.

The following week, I was getting up the nerve to call her at work, but she got to me first. Laurie and her friend called me at home one evening and wanted me to take them to a bar, but I said I would only take Laurie. She was the loyal type and wouldn't leave her friend at home, so my offer was turned down. I just stayed home that night, plotting my next move.

Laurie had given me her phone number, so I called her the next night and we went to a movie. It was a nice date and she even got a goodnight kiss from me. We went to a nightclub the following weekend and got close on the dance floor. I guarantee I ain't John Travolta, but I managed to do what I had to, to impress Laurie.

The relationship started off smoothly but did have its rocky moments as well. Young women go through these crazy emotional phases, and sometimes one little wrong word can set them off. These blow-ups happened from time to time, but in the end I think it made our relationship stronger. When you have an argument with a woman, you learn a lot about her boundaries—and your own. For the most part, we enjoyed each other's company—going to movies, dinners, weekend getaways, and just hanging out. What impressed me most about Laurie, aside from the fact that she was a knockout brunette, was her kind heart and loyal soul. I did tell her during the second week of our relationship that I wanted to marry her (but I'm sure it was only in a joking manner).

Laurie lived with her mother and was from a quiet family, so, no kidding, we were opposites. I am loud, and she was quiet and reserved, but I converted her quickly to being loud . . . then louder. She came out of her shy and quiet shell to compete with me—Mr. Opposite! I often get comments from family members and friends about our being really good together.

— ¤ —

Meanwhile at work, in order to improve my design skills, the branch manager made arrangements to send me to Johnson Controls' head office in Milwaukee, Wisconsin. This course was four weeks in duration: the first three were on system design and the last week was on sales.

By this time, I'd been going out with Laurie for three months. We'd been seeing each other regularly and were growing closer. She wasn't happy I had to leave, but I knew what I had to do to advance in the company. So, no choice!

I was shipped out to Milwaukee in April to spend one month at the Park East Hotel (which is not as fancy as it sounds but was within walking distance from Lake Michigan). According to Lucy, our office manager, I was supposed to share a room with another student. There was no way I'd do that; I value my privacy and I'm a clean-freak. I told Lucy I would pay extra for my own room. She had some good connections at head office, and managed to use my asthma as the reason I needed my own room, without any extra cost to me. (I, of course, bought her a present upon my return. I never forget those who do a favor for me.)

Once there, I discovered I was in a class of fifty or so, with only three fellow Canadians. The days were not so different from university: class time from 8 a.m. until 4:30 p.m., including labs at the Milwaukee School of Engineering. Milwaukee is a nice city: lots of shopping, restaurants, and bars; friendly people; and beautiful Lake Michigan. The highlight of the trip was seeing Ted Nugent in concert with L.A. Guns—and telling the girls in the bars that I was a drummer in a rock band.

Laurie missed me like crazy. Her phone bill had three hundred dollars in long-distance calls that month. I considered marrying her on the spot when I got back to Winnipeg, figuring that if she was willing to rack up a long-distance bill like that for me, she was worth it. However, marrying was too big a step at that time in my life. I was still living at home and only had minimal cash savings in the bank. I wanted to start marriage one step ahead, if you know what I mean!

—¤—

Now it was time to leave Honeywell in the dust; take no prisoners. Work was steady and the economy was booming. Because I didn't have to include design time, project management, or owner training on my estimate sheet, I could get orders on almost every small job I quoted. (Honeywell had to include that overhead on their estimate sheets.) The one major problem was material costs. At Honeywell, the profit center was at branch level, which meant the pricing books showed material prices at cost. At Johnson Controls, the profit center was shared between the corporate head office, Canadian head office, and at branch level. The material prices we had were at least double those on the Honeywell books. Labor rates were the same, since electricians and pneumatic tradespeople were paid union rates. One way to beat Honeywell was by reducing costs by outsourcing equipment such as electric radiation valves and thermostats, and relays from electrical wholesalers. I would do anything to beat Honeywell—legally, of course.

One big problem for the branch's senior salesman and me was that Honeywell had a strong client-base, loyal to the end. If I had a hot price, Honeywell would beat it, even if they lost money. So that became my plan: to quote every job as low as I could. If Honeywell really wanted it, I'd make sure they wouldn't make a profit. I was demonstrating the simple old adage: Don't ever underestimate the little guy—which Honeywell did. They figured: "We'll show that punk. Honeywell is #1." Unfortunately for them, my hard work and killer competitive instinct eventually won out—and did-in my former boss.

About one month after my training, the JC branch purchased AutoCAD Release 9, which Johnson Controls customized for the drafting of control-system schematics. Brand-new IBM 33 MHz PCs and HP pen plotters were installed. This was my chance to learn AutoCAD and plotting. I immediately jumped in, read the manuals, spent time learning DOS, and in a short time I was a competent CAD (computer-aided design) operator. Now I could cut even more cost from my estimate sheets and add just one more nail in Gary's proverbial coffin.

Imagine one man doing sales, specification writing, control-system design, AutoCAD drafting, and project management—a ton of work, but the future rewards would be the payoff.

The most beneficial part of specification-writing for consultants was that I was able to visit almost every consulting engineering firm in Winnipeg and observe their operations in person. While at their offices, my eyes were scanning everything—every single space, person, and piece of paper lying around—for blueprints, letters, number of personnel, office layout, and amount of work on their boards. Sometimes I even overheard telephone conversations. I have an excellent memory and still have much of the information in my head that I gained on these visits. Inadvertently, I was checking out my future competition's operations from the inside.

At Johnson, we had a computer program that tracked every job quoted. After tender, we'd enter our price, also the competition's price, and the identification of the successful mechanical contractor and consulting engineer. At year-end in both 1988 and '89, I printed a summary and discovered that, according to my calculations, Honeywell was losing money. I could also see how many projects my future competitors (other engineers) were designing.

Even after my first full year with Johnson, I could see that I was making a serious dent in Honeywell's profit—or lack thereof. Since Gary was still working there, this added fuel to the fire for my second year. How could I start putting more nails in his coffin—faster?

You may be wondering what the hell fueled this maniacal desire for retribution. Well, here's how I think of it. After flunking out of engineering at university, I just *had* to work harder and graduate; once I did, that was my redemption at the Ivory Towers. Then, because I was fired within sixteen months of my first full-time job, I felt that I'd let my parents down—again. I needed some type of redemption for the Honeywell letdown, so basically that's how I dealt with it—I worked harder than ever to make Gary know that he'd made a big mistake by firing me. Nowadays, I just let the universe unfold as it should and wait to see how people who intentionally screw me get their payback as a result of their own stupid actions. I refuse to waste my energy on any of that revenge-type shit. There are too many good things, especially my family, to focus my energies on.

Chapter 12

Moving Forward

After living with the same six people in the same house for more than two decades, my small space seemed to be shrinking with every passing minute. I was twenty-six years old and pulling in a good salary. It was time to move out of my parents' home.

In December 1988, I purchased a flat in River Heights in a new complex built of concrete and steel, complete with a pool and a duck pond. The place was 700 square feet, with one bedroom and a balcony. I had a nice-sized down payment, about $15,000 from my strict savings regimen, so the mortgage was only about $30,000. My father had instilled in me at an early age the importance of being frugal, so saving money has been really easy for me throughout my life. (*Thanks for that one, Pops!*) With minimal payments and a small monthly common fee, I was now set. The place had previously been an apartment, and I had to wait a month while the tenant, an older woman, moved out. As it turned out, the woman was the aunt of a fellow classmate in engineering who was also a Honeywell coworker. (Winnipeg is a small city.)

The first day of possession Laurie, my mother, and I went to the place in the early evening. It was yellow (smoke-damaged from chain-smoking), the carpet was stained, and the flooring was beaten up, to say the least. I had brought one tool: a utility knife with a new, sharp blade. Within minutes I started to carve up the carpet into strips. Laurie and my mom thought I was crazy. Hey, I couldn't live in someone else's dirt!

We managed to rip out all the carpet, and since the condo was on the second floor, I threw all the shredded carpet pieces off the balcony and into the BFI bin below. The precast concrete floor looked much better than the carpet had.

The building was only ten years old at the time but wear and tear had really taken its toll on the units. It took Laurie and me one month to renovate the place. With three thousand dollars' worth of new flooring, countertops and window coverings, and fresh paint throughout, the place looked just like the display suite we'd seen. I moved in, in January 1989, and purchased new furniture and artwork. The flat was now a cool pad. So I was set: good job, new car, new place, and the best girlfriend ever.

— ¤ —

Meanwhile, at Johnson Controls I was taking on more responsibility as a salesman. The senior salesman was looking to move back to his home province of Ontario. He was offered a job as a branch manager in Hamilton. He stuck around for a few more months so I could make the transition into the senior sales position. After he left, I was the only commercial salesman at the branch. I would have to compete with Honeywell's sales team of Gary, Gord, and my replacement, Darrell— three to one. Not fair? You bet, but I love a challenge.

And so my second year at Johnson Controls began. I was no longer the chief cook and bottle-washer. I was joined by a system-designer, a project manager, and a part-time AutoCAD drafter. This setup provided me with more freedom to concentrate on quoting the larger projects and on writing more control-system specifications for the consulting engineers.

One of the larger projects at the time was the new Winnipeg Free Press Building on Mountain Avenue in Winnipeg's North End. The newspaper had been located downtown in an old and outdated building, the very place where I had dropped off my film of the transformer disaster in 1984. Here was one great opportunity for me to write the control specification and to try to secure a base-bid specification so

Honeywell would have to fight tooth-and-nail to obtain an approved equal from the consultant. (A base-bid is when only one manufacturer is allowed to bid the job, but the other manufacturers may be approved "equal" by the consultant prior to tender-close.) If Honeywell were to get the job, its price would have to be dirt cheap. (I could be such a vindictive bastard. In those days I took everything personally. Nowadays I just don't give a rat's ass, mainly because I've finally figured out that, in the end, it's really not my problem—it's the other guy's.)

The year was 1989, the economy was slowing down, and large multi-million dollar projects in Manitoba were few and far between. A job like this could help a salesman win awards, gold rings with diamonds, maybe even a nice Caribbean vacation! Though I didn't care too much about the bonuses, here was a chance for Johnson to get a big job, the kind that Honeywell secured nearly all the time. I was hell-bent on showing Gary that Honeywell should have signed me up for a lifetime contract.

Fortunately, the engineering company that designed the new Free Press Building was the Austin Group from Toronto, Ontario. If it had been a local engineer, you could have bet on Honeywell securing the base-bid with their written spec. The Johnson Controls branch in Toronto had a great relationship with Austin, so I got a local salesman there to pay them a visit and write up the specs.

So the specs were written, tender documents went out, and the excitement on tender day was driving me crazy. I had worked on the estimate during the week and on weekends, to make sure I had an airtight price so that when the time came, I could blow Honeywell out of the water. Phone bidding started in the morning, and I put out my price early so I could determine which mechanical contractors were shopping my price. It's kind of funny that most contractors didn't know I had a system of determining who was shopping our price, when actually I knew every contractor who was screwing us. (Mind you, they'd lie to my face if I brought it up to them.) So, this time, I used these assholes to help me secure this job. I was quoting higher prices to them than to the honest mechanical contractors, to be sure that Honeywell would have the wrong price, one higher than ours. A tangled web of deceit, I know, but one I had the knack for.

Sometimes the controls quote could help a mechanical contractor secure a project if we gave him preferential pricing. That happened on this job. The best part came even before the tenders closed. I received a phone call from Gary. Yes, believe it or not, my old Honeywell boss called me and begged me to give him the job, so he could beat his year-end quota. He had the nerve to say that I owed him because he taught me everything I knew. He also promised me that I would get the next big job. What a loser, calling me up after firing me a year and a half before, for no reason. I told him that my parents raised me to be honest (true!) and I would not cooperate with his price-fixing scenario.

The happenings that day just confirmed all along that Gary would do almost anything, dirty or not, to get a job. This time I caught him in the act. That was a good feeling, even though the real duty of the day was to secure a large project for JCL.

We ended up with a purchase order for the controls. The price was around $250,000, a fair sum for a controls contract. This was my baby, and I processed the paperwork, designed the controls, ordered the material, and ran the job till it finished. This was my proudest accomplishment while at Johnson Controls. I proved to Dan, the branch manager, that I could close a large project without his help. Going that extra mile to prove my worth to the company and to myself, and wanting acceptance and praise for a job well done, was important to me back then. Maybe most employees strive for the same thing, or maybe I was constantly trying to impress whatever authority figure was in my life at the time. (A hangover from my relationship with my father? Perhaps. It would take a thousand therapists to think that one through.)

— ¤ —

In life, shit seems to find a way of happening. During the last six months at Johnson, things started to derail. I had now found out new meaning in Ozzy's song "Crazy Train." Dan had very poor personal skills. He rarely said a kind word, and put his employees down nearly every day. For the most part I ignored his condescending behavior because I needed the money—and the learning experience. You know, pay your dues.

In July 1989, everyone quit. Our project manager left to attend the University of Manitoba to study Education, our system-designer took a job at Honeywell, and our part-time drafter started school and didn't return. Now I was back in my old position in the small-business unit, but in addition, I was doing the work of four people. I was the small-business guy, the senior salesman, the system-designer, and the project manager. I didn't have any time for AutoCAD drafting, so I sent the drafting out to either the Edmonton or Calgary branch, and had a student come in to assist with drafting whenever he could. This was the start of six months of HELL—so different from my life six months earlier.

I immediately told Dan to hire new staff to replace everyone who'd left. He was a cheap son-of-a-bitch and delayed hiring people to make his bottom line look good. At that time, I was working nonstop, suffering headaches from the stress, and taking six or so painkillers a day just to make it through the workday. My head would start to pound around lunchtime, and got worse when I arrived home at the end of the day. Every morning when I pulled into the parking lot, I felt sick to my stomach. The manager (who didn't even have an engineering degree) would criticize my work and generally nitpick about everything. To this day, I still can't figure out his negative attitude.

It was at this time that my killer instinct seemed to disappear. It was impossible to please or even minimally satisfy Dan, so I figured it was better for me just to hide in my shell for my own protection until the storm passed over—which really meant until Dan was fired.

During the previous few months, Dan had pissed me off so badly that I'd called George, the Canadian president of JCL, at his home in Toronto. It must have been a particular instance of Dan insulting my intelligence that set me off. I explained to George that Dan was a poor manager and that he left me in tears of frustration every day. In fact, I think I may have been crying when I spoke with George on the phone.

He must have taken my call seriously because he informed me he would drop by to see Dan at the branch in a few days. His word was good: he showed up and tore a strip off Dan. He spoke with me briefly prior to his departure and said that Dan needed some coaching. I thought: *Wow, things are finally going to improve.*

Dan was nice for about a week, but then he was back to his old self. Now my patience was wearing thin. I'd worked for two years like a dog, with no recognition of any kind. I knew Honeywell was now hurting, but so was I. Mentally, I was drained.

There was one last large job out for tender. It was for the Agriculture Canada Research Lab in Brandon, a two-hour drive west of Winnipeg. It was to be tendered through the Manitoba bid depository, which meant no price-shopping and low bid gets the job. I told Dan that I was going to get this job. I worked the weekend of the Grey Cup (the Canadian Football League's Super Bowl) and watched the game, surrounded by blueprints and twenty-five or more estimate sheets on my crowded table. But I did it. I knew I had the right price—somewhere around $550,000. That would do it: I would get the gold ring, become a member of "Club d'Excellence," have gold-embossed business cards, and receive a free trip to some exotic location!

One hour before the bids had to go in, Dan reviewed my oh-so-accurate bid and bumped the price up by $5,000. When the bids were opened, we were only $2,000 higher than Honeywell! Dan had screwed me. How bloody close can one be to having the right price? When I saw him later, he made light of it, saying, "On jobs like these, you just throw a dart at it," and mimicked throwing a dart. What an asshole. That was it. *This branch manager knows jack shit about sales,* I thought. *What the hell am I doing here?* In that one bungled deal, everything I'd learned about sales was thrown out the window by this jerk.

I knew then that my remaining time at the company was limited. Things dragged on for a few more weeks, up until I got ill because of the pressures from the previous few months. In the second week of December 1989, I was at home sick when Dan called me and said, "You're not sick. Get your ass to work now. You have a job closing." I could not believe what I was hearing. I calmly hung up the phone and never returned to work at JCL.

Did I quit? Was I fired? Was it job abandonment? Whatever. I just couldn't take the frustration and abuse any longer. I was only concerned with my health, and no amount of money was worth it to work at the Winnipeg branch of Johnson Controls.

The following Sunday evening, there was a clear night sky, a faint breeze, and the ground was covered with freshly fallen snow. Laurie and I drove to the branch office. To my surprise, the locks and alarm code were unchanged. *Did Dan actually think I was coming back? That I needed that lousy job?* Anyway, in about five minutes, we cleaned out my office of all my stuff and loaded the boxes into my car. A beautiful evening to remember.

That was the end. Dan sent me some registered letters, threatening that I would be fired. *Fired? Was he sane? Did he think he was God?* Someone needed to help this man.

— ¤ —

Laurie was a great support to me at that time (and always was, no matter what the situation). She had moved into my condo in the fall of 1989, needing some freedom from the walls of her mother's house. She had been spending more and more time at my place anyway. And after living with six other people while growing up, I hated being alone—the silence killed me. Her company was exactly what I needed. She and I had our share of spats but most of the time they were just plain stupid. One of my friends, Laurence Rosenberg, used to call us "the Bickersons."

Laurie really hated my working at JCL because I would always complain about Dan. So ending my time there was good for our relationship too. We spent lots of time together, shopping and socializing. She was working for Nygard at the time, and things were going well for her. She was really proud of the condo, and all her friends seemed to envy her.

So, contrary to my professional life, my private life was great. Christmas 1989 with my family was a healing time. No work pressure, no worries, a big load off my shoulders. A new year was just around the corner. It was time to turn my life around.

Chapter 13

Learning to Fly

January 1990—a new beginning, another chance to carve out some success in the work world. My first two attempts had bombed, but they were behind me. I was determined to find a way out of the destructive job jungle I'd been struggling in. But first, a detour . . .

On December 31, 1989, Laurie and I, along with my sister Susan and her boyfriend Jason, went skating and tobogganing at St. Vital Park. On my first ride down the toboggan run, I hyperextended and broke my left pinkie finger. If you've ever injured a digit, you know about the pain, and the prolonged healing period. New Year's Eve was a bust. Four painkillers later, the year started.

— ¤ —

After I'd left Johnson Controls, I had applied for UI (unemployment insurance) and was accepted. (Back in those days, it didn't really matter how you became unemployed; if you paid into the system, you were covered.) So I thought that at least I'd have some sort of guaranteed income for 1990. I never did collect because I got a job before the eight-week waiting period was up.

My dad still owned the rooming house on Balmoral and it needed a fire-alarm system installed. The City of Winnipeg had passed a new bylaw for rooming-house life-safety upgrading. Unbeknownst to me, my father was having financial difficulties at the time. That may have been the reason he hadn't yet installed a fire-alarm system in the rooming house, a little slip in procedure that resulted in his having to attend bylaw court. When he asked for my help, I jumped in to assist. I reviewed the bylaw and proceeded to provide the required drawings and obtain permits for the installation. I then ordered all the equipment—conduit, wiring, and the like—and installed the system with my brother Robert. I saved my father the $2,000 he'd have paid an electrician. It was the least I could do, being an unemployed bum-of-a-son at the time.

The work was fun, physical, and required a bit of brainwork. It gave me the idea of starting a company that could do this work for other rooming houses. I proceeded to market my service. The problem was that the balance of rooming houses that needed fire alarms were owned by slum landlords. Not much business in that black hole of greed. (This was my first big lesson in being an entrepreneur. More on that later . . .)

Near the end of January, I received a call from Wardrop Engineering for a job interview. It was for a six-month contract, writing commissioning manuals on the temperature-control system for Limestone Generating Station. I got the job and started work in early February at the Acres Engineering office. (Wardrop had partnered up on this project with Acres.) Three of us shared an office overlooking Portage Avenue across from the University of Winnipeg.

I jumped into the project like a wildcat and wrote five commissioning manuals, one for each part of the station—all in three weeks, even though I had three months to complete the task. When I asked for more work, they gave me some small, boring tasks to complete, which I churned out in record time. Out to prove myself again, I guess, but also, I honestly enjoyed working hard. I think everyone was shocked by the speed of my work. I may have made a few engineers at Acres look really bad and these guys resented me. No apologies from me though; being quick and thorough was the only way I knew how to get things done.

Working at Acres was awesome. Most coworkers were pleasant, coffee breaks were mandatory, nothing was rushed, overtime was paid, and I was treated like a human being. It was quite different from what

I'd experienced at Honeywell and Johnson. *Was this what an engineering job was supposed to be like?*

During my six-month stay at Acres, I still worked weekends on my side-business of installing fire-alarm systems in rooming houses. One time my brother and I installed a system in a rooming house on Banning Street for a guy named Ben. The deposit check was cashed, no problem, but the check for the final $2,000 bounced. I knew that Ben lived on Centennial Street in River Heights because I'd gone to his place to get the contract signed. It was a cool house, built in the late '50s: a four-level split, open plan, really funky, with a studio to boot. It was in need of a total gut-job, but it had potential. When I went back to his house to see him about the check, the only thing I saw was a For Sale sign on the front lawn.

I managed to track this goof down by calling his parents. They told me he had moved to an apartment downtown. I went to see him and we talked for about an hour, during which time he mentioned that his house was for sale, and said he thought that, as a single guy, he didn't need a house. *Yeah, right. Why would someone leave his home prior to selling it to move into an apartment?* I knew something was up. I left with *another* bloody rubber check and went back to his house to take another look.

The real estate agent's pager number was displayed on the sign, so I called him. He told me the house was a mortgage foreclosure. The asking price was $72,900. I found out that Ben had paid $99,999 for the home one year earlier. I phoned my father and told him about the deal.

My dad and I went to the house that evening, during a downpour. He told me to buy the place, even though we couldn't perform a thorough inspection. The next day I bought the house, for $66,000. (The agent couldn't understand why I didn't want to see the inside.)

So, as it turned out, that guy who tried to screw me tipped me off to a great deal. And I did receive my final $2,000 for the fire alarm. I contacted the people at the financial institution that held the mortgage on his rooming house and told them if I wasn't paid in two hours, I was going to rip out all the fire-alarm components I had installed. They told me that would be illegal, so I said, "Try me." A check was waiting for me within two hours. Heck of a deal—I got my money *and* a new "beat-up" home.

I took possession of 639 Centennial Street on my twenty-eighth birthday, June 30, 1990. My condo was only a two-minute walk from the house, a nice short distance while I was doing the renovations. Unknown to me at the time, this would be M^2 Engineering's first office.

My normal workday ended at 4:30 p.m. at Acres. Since I didn't take my work home (in the literal sense), I was free to immediately start the home renovations—a complete gut job. All my time spent watching *This Old House* on TV finally paid off.

The house had a partial basement with only a five-foot ceiling height. The place had sunk at least four inches in the northeast corner, and badly needed some structural work first. By a fluke, my neighbor across the street, Kent Johnson, was a structural engineer. He saw that renovations had started and came over. I guess he was wondering who his new neighbor was and what I was up to. I introduced myself and Laurie, and asked for his advice on the problem. It took him only five minutes to figure it out: "Install three two-by-tens nailed together; install them in two places with four teleposts." Holy shit, five hundred dollars' worth of advice for free—and he even lent me his five-ton bottle jacks for lifting the corner of the house!

Knowing that this was a job for others, I enlisted the help of two of my relatives from Poland, recent immigrants, who were strong enough to do the work. In only a few days I'd rented a Hilti portable handheld jackhammer and purchased all the lumber. Within one day the house was made level, for only $750. Eight years later when I put it up for sale, the house still had not sunk even an inch. Not bad for a bunch of us Polacks.

The process continued with new drywall installed throughout, new electrical devices, new plumbing fixtures, thirty gallons of paint and primer, and new wall-to-wall flooring. We also cleaned up the yard, trimmed the trees, and planted grass seed. (The yard was nothing but mud when I bought the place.) All this work was done in two months with the help of two friends and my Laurie.

The place looked new, and of course I took pictures during the process. Some people at Acres said the house should be featured in the *Homes* section of the *Winnipeg Free Press*. Total cost of the renovations was $20,000. I didn't worry about the money, thinking I had a job for at least another ten years. The new dam we were working on at Acres, Conawapa, was to be built in conjunction with Ontario Hydro and the agreement had been signed. I figured that I'd be "in the money" and could afford this investment.

Laurie and I moved into the house in September 1990, feeling confident that the condo would sell. And normally all would have been well, but at that time there was a glut of homes for sale and I wasn't able to sell it. The sad part was I'd already paid off $25,000 in two years and couldn't benefit from the equity. Plus my credit cards were maxed out from the renovations. In addition, I had to pay my income tax in a lump sum because, as a contract engineer at Acres, I didn't have a regular system of deductions and benefits. Yeah, I'd gone over my head with the home renovation—but at least I'd done the job right!

— ♮ —

Honing my skills as Mr. Do-It-Yourself during the renovations was great, but surviving the process was another matter. At a Hamfest in North Dakota the previous summer, I'd purchased a Heathkit SB1000 linear ham-radio amplifier kit. This amplifier would add punch to my radio signal, and I was up to the challenge of building the kit. Things went well. I soldered the components on the circuit boards, assembled the chassis, wired all the switches, and installed the transformer and tube.

One coiled wire, which acted as a radio-frequency choke, led from the tuning inductor to the top of the tube. This was the last part I needed to finish the kit. I had run out of the heavier-gauge wire, so I used the lighter-gauge wire supplied with the kit, all the while wondering if the wire would get too hot. Anyway, here comes the stupid part . . .

I turned on the amplifier and, without the case on, I pushed in the safety switch on the chassis with my left hand. Then with my right hand I touched the wire . . . *Oouuchhhhhhh*. Five thousand volts of electricity surged into my right index finger, through my heart, and out my left middle finger. What a moron; I knew better. *Jesus!* I couldn't feel my hands. It was like they were on fire, buzzing. I looked at my fingers. *Whew*, they were all still there. I went downstairs to the sink, and for some crazy reason, ran my fingers under ice-cold water. I couldn't feel them for over an hour and I thought for sure they had permanent damage. The tip of my right finger looked like a bullet had hit it and the tip of my left finger looked like it had been sliced open with a razor blade. Luckily, I'd been building the amp on the second floor. If I'd been in the basement, the floor would have acted like a ground, and I may have been more seriously hurt, maybe even fried! (I still have the fuse that may have saved my life.)

Six months prior to this accident, I'd read a story in a ham-radio magazine about a ham who'd been adjusting a linear amplifier in his basement when something went terribly wrong. His runners melted to the floor, his watch melted to the bone, and one of his ears melted off his head. Needless to say, this poor guy didn't stand a chance and he died. The thing was that I knew better; I was just a stupid jerk. I learned an immediate respect for electricity that I have retained to this day.

Anyway, I had been alone at the time—we still had not yet fully moved in to the house. I walked back to the condo, my hands covered in blood, to face Laurie. She asked me what the hell had happened. I lied and said I'd cut my hands on the rain pipes at the house. A few hours later, when I finally regained the feeling in them, I confessed the truth to her. Poor woman—a little taste of what was in store for her as my life's companion. (Oh yeah, I photographed my burned fingers just as a reminder —in case I ever decided to do something stupid with electricity again.)

— ¤ —

My six-month contract with Wardrop Engineering ended and they offered me a full-time job at their office, but the position was mostly a technician's job, which was of no interest to me. Then, I found out by a stroke of luck that Acres had just been awarded the design for a three-unit, hydroelectric generating station in Uganda. That was great for me—they offered me a six-month contract to work with the Winnipeg team as an electrical engineer. That one I took.

The fact that I slid into this job smoothly pissed off a few of the other electrical engineers at the firm who were not asked to work on the project. Like I said before, I work hard and fast, the way I was brought up to do, and I guess for some at Acres, "warming the pine" was the norm. Hey, I just didn't know better.

They shipped me from the sixth floor down to the fourth floor so the entire project team would be together. Things went smoothly and I did the required work without incident. I liked the fact that I had my own CAD drafter, Derwin (who later became one of my employees), and a secretary who would type all my specifications and letters.

During the project, three engineers from Uganda Power were in the office so they could be in on the design and then be able to supervise the construction in Uganda. They were nice, quiet men, extremely polite, although I think the experience of being in our in-your-face culture was a total shock for them.

After that job, Ron Garden, head of the electrical department, asked me to write the preliminary electrical-design criteria for the Conawapa Hydro Station. The time from conception to final commissioning of a ten-unit hydroelectric generating station is about ten years. *Perfect*, I thought, *a guaranteed job for ten years. Let's see . . . average salary of $50,000 per year over ten years . . . that'll be $500,000. I'll be almost a millionaire!* Yeah. Well, sometimes things don't go as planned.

With a few months to go on that contract, bad news hit. Ontario Hydro canceled its deal with Manitoba Hydro, which meant that Conawapa would not be constructed. My time was up. Within a week of the announcement, Ron advised me I should be looking for another job. What a bummer. I'd just spent $20K on home renovations, owed another $6K to Revenue Canada for taxes, and a recession was around the corner. To say the least, I was pissed off—and worried.

On my last day in January 1991, the electrical department took me out for a seven-dollar lunch and gave me a card signed by them all. No gifts or tearful goodbyes, just a punt out the door.

Acres would get really good at punting over the next few years because Canada was on the doorstep of a recession. This was the first of a wave of layoffs there, which I think got the staff worried as well. Some staff were transferred to Wardrop, even some long-term, twenty-years-plus guys. This was a really bad deal for them because as soon as they moved over to Wardrop, they were out the door there as well. I felt sorry for one guy especially: he had spent twenty-five years with Acres as an electrical draftsperson, was never late, did his work, and if he was sick, would take a day of holiday time instead. A model employee. He was sent over to Wardrop and then laid off permanently. He had never married, and took care of his ill mother. I really pitied the guy. It seemed that someone in the past had taken his soul.

Once my fingers were healed, I managed to get hired on with UMA Engineering in February 1991 to work in their electrical department on two Manitoba Hydro projects. This was also a term position, a week-to-week term. The coal-generating plants in Selkirk and Brandon were being modernized, and I was to be the engineer in charge of designing programmable logic controls to replace the mechanical controls, which were almost fifty years old.

UMA in Winnipeg must have had phenomenal growth in the late '80s; their building was filled to capacity with employees. By the time I started working there, the basement, which had been used for storage in the past, was full of work cubicles.

The cubicle I used was not even mine. I had to share it with a recent mechanical-engineering graduate. She worked in the field so I had the space to myself most of the time, but working in close proximity with this female presented its problems. What's a guy to do with a desk full of makeup, nail polish, and paperback novels? When she was in town we had to actually share this space. What an ordeal! I'd had my own desk and phone at my previous jobs, and now I had to share—and with a female, no less. (No offence to females, but this was way out of my comfort zone.) I'd have preferred a desk in the men's washroom or the hallway. (Hallway engineering—that has a nice ring to it, don't you think?)

We had to provide site visits to Selkirk and Brandon so we could determine the exact system conditions. The visits to Selkirk were day trips; with a travel time of only forty-five minutes, they were mostly uneventful. The two-hour trip to Brandon, though, was considered an overnighter. I guess the guys who worked there needed extra time to waste, but I would do my stuff in less than a day, so the second day I'd spend just snooping around the place. If you've ever visited a coal-generating station, you know that the technology used there in the mid-1900s was phenomenal. Most of the systems were mechanical, pure genius in design and execution. I was amazed by the size and height of the plant there, and really enjoyed visiting the tunnels under the station where the cooling water is directed from the water source to the generators.

Having a layover on this trip, I had some extra time to fill, time I could use to hatch up some new schemes—a bloody dangerous situation, as it turned out. One morning when I was eating breakfast poolside at the Red Oak Inn in Brandon, a newspaper item caught my eye. The city councillor in River Heights had resigned and a by-election was in the works. I got the brilliant idea that I should run in the election, and announced that to my coworkers. They all thought I was bullshitting, but people who know me well know that I'm not a bullshitter. Bullshitting is a waste of time and energy. I had sealed the deal when I announced it out loud. That's just the way MM operates.

I was different from these UMA employees, who were probably stuck in the belief that living a mediocre life, clutching onto conformity, and never sticking up for beliefs or voicing opinions was best. Some engineers I've known live their lives like this. In fact, as of today, three engineers I know who are in their forties still live with their moms. This is something I can't understand: three midlife, virginal men still attached to the umbilical cord. (Names withheld to protect their mothers.)

In the following weeks I was terminated at UMA because of a slowdown. I really pitied the engineering manager who had to give me the boot. I was called to his office over the PA system and I knew what was coming. But hey, I was going to be the new River Heights councillor—who needed that frikkin' job anyways? So I watched the manager sweat, shake, and mumble in broken speech as he fired me. I just said, "Yeah, okay," because I wasn't disturbed in the least—well, maybe a little when he told me I had to work out my final two weeks. The previous week I'd had nothing to do and had spent my time reading university textbooks left by my workstation partner—come to think of it, that was when I pretty much taught myself raw HVAC design—so I was pissed off that I had to work those weeks in order to get my pay. And I didn't much like the prospect of being the object of the buzz on the office grapevine. Everyone would figure that, seeing I was leaving after only two months, I must have been fired. I wanted to make my exit as quickly as possible. I went to the manager's boss and told him I wanted my two weeks' pay and then I would leave. When he refused, I found a cardboard box in the blueprint shop and packed up my stuff and left. (I was becoming a damn good escape artist.)

I knew I didn't have enough weeks of work to collect free money from the Government of Canada, so I felt justified in saying "Screw it." Besides, the sooner I got out, the sooner I could start my election campaign and get into a cushy position with a $40,000 per year salary. What the hell, engineering jobs were almost nonexistent in 1991, so maybe a career change would be just the ticket.

Chapter 14

Dancing On My Own

Sometimes being gullible and blind to reality is a protection—for a while. I really thought I could win that city election of 1991 and go on to become a local bigwig. Boy, was I a dreamer. Still, I had to try. I'd told those clowns from UMA that I would run, so I *had* to run. I'm just that way.

I hired Ralph Mayer, a boyfriend of one of Laurie's friends, to help me. Ralph was a graphic designer with all the new Mac computer gear, including a 1200-dpi laser printer—the best stuff in 1991. We did up two handouts stating my credentials.

I got the twenty-five signatures required to run for council by trudging through the snow in the bitterly cold weather of a no-spring April. I should have taken Mother Nature's hint not to waste my time; it was a battle just to get the stupid nominations! When I handed them in at City Hall, I learned I was the second candidate to qualify. Not a good omen—I don't like to be second at anything.

For over two weeks, I visited almost every home and apartment in the River Heights electoral area. My feet were dead, my body was sore, and I knew I was crazy. I met a lot of really nice people, especially on Wellington Crescent, mainly stay-at-home moms who loved to chat. I bet all my votes came from these women.

One of the female candidates had the support of a lobby group. Because of my naivety, I didn't know she had hundreds of volunteers and thousands of campaign dollars backing her. Her campaign headquarters was only fifteen houses away from my home at 639 Centennial. As you can imagine, my campaign team was a little sparser than hers. Laurie, my mother, and my Aunt Julie all helped me go door to door, to deliver my flyers and speak with the voters. It was tiring because that was my whole slate of volunteers: three people, and they were all just part-time. Most of my family and friends supported me and I really thought I had a chance. Stupid thing was that neither I nor the frontrunner, the woman, lived in the River Heights ward that we were running in. I did live in River Heights—but a block away from the boundary. That meant that neither one of us could even vote!

The woman candidate won the election by a landslide, with over a thousand votes. I was dead last with 203 votes. What a waste of $1,500 and three weeks of my life. I'm still not sure that I gained anything qualitative from the experience, at least not then. I was bitter: no money, no job, no nothing. I felt doomed.

It was now May 1991. I still owed Revenue Canada the $6,000 for back taxes, owed my sister Susan $5,000 for the house down payment a year earlier, had a Visa bill in the thousands, as well as many unpaid utility bills. The recession of the 1990s was upon me too: interest rates were hovering around 16 percent for mortgages and 20 percent for credit-card spending. Layoffs were happening across Canada, and of course construction was almost at a standstill. I sure could have made better use of the $1,500 I had flushed down that election toilet.

Seeing no city councillor paycheck would be coming my way, I needed to find work. I applied for the few entry-level jobs that were available. One was as an energy-audit technician and the other was as a meter technician. They each paid around $30,000 per year. I had been making $40,000 per year at Acres, and to take a pay-cut like that was demeaning.

I went for the interviews and realized that neither position was challenging enough for me. Minimal or no engineering experience was required, and they were more suited to technicians. The idea of going backwards in my career did not appeal to me, so I didn't take either job. I decided to tough it out on my own.

— ¤ —

I had no real plans to start an engineering firm, but I had to make some money so I wouldn't lose my house. The venture into self-employed consulting engineering was then actually a spur-of-the-moment idea. One of my best, as it turned out.

Once I'd made this decision, the name for my firm came to me really easily. When I worked at Honeywell, the secretaries called me "M-Squared" because of my initials. On all messages they would write M^2. I didn't want to use my name for my company title—too obvious. I wanted something unique, but simple and easy to remember.

I then hired Ralph, the commercial designer, to come up with a logo. For a measly two hundred dollars (which I probably didn't have at the time), he worked out a logo and the color and font for the text.

The logo is basically two squares, the outer one at an angle with the inner one offset from the outer. The idea was that, if you look carefully, you can see the letter M twice. The red color (actually pantone red) was neutral, and the font was Helvetica Bold at an angle—simple, meaningful, easy to remember, and, in my opinion, inspired and artistic. It remains the same today, other than I have changed the font of the lettering to mimic eBay's logo, one of my favorites. (I wish I had bought some eBay stock. I'd be off on a Caribbean island somewhere doing something other than writing this book!)

I set up a makeshift office in a bedroom off the kitchen at 639 Centennial. I purchased a Canon fax machine and used the new phone number I'd acquired for my less-than-glorious election-campaigning days. By May 1991, I had my logo, letterhead, envelopes, and business cards designed and ready to roll.

I had purchased a computer the month before while I was at the Dayton Hamfest, in Ohio, with my old childhood friend James. (Being with 30,000 crazy hams, wall-to-wall in the arena, buying stuff—that was cool, and crazy.) James and I had stopped by a computer-clone booth, and I was debating about whether to buy a radio or a computer. I didn't have a PC at the time and knew I was going to need one for my business, but US$900 was a lot of dough, especially for a Canadian. The machine was an Intel 386SX-16, with 2 meg of RAM and a 40-meg hard drive. This was almost the best machine at the time. It came with boot-legged DOS 5.0 and a thirteen-inch color monitor. There was no math coprocessor so I knew that any CAD program would run at a snail's pace. There was no mouse and no Windows—a dinosaur operating system—but you know what? I still use DOS today from time to time.

I knew that buying this computer would be a gamble. After all, these guys had even ripped off Bill Gates. (Impressive!) The cost of the machine was the equivalent to C$1,300, and would have been even more (about $2,000) if I'd bought it in Winnipeg. I knew I was almost maxed-out on my Visa and didn't know when I would be able to pay the machine off. Still, James convinced me to buy the thing by saying, "I guarantee that this purchase will provide a big payoff in the future and you'll thank me later in life." Done deal! I gave the vendor my Visa card and became the proud owner of my first PC. I lugged the stuff back to Winnipeg with all the other radio gear I had purchased.

Back at home, I set up the machine and started teaching myself DOS. I purchased a copy of WordPerfect for DOS for $100. Because I couldn't afford the $4,000 AutoCAD program, I was on the search for a low-cost CAD program.

By some sort of fluke, I ran into an old university buddy, Dean Weiten, who was working for a firm called Vansco. I mentioned that I was looking for a CAD program, really cheap. He had Generic CAD and said he would part with it for something like $50. What a deal; I'd struck gold—and for $50 I was running a CAD program. At that time, most consultants were still drafting on the board, but I have the worst, and I mean THE WORST, lettering and drafting skills. I needed this program so my drawings didn't look like chicken scratch on a napkin.

Seeing I'd learned AutoCAD at Johnson Controls, it was a breeze for me to come up to speed with Generic CAD. I also taught myself WordPerfect so I could produce neat and tidy drawings and my documents would not be covered in White-Out or Liquid Paper.

The next step was to find clients. I contacted the mechanical contractors I knew from my Honeywell and Johnson days. Some of these guys provided design-build installations for general contractors. (Traditionally, an architect and consultant designed the project. Design-build installations, meaning the mechanical or electrical contractors assisted with the designs, made more sense.) That would be a good place to start. I'd already developed a rapport with most of the mechanical trades in Winnipeg from my two prior jobs. They knew they could count on me for a price for every job, and if there was a problem with the installation, I could always rectify the situation in a timely manner. Plus they knew I was an engineer, which of course was a big asset.

The jobs required tight teamwork. Most HVAC drawings are required to be sealed by an engineer for a building permit. The mechanical contractors would have a concept and either draft it up themselves (or hire me for the drafting) and pay me to check and seal the drawings. I would then provide inspections and a letter of certification when the job was completed.

These guys always provided a good installation, and if there were any problems they would take care of it so as not to inconvenience the engineer. If they looked good, then the engineer looked good. With them, it really was a team effort, with a common goal at the end of the project.

I really flew by the seat of my pants back then. I'd never before worked in the capacity of a consultant who provided designs for electrical and mechanical commercial projects. To say that I didn't know what I was doing at the time would be correct, in a way. However, I had looked at or reviewed about eight thousand sets of plans during my tenure at Honeywell and Johnson, so I knew the basic design elements of electrical and mechanical work, and also which engineer's designs were in tune with the KISS method. (And I don't mean the rock band; I mean Keep it Simple, Stupid.)

Within about a week of starting my little business I received my first project. It was for John, who worked for the design builder, CB Builders. He'd gotten my name from a sheet-metal contractor. The job was a small maintenance garage. My total fee for the electrical and mechanical work was five hundred dollars. Nowadays, for a job like that I'd charge at least two thousand.

Word-of-mouth was working for me. John gave my name—and a recommendation, I assume—to the people at CB Builders. The next job was actually too big for me. It was for a renovation and addition to a golf-course clubhouse. Renovations have twice the difficulty of new construction, and this one was difficult to the max. I knew I needed more manpower than I myself could provide, so I hired Derwin, my CAD drafter at Acres, to do the electrical design and drafting. Derwin had worked for many years at other engineering firms as an electrical design/drafter and had lots of experience with commercial projects. I opted to do the mechanical design and drafting myself.

I did the preliminary site visits to determine what we had to work with. It was a nightmare—multi-levels, basement, change rooms, meeting rooms, commercial kitchen—a real mix of systems. For the plumbing, I went to my buddy Trevor who owned Community Plumbing & Heating, and he basically designed the plumbing for me. Necessary, because I had minimal experience in that area.

The deadline was impossible. Bob, the owner of CB Builders, needed everything done in five working days. Holy sheep shit, what a nightmare I'd gotten myself into! I didn't panic though. I called the architect and got the floor plans I needed for this hand-drafted job, and went to work.

I set up my workstation in the living room of my house with a drafting board that my father had bought for me during my university days. I worked on the mechanical design during the day. The carpet underneath got covered in eraser dust. I didn't expect Laurie to clean up that mess, so I vacuumed it up each day. I also spent two nights in a row working on the electrical design with Derwin at his house, which was a half-hour drive from my place. He was still working at Acres, so for him moonlighting started at 6 p.m. We didn't end until about 3 a.m., which was pure hell, at least for me. I had never worked that late, and I could barely function the following days. All that sweat equity paid off though; I did meet the deadline.

Still to this day I don't know how we pumped out something like sixteen hand-drafted drawings in only five days. I'm not sure I could do that today! The job was completed about a year later—under budget, and with only slight changes to our design. That job remains one of my proudest accomplishments from my early days as an entrepreneur. I guess I proved to myself that I could take on big jobs and succeed. *Whew!* It was a tremendous treat to attend my sister Susan's wedding reception at the same golf-course clubhouse one year later.

The third job, for Motor Coach Industries in Fort Garry, was also with CB Builders. The project was for a two-story addition and the renovation of an engineering R & D lab and office. Same deal as the previous one—five days, lots of hand-drafted drawings, and I met the deadline. This job was straightforward and was ultimately completed pretty much as I designed it. Fifteen years later, the building is still standing and I drive by it weekly when I take my kids skating on Sundays. For obvious reasons I still have a soft spot in my heart for that place.

Those early days were not without mentors. One was Bob, the owner of CB Builders. Even though he presented himself as gruff and demanding on the surface, he had a good heart and took me under his wing and helped to guide my career. I remember one thing he said after I had finished the two jobs for him: "You just made $7,000 in two weeks. One day you'll make over $200,000 in a year." I thought to myself, *What is this guy talking about? That will never happen.* Well, he was right; a hundred percent correct. How did he know this? At that time, I was just happy to make a living. He must have had laser perception or something to be able to see qualities in me that I hadn't yet realized.

I needed that $7,000 in a big way. I was barely making the mortgage payments, the Visa interest at 20 percent was killing me, and the utility companies were ready to cut me off. That cash would come in the nick of time. I got paid for one of the jobs right away, but the other payment was slow in coming. (At that time, I honestly thought that thirty-day terms meant that payment would be made within thirty days. I've come to discover that in this industry, thirty-day terms mean nothing—and if you try to charge interest for overdue accounts, the client laughs in your face.) Well, I needed to be paid for that work immediately. I called the payroll person at CB Builders asking that the company pay my bill. The person on the phone told me in a bossy, sharp voice that I'd made too many mistakes on the drawings and therefore I wasn't going to be paid. She must have thought she was an engineer, given the know-it-all tone she used with me. I was royally peed off. I immediately faxed her a letter stating that if I was not paid by the next day at noon, I would file a lawsuit in Small Claims Court. The next day came and I found myself at Small Claims Court doing exactly what I told her I would do.

I filled out the required paperwork and launched a lawsuit against the firm. For a one-dollar fee, I was able to look up the firm in the Province of Manitoba Company Registry, which showed all the owners, partners, and directors of the firm. So I sued all of them too. That payroll person with her pompous attitude caused ultimate shit for the owners of CB Builders. Remember, I told you that my word is good— if I say I'll do something, I *will* do it. No idle threats by Mike Mark.

By the time I got home at around two o'clock, a check for the whole amount was in my mailbox. I cashed the check and the next day I dropped the suit. However, it was mentioned in the Business & Law Digest the next week. That suit ended up haunting CB Builders years down the road, but that was nothing to me because my relationship with them had basically ended, thanks to that fiasco.

Chapter 15

A Guy's Gotta Eat

It was now the fall of 1991, and after banging out these few good-paying jobs for CB Builders, I had nothing on the boards. It was time to do some self-promotion. Ralph helped me make up an introduction portfolio, and with that I started to call on architects, design-build contractors, and HVAC contractors.

I actually wore a suit and tie for these visits—one of the last few times I ever did. One great thing about being my own boss now is that I wear what I like—Levi's jeans and semi-dress shirts without a tie. Oh yeah, no dress shoes either, just running shoes. This is my trademark now: no dressing up—ever. I work better in casual clothes. (I was ten years ahead of my time; many workplaces nowadays let their employees wear casual attire.)

At first, it was tough to break in with the architects. They had their usual consultants and I knew who they were from working at Johnson and Honeywell. I would call and make appointments, see the required person, make my sales pitch, and leave. I remember calling on architect Harold Funk in 1991. He was known as the Church Architect, having designed some phenomenal churches in and around Winnipeg (including the huge Immanuel Pentecostal Church on Wilkes Avenue with its distinctive blue roof). When I was younger, men like Harold were like gods to me because of their work. An even crazier thing is that some of them actually thought they *were* gods, or at least godlike. Anyway, after speaking with "the Funkster," I thought: *Well, I'll see ya never!* But as it turned out, in 1993 he actually gave me my first big job, designing the electrical systems for an apartment building, probably because my fee was almost free. (I learned early that to develop relationships and build up my portfolio, I had to almost give up on fees. You know—paying my dues.)

— ¤ —

During this time I was in a real cash-strapped mess. Laurie was working at Nygard making around $20,000 a year, although after Revenue Canada got finished with her, her take-home pay was about $14,000. Not much, if you ask me, but she was the one keeping us afloat. We managed not to miss a mortgage payment, but the utility bills were piling up. While Laurie was at work, I kept the house at 60°F and wore my winter jacket inside to keep warm. At night, I would shut the furnace off when we were sleeping, and the house would dip down to 50°F. The house had only R1 insulation and it cost a small fortune to heat. During the winter months, this routine was the pits. Laurie and I were freezing like a couple of popsicles in our own home.

I felt poor—dirt poor—and helpless. I'd grown up in Tuxedo, the upscale area in Winnipeg, had obtained an engineering degree, and I couldn't believe what the hell was happening to me. We did our laundry during this time at my parents' home at 518 Laidlaw Boulevard, which was only a two-minute drive from my place. We also did our "grocery shopping" there too. Four of my younger siblings were still living at home, so in their basement storage room my parents kept a huge stock of groceries—Kraft Dinner, crackers, and a variety of canned soups. I didn't realize it at the time, but my father was still having financial troubles, not to mention he was a diabetic and extremely ill. I feel pretty guilty today about how I mooched from my parents. Laurie's mother didn't help us out one bit, but my parents never once complained about helping us out with food when we were broke.

I couldn't collect unemployment insurance because at Acres I'd been hired on contract. They'd actually offered me $19 per hour on contract, or $15 per hour on payroll. *What—only $29,250 per year on salary? Forget it.* (After all, I'd been making $36,000 at Johnson Controls a few months earlier.) Yes, they got the best out of me, and gave back diddly-squat—no benefits, no Canada Pension Plan contributions, no unemployment contributions; nothing. I saved those cheapskates thousands of dollars because I wasn't hired on as an employee. Then when they let me go, I had nothing to fall back on. *Thanks guys; I work my ass off for you, and then you kick me out on the street.*

— ¤ —

During the Christmas holidays I called the provincial government's welfare department—this is true—and asked for assistance. The first question they asked was, "Do you own a car?" I said yes. "Then, sell it," was their response. *Thanks for nothing.* I'd paid income taxes for over twenty years, and the only time I tried to use some of the services I'd been paying for, I was told, basically, to screw off. And here I had thought that Canada was a socialist, caring place to live. Wrong!

I still owned that stupid condo. It was now rented, so I wasn't able to sell it to recoup my $20,000 equity. And I was really counting on selling it so I could repay all my debts—except my mortgage, of course—and have a little bit left for us to get by on for a while.

So I figured that, seeing our home showed so well, we could sell it instead. But there was the dilemma of where we would go. Because I had signed a one-year lease on the condo, we had nowhere else to live. Our only resort was my father's rooming house. It had a nice 450-square-foot, self-contained suite, the one I'd lived in during my first two years of life. I told Laurie that we could move into the suite if we sold the house. That was it, the best plan I could come up with: sell the house, move into a West Broadway rooming house, and spend our time having coffee and watching black-and-white TV with our new best buddies: nine other roomers on welfare. Wow, my life would be set! No air conditioning, a common front door, a musty basement, an old, only-sometimes-functioning boiler—and, of course, wild parties every weekend! Shit no, I just couldn't do that.

If we were going to hang on to our house, every penny counted. When we'd moved in, the year before, we'd managed to purchase a lousy old stove for $150 from a guy on Elgin Avenue and had borrowed a bar fridge from my father. Of course, we still had no washer and dryer; that's why we used the ones at my parents' place. At least I'd had the luck of finding a used math coprocessor for my computer for only $100, from a young computer geek in south St. Vital. Now my computer was like a rocket: fast on the takeoff. My CAD program was speeded up at least a thousand percent, or so it seemed to me.

During the marketing of my firm, I spent a lot of money on postage. But during the winter of 1991, Canada Post issued defective stamps. I don't know what type of coating they used on those stamps, but the ink from the Canada Post machine that canceled the stamps rubbed off on your fingers. By some fluke, I figured out this design flaw. So I collected the envelopes from every Christmas card Laurie and I received, removed the stamp, and reused it. When I asked my relatives for their envelopes too, they were all somewhat puzzled. I showed my grandmother what I was doing and she scolded me about being dishonest. (*Sorry, Granny; necessity dictates.*) Jim Pattison, a Canadian self-made billionaire, looks for quarters in payphones—and Michael Mark looks for uncanceled stamps on envelopes. (I guess we billionaires and potential billionaires are alike in our money-saving habits!)

— ¤ —

I had a depressing Christmas that year. It seemed like everything was going downhill. Work was almost nonexistent. I managed to get a few jobs with some small architectural firms and mechanical contractors by charging rock-bottom fees: between $500 and $1,250 for jobs I'd bill three to four times that amount today. Those contracts just barely kept the gas on. I was preparing for the worst—losing or selling the house, and maybe leaving Manitoba for greener pastures.

By some sort of magical power from above, I received a phone call in late December from Cy Howard, an engineer with the Manitoba government. Months before, I'd sent in a résumé for a position advertised in the *Winnipeg Free Press,* but had not been called for an interview. Apparently my résumé had been kept on file. (Hey, sometimes they don't lie!) Cy told me there was an opening in the maintenance department of Government Services for an electrical engineer and called me down for an interview. Pay dirt! After the interview, they offered me a two-month contract, but this time as an employee, making seventeen dollars an hour. Wow, this was my saving grace. There *was* a God! My house would be saved—at least for a few months.

I took the job and reported to work in January 1992 in my Sunday best—yes, suit, tie, and leather shoes. The year I'd spent in jeans was really good but, what the heck, I would put up with the dress code for those essential bucks.

The job entailed looking after the electrical systems in all provincially owned buildings and at a few leased sites. At least I would get to see some cool places that most people couldn't visit. I made sure I went to the top of the Legislative Building in downtown Winnipeg. I made my way up the spiral stairs and to the top where the famous Golden Boy stands. I opened the hatch and shot off two dozen pictures with my camera. I also remembered to bring a new, fat, felt marker, and I signed and dated my name on one of the steel dome supports near the top hatch. Now I really did have some political prominence—only in name, though.

I was a diligent employee, always on time and I never left early. My supervisor was a woman who was a mechanical engineer. She was a nice person with a somewhat reserved manner; soft-spoken and easy to get along with. She had been recently promoted, and I guess she didn't like being in management because a few months later she took a new job with the City of Winnipeg. This was unfortunately the Province's loss, but the City's gain.

I was starting to feel stifled, wearing a suit every day, but I was receiving a regular paycheck and could still run my own engineering practice at night and on weekends. I made it very clear to Mr. Howard that because I was only on a two-month contract I planned to keep up my private practice. I did not use government time for my business activities. I carried a pager with a personal greeting by a female employee of the paging company, which made my small business seem more legitimate. Some clients actually thought that the woman answering the call was my receptionist.

I went home for lunch every day. I couldn't afford to buy food in the cafeteria, so when I arrived home at 12:03 p.m. I would turn the heat up, make a sandwich, and return all my pager messages. My lunch break was the only time I could run my practice during normal business hours. This was tricky, as I normally would return pages within five minutes. So when clients asked, "What took you so long?" I'd say I'd been in a meeting. At home, the temperature never reached any higher than 65°F, so I'd go back to work to warm up.

At the end of my two-month term, Mr. Howard told me he was very satisfied with my performance and offered me another two-month term. I gladly accepted his offer and signed the required documentation. This was a happy day: two months more of paychecks! I was slowly paying off my debts and sending Revenue Canada some income tax money as well.

I met some really nice people at this job. One of my old university buddies, Dennis Krahn, a computer genius, was working there in maintenance on mechanical systems. A recent older graduate from Electrical Engineering, Brian Kautz, was also on staff. I signed some papers for Brian to help him obtain his professional engineering designation. He appreciated my help on this, but I thought nothing of it.

During my second contract, a recent male graduate from Mechanical Engineering replaced the female manager. I'll just refer to him as GB (Goof-Ball) from now on.

This guy, who was five or so years older than I was, received his degree later in life (four years after my graduation) and for some reason he figured his shit didn't stink. He'd been pointed out to me by one of the other employees prior to his becoming a manager. I was told he was an asshole and to avoid him as much as possible. I guess GB thought that because he was a graduate engineer he automatically deserved respect from the entire world, no matter how much of a jerk he was.

Nobody in the office liked GB and I suspect he knew that. When we had our weekly meetings, he pretty much gave all of us his negative attitude. Each meeting was an uncomfortable session, with him always criticising our work—like Dan at Johnson Controls did, but ten times worse.

With GB as our boss, I felt more uncomfortable with each passing day. It was not a happy place to work. You must understand that when working for the Government, office politics is part of the game. Most of the staff were looking for other means of employment in order to get out of Government Services. One employee actually had a clock that ran backwards. (You set the date and time of your retirement day, and the clock tracks the time you have left in your lousy job.) This guy was pathetic, hated his job, hated the staff, and probably hated himself. This was a wake-up call for me.

With GB present, the atmosphere was dismal. I was there only for the money. During the summer of 1992 (yes, my third and fourth contract extensions), we had a summer student who wore casual clothing —nice jeans, semi-dress shirt, and casual shoes. He looked pretty stylish and I felt that if this was okay for a summer student, it was okay for me. My youngest sister Heather was working part-time at the Gap clothing store in Polo Park. When there was a family-day sale, I thought I'd stock up on some Gap jeans and shirts for a 30 percent discount, buy some funky shoes, and start to wear that stuff to work. I knew I'd feel more comfortable and would then be more productive at work.

As soon as I started to wear the Gap fashions, GB took notice, and I don't think he liked it. I'm sure he had only one suit, but that was not my problem. I was not going to wear a suit to work again, and there was no dress code as far as I was aware.

During July and August that year, I spent most of my time at the new Provincial Remand Centre, a Tyndall-stone building with lots of glazing, located in downtown Winnipeg across from the Law Courts building. It was a new state-of-the-art correction facility designed by Gaboury Architects, and a far cry from the old jailhouse where the cells were in a dimly lit, musty basement that reeked of body odor years after the inmates had departed.

I was commissioned to check the entire electrical system with the help of one of the staff electricians. This was great: I was out of the office, not wearing a suit, and able to explore every nook and cranny of a high-security environment with guards and locked doors all around. I had tons of freedom—and also found numerous electrical problems, which we were able to remedy.

The one irritating thing about working at the new Remand Centre was that they wouldn't give me a parking pass. Since I didn't want to charge the taxpayer for parking, I found a Johnson Controls decal and put it on the dash of my car. This sticker was big, about six by twenty-four inches. The parking commissionaires thought I was a service technician, and in this way I was able to park on site and at other locations for free. I saved the Government at least two hundred dollars in parking costs. I learned this trick from a Johnson Controls technician who did it all the time, and his car was never towed.

The most rewarding part of my time there was helping a young, deaf summer student learn Generic CAD. Since the department was on a tight budget and AutoCAD still cost around $4,000 (plus, earlier in the year, the department had been busted for copying software), I recommended they purchase Generic CAD 6.0 for him. They took my advice, and in a few days, he was up and running, and doing drafting for some of the staff. He wrote me a letter after I left, thanking me for taking the time to lend a hand. That was all the payment I needed.

Around this time, I sealed HVAC drawings relating to a tenant improvement in a strip mall, for a plumbing and heating contractor based out of Portage la Prairie, Manitoba. The mall had been built by CB Builders; the tenant was Manitoba Crop Insurance. One day, GB called me into his office and pulled out the sealed drawings for this job (in rural Manitoba), and asked if it was my seal. Well, no shit; it was my name: M.J. Mark. He went on to say that I had used my position with the government to get the work and was therefore in a conflict of interest position. *Now, why would I risk my job for the lousy $500 I charged for that project anyway?* He said he was going to fire me, but suggested I resign instead. He tried to get me to admit he was right, but I'm not a liar and I refused on principle. *To hell with you,* I thought. *Why would I resign when I have another month on my contract?* Even though the job was not the most enjoyable, I still needed the money. That cheap bugger wanted me to resign so he wouldn't have to pay my contract out.

I immediately went back to my workstation and made a call to the Office of the Ombudsman. They faxed me the conflict of interest guidelines. I reviewed the document and determined I was not in a conflict of interest: I had not used my position with the Government to obtain any work, nor for any personal, financial, or other gain. GB was either jealous or wanted to shove his weight around since he had just received his professional designation.

I knew I was not in the wrong, and there was no way I was going to make my departure easy for that jackass. I found some boxes, packed up my stuff, and went home. My coworkers near my workstation couldn't believe their eyes. "Yup, I've been fired, so I'm going home," I told them. It took five minutes and two trips to my car to put that workplace and that pathetic boss behind me.

I spent the next few days at home, but GB wasn't finished with me. He left numerous messages on my pager, sent registered mail, and had government employees wait in front of my house to drop off letters to me personally. I avoided the drop-offs for a while, but then I just accepted the stuff at the door. The letters stated that I would be guilty of job abandonment if I didn't show up for work. What a pack of crap! He had told me I was going to be fired unless I resigned. Since I didn't resign, to my mind it was plain and simple—I had been fired.

However, I decided to show up at work at the Remand Centre a few days later so I wouldn't be fired for job abandonment. When GB found out I was there, he immediately came down and had me escorted out of the building by armed guards. I had brought along a pocket tape recorder, and just before he started speaking to me, I held the machine up to his face so I could record his every word, in case I needed it in court. I forget what he said, but I know I still have this recording, even though I don't plan on listening to it anytime soon—too many bad memories.

I then went down to the Manitoba Government Employees Association, the union a person automatically joins when hired by the province. I thought this would be a good opportunity to make the dues I had paid work for me. I explained to the receptionist (in a heated way, I suppose) what had happened and said that I wanted severance pay. I was told later by the worker assigned to me that a note on my file indicated I had been rude to the receptionist. (*Well, sorry to those who have no stress in their lives and can only deal in niceties. Excuse me for living in the real world, Ms. Civil Servant Receptionist.*)

In spite of all that hassle, my caseworker was nice and helped me out. I had a meeting with her, the personnel manager, and GB. I knew that those three government-types were in cahoots, but this was about money for me, and nothing else. I did manage to get a couple of thousand from them, as well as an honorable discharge—just like in the Army. (And I made good use of the severance package money: in December, I took Laurie to Hawaii for a week and had a fine time lazing in the sun, happy that I had stood up for my rights.)

The story about GB is not over. I did not like the treatment I received from him and, as I've likely demonstrated already, in those days I needed to see that those who were bloody unfair to me got paid back. I'm not sure why I was that way. Maybe it was wounded pride, maybe it was a sense of moral justice, or a combination. Whatever the reason, I looked for an opportunity to repay GB. I'm a bit ashamed now to admit that I pulled a few political strings—after all, I was from a family in Tuxedo with Progressive Conservative allegiances, and the premier of Manitoba was our MLA. I wrote a few letters and lobbied as hard and effectively as I could. Needless to say, GB was no longer working for the government a few months later. There's a saying: "Treat people the way you want to be treated." GB obviously got what he wanted!

Maybe I'd just been unlucky with the supervisors I'd had in my previous jobs. Maybe these people were never properly trained to be managers. Or maybe they were threatened by my work ethic or the fact that I was smarter than they were. I guess I was just not cut out to be supervised by these boneheads. Whatever. It was becoming more and more obvious to me that being on my own was the only way to go!

Chapter 16

No Looking Back

In October 1992, I was officially self-employed. It was time to seriously work on M² Engineering full-time and make a go of it.

First, I made a few improvements to my bedroom office. I purchased two cheap tables for forty dollars each at Office Depot, bought a used leather chair from a ham-radio buddy, and installed shelving for my books and manufacturers' binders. I also had a little M² Engineering sign made and put it in the bedroom window.

There was no looking back. And since I could collect unemployment insurance while still applying for jobs, I really had nothing to lose.

I look back on that decision to strike out on my own as one of the best I've ever made. It had been coming for a long time. Working for others, as you've likely figured out by now, had been a total bust. Either they were crazy or control freaks, or I was unmanageable. (I prefer to think that *they* were the lunatics.) I'd also been presented with a few opportunities to partner up, but these were dead ends too. One of those had occurred back in March or April of 1992 while I was still on contract with Government Services. I received a phone call at home from an acquaintance who owned a small consulting engineering firm in Winnipeg. Dave Balderman (not his real name) and his other partner, Bill, were looking for the right person to build up their firm, and he asked if I would be interested. I like to be open-minded, so I said I would meet with him at his office the following Saturday morning.

His office was a small, dingy place above a Chinese restaurant in downtown Winnipeg. The temperature in the office was just above freezing, and he was using a small portable electric heater from the '60s to heat the room we met in. The furniture must have been from World War II, and there was no carpet (or maybe it was just so worn that it looked like tile). What a mess—books and dust everywhere; not exactly the image of a successful business. (And remember, I'd seen the insides of most engineering firms in Winnipeg.)

Hey, I had nothing to lose, right? *Wrong!* I knew from the engineers' grapevine that his firm was a revolving door for young engineers. In fact, I knew two of their most recent partners—and they'd quit and gone to work for UMA and Manitoba Hydro. Bill was about my age, a mechanical engineer and someone I could probably partner up with, but Dave presented the problem.

Dave was in his mid-50s, short, white as a ghost, with a shiny, bald head and a whiny, high-pitched voice. (I wondered if he could have had any girlfriends in his younger years.) He made his case, stating that his firm was financially stable and times were good. He mentioned that he did not work for architects and preferred to work for building owners. (My business philosophy at the time was to work for everyone.) He told me I would have to quit my government contract and close M^2 Engineering. *Fat chance!* Still, I thought I'd check his offer out. My only demand was that I be guaranteed $50,000 minimum per year. Balderman said he couldn't guarantee that amount, which pretty much helped me to make up my mind on the spot. I thanked him and Bill sincerely for the opportunity to meet with them, shook their hands, and left. I didn't have to put my coat on because I hadn't even taken it off.

The next week, Dave called me at home and asked when I would be starting with them. I told him I was flattered that he called, but if he couldn't meet my salary expectations it would be a no-go. He was totally shocked that I rejected him—the shithead took it personally. He said I was making the biggest mistake of my life. And he must have lain in wait to make sure that was true, because years later he wrote a report on one of my designs, resulting in my engineering license being suspended and my having to pay $9,000 in fines. I bet he was in heaven. (I'll fill you in on that unjustified suspension later.)

So here I was, in a little office in my house. Humble beginnings, but I had the grit and determination to rise up and prove the skeptics wrong.

Now, Winnipeg is a one-horse town, which means that if you say something, most people in your circles will hear what you've said. (For example, everyone knows I have sex every day and three times on Sunday. Ha ha.) Well, during this time I heard that some of my competition was making fun of me, saying mine was not a real company because I didn't have an office in a building. I also heard via this engineers' grapevine that Balderman said I wouldn't last more that six months. That only fueled my determination.

I realize now that it was my competition that actually started M^2 Engineering. Makes no sense, you say? Well, this is how it worked. I had applied for jobs with most of the firms and was not hired. None of them even called me for an interview. *No job, no money. Hmmm . . . they're telling me to start up my own firm to compete with them,* was what I heard. Just imagine the millions of dollars in fees I could have earned to the benefit of a larger firm. *Thanks to all you big firms out there that snubbed me, now I've earned all that money for myself. I love you all—and I say that with the greatest of sincerity!*

The challenges of striking out on one's own are endless. Marketing was my first priority: without clients, there's no work. I assembled a small portfolio, similar to the one I'd done in 1991 but with a small list of additional clients and projects I'd designed. I also ordered snazzy two-color coffee mugs imprinted with my logo and phone number. I figured that a mug could be used either for coffee or as a pencil holder (just not at the same time!). My marketing ploy was to give clients these mugs to put on their desks. Then they would have easy access to my phone number if a job came up where they would need an engineer. I purchased the mugs from my brother who'd just started a trophy business; I only paid two bucks for each. This was a cheap promo and, unlike pens or calendars, the mugs would stay around for many years.

Check one off for Mike's marketing savvy! (I have since reordered many more, and have handed out over a thousand M^2 Engineering mugs around Winnipeg.)

My next best strategy was to work for nearly nothing. Most of the potential clients already had close working relationships with their preferred consultants, so to break in, I had to ensure that I could improve their bottom line by charging low fees.

What was a break for them was tough for me, really tough. I had doled out money to pay off the debts I had accumulated from the home renovation and back taxes. Laurie had obtained her medical-assistant papers and was working at a medical clinic by then, but her pay was brutally low. We had few luxuries (the trip to Hawaii being one of them), but in some cases we didn't even have essentials. We did laundry at my parents, our fridge was still the bar model I'd borrowed from my dad's office, and because I didn't own a lawn mower, I used my father's on weekends. (After a while, the weather stripping lining the trunk of my Beretta was worn out from transporting that lawnmower around.)

Obtaining work was slow but, little by little, I started providing electrical and mechanical designs for smaller companies. About this time I began using the Generic CAD program for all of my drafting. I took the drawing files to Central Graphics, the only place in town that would plot Generic CAD files. It cost $15 for each 24" x 36" (D-size) drawing, and $7.50 for an 11" x 17" drawing. I'm sure I was the only engineer who brought his drawings in for plotting, Most engineers were able to buy their own plotters, but that wasn't me at the time. Also, I knew that any plotter that could handle D-size paper would cost a small fortune, and I had no cash to spare.

I subcontracted the mechanical design and drafting to a young mechanical designer. He was a good designer/drafter who had been laid off by a local firm due to the recession. He had used the AutoCAD program previously, but because I only had Generic CAD, he had to convert his drawing files to import them into my Generic CAD program. The process was not seamless, and I had to clean them up a lot before they were ready for plotting.

This designer lived about a forty-five-minute drive from the city. He didn't have a modem, which meant we had to meet somewhere to exchange disks and checks. There was no Internet in those days, but I did have a modem and knew how to send and receive files with the ProComm or PC Plus program by dialing up computer-to-computer. (This data-transfer system was used before e-mail became common place.) To save on travel, I transferred files electronically with other subcontractor designers.

This was during the transition period when most engineering firms moved from manual to CAD drafting. I had never taken any courses on CAD, computer communications, DOS, or plotting. I was self-taught in all those areas—no courses, no mentors, no help. Once again, flying by the seat of my pants.

By Christmas of 1992, I was into the swing of things: a little bit of money in the bank, a trickle of jobs coming in, and the end of one full year of having my own business up and running.

—¤—

The new year started off with a great surprise. I received a phone call from Defence Construction Canada, a federal government agency responsible for construction projects on military bases in Canada. My company had been selected for an engineering project at CFB Shilo. *Holy shit; what luck!*

The project was the design of a high-voltage electrical system to distribute power to some of the buildings on the Base. The fee was already set—and boy, did it pay well! I made my visit to CFB Shilo, a two-hour drive from Winnipeg, for a briefing. This was the big league! There were three Base staff waiting for me in the conference room (lucky I was on time). I received the information, made a site tour, picked up the contract paperwork, and headed home to work.

When I went to the Winnipeg office of Defence Construction to return the signed contract, I brought in a few coffee mugs to give to the project officer who had retained my services. When I told the receptionist who they were for, she stared at me like I was an idiot. I asked, "What's wrong?" It turned out that she had just heard that the project officer had died the evening before. I expressed my condolences and asked her to leave the mugs in the coffee room. I guess I have one of the last letters he ever wrote.

As more projects came in, I found myself spending too much time and money at Central Graphics plotting my drawings. I really needed my own plotter. I did some research and ordered a CalComp Design-Mate 8-pen D-Size plotter with a stand, for about $2,500. The money I'd earned from the Shilo job allowed me to purchase it with cash. (I was approved for a bank loan earlier but I prefer to pay cash whenever I can.) That job gave me a big boost. I later wrote a letter to Defence Construction, thanking them for the project and telling them that they had helped pay for a plotter. To this day I am still grateful to them.

That plotter proved to be a worthwhile piece of equipment. I would design the jobs in the day and plot them at night. A pen plot would take between thirty and forty-five minutes, depending on the size of the CAD file. Laurie and I would watch a movie or TV while the plotter did its work. It was mesmerizing to watch the pen moving side-to-side and up-and-down as the roller moved the paper back and forth. The sounds it made were just as amazing. Our guests would watch it operate purely for the entertainment value. Whoever designed and built this machine was brilliant. This plotter is now in storage in one of my buildings. Despite many offers to purchase, I can't allow myself to part with this piece of M^2 history.

While I was building up my clientele, I watched for role models of smart business practices. One came via a phone call from the CalComp's sales manager in Toronto, Ontario. His name was Charles Potter. He called to see if I needed pens and paper for my newly purchased plotter. I asked him why he would call a company with zero employees. He said that every customer, no matter how small an operation, deserved the same attention as a large firm. This was a good lesson (and he was a hundred percent correct). When I told him I didn't have much money for supplies, he offered to cut me the same deal that large firms got. He also threw in free shipping all the time. (And because they didn't charge Manitoba's provincial sales tax, I was saving 7 percent off the top.)

I ordered pens and paper in minimal quantities on a just-in-time basis. I still do this today. Charles and I developed a good relationship on the phone. I was, and still am, a salesman, and my gift of the gab helped in getting the deals and letting him know more about me personally. I told him that I was a typical Winnipegger—cheap—and from what I had learned from my father, "retail" was not part of my vocabulary. I told him that if there were any deals on supplies or equipment, to call me first. He liked me so much that he sent me a CalComp sweatshirt, gratis. Sometimes he even called me just to shoot the breeze. I ended up purchasing seven plotters from him during our five-year relationship.

Just before Charles left CalComp for another job, he told me that in his marketing seminars for CalComp salespersons, he would use me as an example of how a small firm could grow and possibly turn into a good customer. The moral is, again, that no customer or potential customer, no matter how small, should be overlooked. I think I've spent over $25,000 with CalComp—yes, ten times the amount of my original purchase. Charles was a top-notch salesman and I've never forgotten the lessons my association with him taught me.

Chapter 17

Worlds Away

The year 1993 was steady, no major projects, mostly small stinkers, but they paid the bills. Laurie and I were at a crossroads in our relationship at this time. I was finally making a living on my own and, seeing I was thirty years old and Laurie was twenty-five, we decided that it was about the right time to start a family. We had dated for five years, and for most of them we were shacked-up anyways.

I thought Laurie was the best, and agreed that we should be married before having kids. We were both from traditional families and wanted to continue that way in our lives. We felt it was okay to live together, but it was the kid thing that actually got us hitched. I'm not the romantic type, so there was no down-on-your-knees proposal; we just agreed to get married. Laurie still bugs me to this day that I didn't really propose to her. (Maybe I'm just too much of a goof to know how to play the romantic role.)

We picked our wedding bands together and the total bill was about a thousand dollars. (Okay, okay—give me a break. I wasn't rich at the time and that's all I could afford.) On our 10th anniversary I bought her a nice pair of diamond earrings, which may have made up for her inexpensive wedding band. I'll have to buy her a "real" diamond band one day!

We set a date of June 5, 1993, for the big day. The event was staged in my parents' backyard with our guests seated around the swimming pool. Neither Laurie nor I is strongly religious, so a justice of the peace married us. There were about fifty people in attendance, including my two childhood friends, Steve Dubois and James Inco. Both my grandmothers were there, as well as a few of Laurie's relatives. Laurie looked great! We were not nervous, just having a good time. We both laughed like crazy during the ceremony when the JP's hair—a four-foot comb-over—blew like a flag in the wind.

My brother Robert gave the toast, and over the stereo system outside he played a cassette tape of me with Steve from some twenty years earlier. The tape captured our play-by-play commentary during a game of table-top hockey. (We loved hockey and wanted to be sportscasters later in life.) Everyone had a good laugh.

We had a Texas-style barbeque and everyone had a blast, especially James's wife. She was enjoying the free booze, and was dancing with all the single guys, and it seemed she wanted to take Steve home. (Steve was a good-looking charmer, Winnipeg's answer to movie star Don Johnson.) One of Laurie's single girlfriends also tried to make it with Steve but he told her to find her broom and fly home. (Brutal, yes, but she was being obnoxious to everyone there.)

The wedding ended at about midnight—with no casualties.

— ♮ —

So there I was: married. Nothing seemed much different; everything was still kinda boring. (Ha ha.) Well, within two months, things picked up: Laurie was carrying our first child, the first grandchild for my parents. Everyone in both our families was really excited. Two of my sisters, though married, had not had children, so for us to give my parents their first grandkid made it more special.

Laurie did really well carrying the baby. But from the results of her blood test, the doctor learned she was Rh-negative. Now I had to be tested to find out what my Rh type was. There's only one thing I'm scared of, and that's blood tests. (Maybe because in the '60s my mom took me to the worst butcher medical doctors—and whenever I was given a needle, it felt like a nail was being pounded into my arm.) My youngest sister's boyfriend at the time was an emergency doctor, so I asked him to come to the house to draw the blood for the test. He came over with a fresh blood-taking kit. I lay my left arm on a dining room chair and closed my eyes. He jabbed my vein and took three vials of blood. (My mom had asked him to test my blood for other things, including diabetes. *Thanks a bunch, Mom.*) All the tests came back negative except the Rh . . . I was Rh-positive. Bummer. This meant that, to have a healthy baby, Laurie had to go a few times to the Health Sciences Centre to have a locally invented drug, WinRho, injected into her arm. (Luckily, Laurie is braver than I am. Actually, she's not scared of anything. Hell, she married me, didn't she?)

This time was one of the high points in my "domesticated" life. Laurie and I would sit in bed at night talking about baby names. We didn't argue too much about names, and decided on Alex for a boy and Kaitlin for a girl. We decorated the spare bedroom in neutral colors because we didn't know the baby's sex. A few months before the birth, I bought a little pillow that had a place to add the new baby's name, plus stats such as birthdate and weight. I thought it was a neat thing and would be a nice memento for our child-to-be.

— ♮ —

Working at home started to become dead boring. If the phones were quiet and the work was done, the empty space in front of me drove me crazy. I liked to get out of the house for lunch. I had become friends with one of Laurie's childhood friends, Ray, a jack-of-all-trades. I would usually visit him and his coworker Peter at their home-renovation job sites, and we'd go for a bite and shoot the shit. It was good therapy.

Sticking to being self-employed isn't always easy, especially if an attractive offer pops up. During the last months of 1993, I received a phone call from Assiniboine Community College in Brandon, Manitoba. They had received my name from a résumé I'd submitted about a year earlier to Red River Community College in Winnipeg, and were offering me a teaching job in their Electrical Technology department. They needed a replacement quickly for an instructor who was about to undergo cancer treatments. I told the department head that I would gladly meet him on campus after my final inspection on the CFB Shilo project, which was to happen the following week. I went to the college and toured the facility, grabbed lunch at the cafeteria, and told him I would think about the offer.

Leaving Winnipeg for a small center was not in my best interest, even though the offer was attractive—and ego boosting. (*A college teacher; what a gas!*) But I had to look at things from a practical point of view. (That's what settling down does to a man, I guess. I'm sure glad I'd been wild when I could be.) My company was slowly growing, and I was meeting all my financial obligations. Laurie and I talked about my renting an apartment in Brandon and traveling home on weekends, but the question was how could I keep my engineering practice alive while working 125 miles from home. As well, Laurie was expecting and I couldn't just leave her to have the baby alone. So, with some regret, I contacted the department head at the college and expressed my greatest thanks for the offer but explained that the timing was off. If it had been a year or so earlier, I might now be working as an instructor for a college—maybe even wearing a tweed jacket with elbow patches, and smoking a pipe!

The year ended with a few job problems. One was a bad layout of a laundromat by an architect, which caused major HVAC problems—but, of course, according to Mr. Big-Ego Architect, all the troubles were mine. I ended up paying a few thousand dollars for the repairs. Another client owed me $4,000 for a design. I suspected he spent my fees on his debts (the rob-Peter-to-pay-Paul syndrome). I put a lien on the building and the owner blew her lid. I ended up getting paid, but it created bad feelings between me and the client and owner. Funny thing, I've heard it said that engineers can't place liens on buildings, but I did it then and have done it other times as well. I guess Land Titles employees aren't aware of this, because the liens I've placed have all been registered without incident and not one has been rejected. (I will never understand why engineers gave up their lien rights—stupid, if you ask me.)

In short order I learned that if there is a problem on a job, the engineer is the first to be blamed. Now, older and wiser—forty-three at the time of this writing (with an IQ in the thousands!)—I know how to keep the horse in the stable. A few times prior to this, I had been fingered for mechanical contractor screw-ups, which cost me tons of money. You'll read later about one project that will blow your #%$#@ mind and I guarantee that you won't believe what you read.

—¤—

The year 1994 started busy and ended busy. Daytime was for taking phone calls and coordinating the jobs for my moonlighters, which meant picking up the disks with the CAD files, plotting a few blank floor plans, and writing a brief description of the work. At night I would visit the moonlighters, drop off the stuff, and pick up designs that were complete. Most of my guys lived in the north and northeast part of Winnipeg, the other end of the city from me. I sure racked up a lot of miles on the Beretta.

Evenings would also be spent plotting drawings and checking details. I had to ensure that the electrical and mechanical designs were in proper coordination, and also that the designers followed my criteria for simplicity and for budget concerns. Everyone makes mistakes—even marvellous Mike—so double- and triple-checking was the norm. (I hate to issue addendums or PCNs: proposed-change notices.)

That year I designed about a hundred projects, incorporating both electrical and mechanical aspects. I can hardly believe it today that I pumped out all those projects from a 120-square-foot bedroom cramped with a desk, computer, fax, photocopier, plotter, plus two hundred manufacturers' catalogs crowded on bookshelves, and only one phone line. It was challenging, to put it mildly. Despite the fourteen- to sixteen-hour days, it was fun; there was minimal politics, and I loved every minute of it.

There was joy on the personal front too. The evening of March 30, 1994, at 10:30 p.m., Laurie's water broke. Within one hour we were on the way to St. Boniface Hospital. Once the check-in and other medical details were looked after, she was wheeled into a nice private birthing room. While waiting, I tried to sleep on a chair—not my idea of comfort. I finally went home at 3:30 a.m., but promised Laurie I would be back in the morning.

After a short sleep, red-eyed and with a headache, I arrived back at the hospital. Laurie was in labor for thirty or so hours, and I was by her side during the last few hours prior to the birth. We had taken prenatal classes so I knew my part in the deal. A lot goes on for a woman in the birthing process. Laurie had an epidural in her spine to alleviate some of the pain. (I hated watching that procedure!) But it worked, and she was more relaxed the rest of the way. At 3:17 p.m., our baby boy was pulled out—yes, pulled out—with what looked like stainless-steel cooking tongs. He had a battle scar to prove it. As he came out, blood and guts spilled all over the place, and when the nurse cut the cord, some of the fluid spurted into my eyes. (A great intro to the joys of parenthood.)

Laurie looked great, and I snapped a few pics of her and our son Alex within thirty seconds of his entry into the world. (I thought that a video camera in the delivery room would be too much and had left it at home.) That evening, most of our family came to the hospital to visit and see our new package. By this time, Laurie was really tired, but we were both happy that our baby was healthy—and good-looking! Although the sex of our child wasn't a concern to me, I must admit that our firstborn being a boy did seem like a bonus. It really was a proud time for me. I know kids are born every second in the world and to some men it's no big deal, but to me it *was* a big deal. And now I had not just my wife to care for, but another human being as well.

When I got home, I plotted an announcement in multicolor that read: IT'S A BOY! ALEX MICHAEL MARK, MARCH 31, 1994. PROUD PARENTS LAURIE AND MICHAEL. I put up the 24" x 36" poster in our second-floor bedroom window facing the street. I figure hundreds of people saw it, because I kept it there for six months, until it started to fade.

That was it. Laurie was now to become a full-time mother and, unless she wanted to, would not have to work again. Back in the 1960s most mothers stayed at home, including mine. My four brothers and sisters and I were blessed to have our mom at home all the time, and we all turned out okay. Besides, there was no way that *my* kids would be raised in a daycare. I was making a decent living and, because Canada Revenue did not allow income-splitting between spouses, if Laurie worked at a job, any money she made would have been negated by income taxes anyway.

— ¤ —

But my happiness at the birth of our son was dimmed by the grief I felt when my beloved Granny was taken from me on June 20th. Losing my dad's mom was a huge blow to me. She was a constant bright spot in my life, especially when everything else seemed to go wrong. Of every living soul on earth, she loved me the most. (At least, that's how it felt when I was with her.)

Her home was always open to everyone, and I mean EVERYONE— the whole neighborhood, kids and adults alike. The neighbors would come to visit her often, or walk over to her yard just to chat. (It seemed to me that she was always in her garden, or else hanging wash outside on the clothesline.) Her carefully maintained tiger lilies bordered her front yard along the city sidewalk. More than ten years after her passing, those tiger lilies grow back each spring. Whenever I drive by the house, they remind me of her and my childhood days. It seems as if she really did leave part of her soul in Fort Rouge.

In her last days at the hospital, Granny was in and out of consciousness. I went to visit one day, but when she spoke, it was hard for me to understand her; it seemed she was living out her past, talking to people who weren't there. It was really weird for me to see her like that, and I didn't know what to think. I just sat beside her and kissed her forehead. She passed away the following day.

Granny's influence will always be with me. (A lesson here: the effects of great people outlast those of mean, miserable ones.) I always wanted to make my granny proud of me, and I know that she was. When I graduated from engineering, that was the best. I know for a fact she told all her friends that her grandson was an engineer. I still miss Granny—we all do. Laurie loved her as much as I did. I'm just sorry that my boys will never know her.

— ¤ —

The responsibility of being a family man had its effects on my business. In 1994, I started to apply for membership in many of the engineering associations across Canada, including in western Canada, Northwest Territories, Yukon, and Ontario. I didn't want to have to turn away business because I wasn't eligible to practice in those areas. The costs of the memberships were high, but I figured that if I was able to obtain even one out-of-province project, the annual fees would be covered.

Attaining membership with APEO (Association of Professional Engineers of Ontario) proved to be difficult. I had to write their exam four—yes, an unbelievable four!—times. (I could insert some profanity here, but I'll just let the words float around in my head.) I had to read APEO's code of ethics, a whole bunch of bylaws, and two recommended books on engineering law and ethics, at least ten times each. I wrote the exams at APEM (Association of Professional Engineers of Manitoba). I felt like a moron each time I went in to write. Mr. Dennis, the registrar, must have thought I couldn't read or something.

Each time I wrote the exam, I'd pass either the law part or the ethics part. But if you didn't pass both at the same time, you had to write the entire thing again. It seemed to me that APEO didn't want out-of-province engineers to be licensed in Ontario, maybe because it would take jobs away from the locals. (That's the closed mentality of Ontario. I've never liked that province, in general, since I was nine years old because of the uppity attitude of my father's eldest sister who, after moving there, figured Ontario was the trendsetter capital of the world.) Finally, after bugging them via phone as to why they kept failing me, I received a call from APEO's legal counsel, stating they were sorry for the treatment by APEO and that the error I was making was in simply not stating the numbers from each bylaw and code item. They then sent me a sample exam, with answers showing what they were looking for.

On July 12, 1994, I sent them yet another check for $100 for the exam fee. This was no laughing matter: APEO stated very emphatically that I had one more shot at writing the exam, or no dice in ever obtaining a license in Ontario. I was pretty much terrified that the door would close and never open again.

I studied like a maniac every evening after work, and wrote the exam for the fourth and final time. Man, I felt like I must have been the dumbest engineer in Manitoba and imagined the headline: "World Record for Most Times Writing APEO Exam." (Well, at least I would be remembered for something.)

About two months passed with no word on my results. I finally called APEO, reluctantly, as I was sure I'd failed. The man I spoke with said he would go to my file room. *My file room!* He told me my file was so thick they needed a separate room just for my stuff. *Really? Did I fax them that many pages?* The pressure was so intense I could hardly stand it. What if I failed again? I debated between blowing my head off or, less drastically, leaving town and changing my name. After what seemed like an eternity, the man came back on the line and said I had passed. *Holy shit, I couldn't believe it; I had passed!* So why did they delay my licensure for two months? You know why? They probably thought I was just a young punk with a bad attitude! I still have bad feelings toward APEO. (Another reason may be that when I visited my sister Susan in Toronto in the fall of 1995, I went to APEO's new office on Sheppard Avenue and dropped off two M^2 Engineering coffee mugs to the registrar as a gift. He didn't even call to thank me. I wasn't surprised.)

The thing that really pisses me off is that if I'd waited one stinking year, I wouldn't have had to write the exam—just pay the money and I would have been in. (If you're a member of another Canadian engineering licensing body for five years or more, you can apply for licensure in Ontario without writing the exams.) All that unbelievable crap for nothing.

However, once again my stubborn streak paid off. By the end of

1994 , I was licensed in seven provinces and territories. I could then do work for local clients who had out-of-province contracts.

— ¤ —

One of the projects I worked on in 1994 was at an apartment building where a sprinkler service had failed. The apartment in question had a 6-inch PVC incoming water service and the vertical ready rods holding the assembly had rotted and failed. The basement, crawlspace, and the main floor filled up with water and it was pouring out the front doors. One of the tenants stated she had felt the building shaking, like in an earthquake.

I was called in by Manitoba Housing, the building's owner, to inspect the damage and provide a repair specification so the repairs could be tendered. I arrived—in rubber boots—to a sorry sight. All equipment, including the make-up air unit in the crawlspace and some electrical distribution, was under water and covered in mud. What I found out was that the ready rods were not of the stainless steel variety and that the main electrical ground had actually been tied into these rods. Because of the crawlspace humidity and the improper installation of the electrical ground, the rods had corroded. The design engineer must have missed this on his inspections.

As it turned out, the electrical and mechanical systems had been designed by Dave Balderman's firm a few years earlier. *Hmmmmm, interesting.*

The repair cost was around $100,000, paid by insurance. The insurer wanted me to provide an explanation of the cause, but I didn't want to finger a fellow engineer. I sent a letter to the insurance company and, in doing so, I purposely saved Balderman's ass! If I had the chance again, I would have written an entirely different letter— because, as you'll read later, ol' Dave was waiting in the wings to put the screws to me when he got the chance. Maybe there is some truth that "nice guys finish last." So much for being considerate.

With each new contract, I was gaining the knowledge and experience I needed to expand my business. Sometimes I learned by seeing the stupid mistakes of other engineers, the incident above being an example. And sometimes I was expanding my skills, trying things that were new and challenging. And I guess my work was being noticed, because in 1994, I obtained another contract at Shilo—a two-year retainer with National Defence for mechanical engineering work. They were satisfied with my work and I rated between 80 and 90 percent on their performance reviews. I traveled to Shilo quite a bit and would then go on to attend to my projects in Brandon. The CFB Shilo design department had very strict standards and it provided me with good design skills and patience for detailing drawings and writing specifications.

I finished off 1994 with 131 invoices. Hard to imagine that in less than three years I'd actually created a *real* business.

Chapter 18

Built for the Future

Alex was growing, and I had my share of diaper changes, bath times, and burping sessions. At family gatherings, he would be passed around more than a football at an NFL game. I was a proud father, really happy—and the positive comments about Alex were not too hard to take either!

Watching him grow was like seeing a real miracle happen. I'm glad I was working at home in those days because I got to see him develop (and puke and poop!) every day. I was always wondering if he would be like me. Would he be smart? Good-looking? Have some sort of hidden talent? He was full of wonderment. Laurie and I would get a kick out of watching him do just about anything. I loved hugging him all the time, or just lying with him on the sofa or in our bed. We would both tuck him into his crib each night and talk about what a beautiful child we'd created. Mushy, I know, but this is what life is all about!

Yet, at the same time, with Laurie at home with Alex, working from the house started to be more difficult for me. Sometimes Alex would crawl into my bedroom office and under my desk, vying for my attention while I was on the phone. If Laurie went out on an errand, I had to watch Alex while trying to work. Not that I was complaining, but I felt that in a year or so, I'd need an office outside our home. The planning stages of a "real" office began forming inside my head.

— ¤ —

In January 1995 I was browsing through the *Winnipeg Real Estate Guide*, a weekly paper that lists properties for sale, with photographs and prices. I was interested in purchasing some land so I could construct an office building for my business. I hit pay dirt when I stumbled upon a listing for a derelict building at 1050 St. Mary's Road in South Winnipeg. The place was boarded up and all utilities had been cut off from the building. It would be cheap, I thought, with lots of potential. The 50' x 100' lot was zoned C1 (light commercial use within a neighborhood), which meant I could demolish the old structure and construct a small commercial building to accommodate my office and a few tenant spaces that I could rent out.

I realized that it was time to move my office out of the house. My family was growing and I needed to set up my business in a more professional location. I didn't want to rent space and have someone else rake in the dough. If I had a building with a tenant (someone else picking up the tab), I would be able to have a free office as well as pay down a mortgage. That way I could also build up my net worth.

I went to look at the property and felt my enthusiasm plummet. The place was a worse dump than I had anticipated. That winter of 1995 was brutally cold. Going inside the building, where it was even colder than outside, was like walking into a messy igloo. The interior walls were covered in ice crystals. It had been a hair salon and residence, and thrown about the place were clothes, dishes, towels, hair salon products, bills, paperwork, and other miscellaneous items. The salon owner was in arrears to the tune of $36,000 for back taxes on the property. Apparently, she used to stand on the center boulevard on St. Mary's Road and wave her hands, motioning at people driving by to come in for a haircut. The poor lady was in a sad a state of affairs. She had eventually been evicted and placed in a seniors' home, and Manitoba's Public Trustee had taken over possession on her behalf.

Laurie and I went to look at the decrepit place no less than ten times. With each visit, I felt worse. The thought of purchasing a nightmare was not appealing. Still, I thought that the investment might be worth it. The asking price was around $50,000 and I figured that the land alone, with the C1 zoning, had to be worth $40,000. I managed to draft some building designs on the computer and, as time passed, the site was looking pretty good in my mind. About a week later I made an offer, and when a counter came back, I signed on the dotted line. (My home on Centennial Street was almost clear title, so I used the equity in my home to pay $40,000 cash.)

But the story about the purchase is not over. When I obtained the land tax assessment, I realized that the property had been overvalued. I appealed the assessment in the spring, thinking I would benefit from my action. When I won the appeal, a check for $750 was mailed—to the former owner, seeing she had owned the place in 1994. Can you believe that? I got nothing. Boy, did I feel ripped off. (And she never even called to thank me for the bonus cash.)

— ♮ —

After the purchase of 1050 St. Mary's Road, I decided I deserved a new car as a reward for becoming a big-time real-estate baron (just like jazz musician Herbie Hancock: after his first hit "Watermelon Man" in 1963, he bought a new Shelby Cobra CSX-2006, and paid $5,825 cash). I'd been looking for a new set of wheels for some time but couldn't find one I liked or could afford. The BMW 318 series was nice, but the design was still new and the cars, even used, fetched a high price. I had always been a GM man, but that was about to change.

One Sunday evening, while out for a drive with Laurie and eleven-month-old Alex, I drove into Keystone Ford's car lot. A 1994 forest-green Ford Mustang GT was sitting there. (I really liked the new design of the 'Stang. It had been unveiled in 1994 and had won Motor Trend's Car of the Year award.) This car was loaded: leather seats, 5.0-liter engine, automatic, power everything. The best part was that it only had 4,600 miles on the odometer. The car, new, sold for $27,000 and they were asking a mere $21,000. The best price advertised in other car lots was $23,000. I wasn't too fussy about the color, but I sure liked the car. The following Monday I called to set up a test drive, and went with my old friend, James Inco, to check it out.

The Mustang still had that new-car smell, especially with the leather interior. My 1988 Chevy Beretta was a front-wheel drive so the traction in winter was good. The 'Stang, on the other hand, had rear-wheel drive. Like I said before, that particular Winnipeg winter was a bitch—cold, cold, cold, with roads like a butchered ice rink. I had a tough time test-driving the car. High-performance, low-profile tires didn't help either.

By the time I'd made it to the local Esso station (the car was running on fumes), I'd decided to make an offer. After some haggling and the usual BS on the part of the salesman—"I have to take your offer to the sales manager, blah blah blah . . ." (which really meant the salesman had to take a leak)—I managed to get them down to $20,000. I also told them I wouldn't pay the tire tax and documentation fees. And, what d'ya know, they agreed. I got a loan from the Royal Bank (that I paid off in five months—not as quick in paying as Herbie Hancock was, but still not bad.) When I picked up the car on Valentine's Day, I vowed to never sell it. Today, that car sits in my driveway in the summer, and in my front yard in the winter. (My neighbors really love me!)

— ♮ —

Meanwhile, work was picking up. I managed to design ten projects for National Defence, one of which was a new hot-water heating system at Brandon Armouries, a job worth about $250,000. Mohan, my mechanical-engineer friend, did the mechanical design and AutoCAD drafting while I designed the electrical part. Everything went perfectly—not one dime in extras, and almost a perfect score from my client for our work. Now that's the way I like a job done!

I had obtained this contract because it turned out the engineer originally chosen for the work, according to Defence Construction sources, was nearly insane. When I guessed who it was, they couldn't believe I knew. However, I'd heard a few months earlier about that engineer pulling out a rifle when a real estate agent approached his home (he was truly crazy, I guess), and the incident had made the national news. Anyway, they called me and offered me the job, and the rest, as they say, is history (at least, a part of *my* history).

The projects started to get larger. I managed to design electrical and mechanical systems for a new Manitoba Hydro maintenance facility, a couple of churches, and a few apartment blocks. I also did a project for one of the wealthiest families in Brandon (which wouldn't hurt anyone in a small business wanting to "get connected"). The reason I was able to grow my business was that I kept my fees low. When you're still small, you need new clients to build up a base, and low fees are one way to get those new clients. I guess my competitors were pissed off, but hey, as I've indicated before, they were the guys who started M^2 Engineering—my founders, by default. I have to thank them for placing my résumé in File 13 (a.k.a. the trash can) and giving me the boot, which was the impetus I needed to go out on my own. But in those days I was still stupid to the fact that there's a price to pay for success, no matter how small (and, boy, was I small).

— ¤ —

Back to my real estate venture . . . Since I was then the proud owner of a dump, it was time to get busy. I had fun rummaging through the hair salon stuff; then I held a garage sale in the place on a day it was −30°F, and sold the sinks, hair dryers, and mirrors (and a basketball) for a couple hundred bucks. I really couldn't do much else, seeing it was still February and I didn't have a tenant. Then a brilliant idea hit me. I contacted some outdoor advertising firms and inquired about installing a billboard on the property. I had a man from Mediacom and a woman from Hook Sign come down to the site, separately, to see if they were interested. They both loved the site (the west side of St. Mary's Road, just half a mile north of St. Vital Centre shopping mall). With over 30,000 cars passing each workday, it was a great exposure that neither of them had before.

Mediacom came in with its offer first, about $3,000 per year, which I thought was great, considering my father was receiving $1,200 per year rent for a billboard on McPhillips Street in the west end. Then the woman from Hook Sign came to my home office later that afternoon and presented an envelope with an offer. She said it would be her only offer and I had to accept it that day, complete with my signature, or no dice (which meant I couldn't shop her price to Mediacom. She was a smart lady). It was to be a now-or-never deal. She explained that the price was the highest ever offered for a billboard in Manitoba: $4,200 per year. Hot damn, $100 a month more than Mediacom!

Without hesitation, I signed the five-year deal with Hook Sign. That income would pay the property taxes while the land was vacant. Then, once I had my building constructed, it would just add more income. The billboard was erected in July 1995 after a variance hearing with the City of Winnipeg Property and Development branch. We ended up receiving the variance without any hassles, but that was my first experience with the red tape a person has to put up with to develop property in Winnipeg. (And it was nothing compared to the real bullshit that goes on when someone wants to invest hard-earned money in this city.)

—¤—

Let me backtrack a bit. Prior to the erection of the billboard, I had to demolish the existing structure. I had some quotes from local demolition contractors, but the amounts ran up to $9,000 for the job, which I couldn't afford. I decided to do the demo on my own. I hired a guy named Bill who did demo, garbage removal, and odd jobs. For $2,000 he agreed to clear the site, but I had to apply for the permit, get the gas disconnected, install safety fencing, obtain insurance, pay the damage deposits to the City, and handle the hassles with the inspector. No problem, right?

Centra Gas disconnected the gas for $500. The City took $1,000 for the damage deposit. Permits were issued, safety fencing installed, and we were ready to go. Bill took the roof down, board by board, and sold the used lumber to some Hutterites. Unfortunately, Bill left some boards at the rear of the building outside of the fenced area, and the bloody inspector issued a violation and shut down the job site. He also complained that we had a few feet of four-foot fence that should be six feet. A real nitpicker. He even stated on the violation notice that he was going to take me to court. What an asshole. There must have been some reason the guy was so anal. Maybe some demolition contractor complained that I was doing the demo myself. Anyway, I called his superior to protest, and the mess was cleared up. I didn't have to go to court because the supervisor thought the violation was trivial. (It pays to go to the top when you have to deal with a tight-assed bureaucrat.)

With the dumpy building gone, the site looked great—clean and orderly. I figure I saved at least $6,000 on the demo, since I eventually got the $1,000 damage deposit back from the City, and Centra Gas refunded my $500 after I reconnected the gas to the new building.

The next step was to find a tenant. The Royal Bank wouldn't lend me money for the new place even though the land was clear title. With the old building gone, the land was valued at $67,000, an increase of $27,000 in equity. I was really impressed with my investment savvy!

I hired a real estate agent to find a tenant, but as it turned out, the wife of a friend of my old buddy Ray found the tenant. An esthetics services place just down the street, Alexandria Body Sugaring, was looking to move to a larger space. I met with the owners, Rob and Glory, and they signed a three-year lease for an "air" building. Boy, was I happy. I couldn't wait to start on my first building. Unfortunately, I still had to pay the agent $2,500—for nothing. I was really pissed off. He'd done jack shit for me, but I had a contract, and I always look after my obligations. (I also gave $500 to Ray's buddy for the lead.)

Alexandria Body Sugaring wanted 2,500 square feet of space. The design was for a 3,000-square-foot building broken up into three 1,000-square-foot rental units. I really wanted a thousand square feet for myself, but Glory would not ink the deal unless she got two-and-a-half tenant spaces. So I gave in and ended up with a 500-square-foot storefront for my own office. Whatever . . . I figured a move from 120 square feet to 500 square feet was a good jump, so that was that.

Lease in hand, I went to the Royal Bank and obtained a $110,000 construction loan. It was pretty easy in 1995. I hired my friend of four years, Percy Beach, a structural engineer whose office was just two blocks from my site, to design the building. He gave me a hell of a deal because earlier in the summer I'd provided the electrical and mechanical design, gratis, for an addition to the Jamaican Centre where he was a volunteer.

I thought it would be a piece of cake to obtain a building permit since the City of Winnipeg had just implemented the One-Stop Shop building permit process. Whoever named it must have been on drugs. It was more like "You want to invest here? Count on us to make it hard as hell for you to get a permit."

Oh, yeah, I learned quickly how the City of Winnipeg makes it so fucking hard to invest that it's a wonder anyone would ever want to improve a place. I did the City a big favor: I took down an old building that had been boarded up for many years. All the proceeds from the sale went directly to them, since the $40,000 purchase price was for payment of back taxes. I thought the City would be kissing my ass when I built a new structure (which would mean more property and business taxes for them), and created employment opportunities as a result. Boy, was I naive.

Because of Plan Winnipeg, a document written back in the stone ages, I had to apply for a variance. In my design plans, my building was too close to the back lane and I was short a few parking spaces. I paid the $1,000 fee, waited a few months, and after receiving a negative planner's report (the report stated that the development did not fit in with the neighborhood), I went to the public meeting. I guess I got lucky. There were no opponents to the application and I pretty much breezed through the process. I was then allowed to build. But by this time it was September, the end of construction season, and I had a tenant waiting for her space.

I managed to get the building permits, but our anti-business city wanted another $5,000, this time in damage deposits. Yup, another thing just to piss a guy off. I was at a point where I almost said fuck it already, but I'm stubborn, and I hung in when others would have quit.

I managed to get the plumbing roughed in and the piles and slab done really quickly. But the concrete contractor didn't pay the supplier for all the concrete he'd bought, and a builder's lien was slapped on my site. The bank called and asked me what the hell was going on. This was just another bunch of crap that held up the project. The concrete supplier had called me prior to processing the lien, asking for payment of $7,500. I told them no dice. I was smart, though, to still have the 7 percent holdback in the bank. I knew that all I had to do was to pay the holdback monies to the supplier and, by law, they had to drop the lien, which is, of course, exactly what I wanted.

A few fortunate things do pop up every once in a while. As it turned out, the concrete supplier and I both used the same law firm, and our respective lawyers had offices across from each other. The paperwork was done easily, and within a few days the lien was released. In this case, hanging in paid off. (It doesn't always, I've learned.)

Things started moving after that. The framing went up fast; electrical and HVAC too. Prior to snowfall, the building was closed in. I was at the job site every day and ran my engineering business from my pager and cellphone. At first I just cleaned up the site each day and made sure there was no debris on the streets and sidewalks. Then I got into some major hard labor: I spent two days installing the entire roof sheathing. Exactly a hundred 4' x 8' sheets of 5/8" plywood and five thousand air staples later, I had a roof—but I was sore for weeks. (I had all the sheeting craned up, which was smart because I would not have survived otherwise!)

I also did some electrical roughing-in and all the drywall finishing and priming. To this day, I'm one hell of a drywaller. Two coats, then sanding, and it's a perfect job, even in the corners. I did the same for my second building.

I found a framer—a middle-aged, rough-around-the-edges guy—at a job site I was inspecting. Mitch had overheard me talking to another person at the site and called me later that week. I should have known better—he had been fired from that job. He came to my house in River Heights and looked over my plan. He gave me an incredibly low quote, so I hired him on the spot.

Things started okay, and he even brought a helper. A few weeks later, things started to fall apart. First, his truck broke down, so his stepson started to drive him to the job site. He was kinda slow but I had Ray on the site to keep things in order. Every Friday was payday, and at lunchtime Mitch would walk to the Dakota Hotel across the street for a "barley sandwich" and a little bit of eye candy.

Needless to say, on Friday afternoons his work speed was slow. One day he fell asleep on a pile of drywall, using some two-by-four waste for a pillow. So Ray and I dragged a scaffold without wheels across the concrete, at a noise pressure of over a hundred decibels—but he didn't even wake up. I laughed so hard that I almost split a gut. I quickly snapped a few pics to put in my 1050 St. Mary's Road photo album. Whenever I show clients these pics, they laugh too. Let me tell you, those images are priceless.

That story is funny, I know, but at the time the circumstances were pretty serious. When my tenant's husband, Rob, laid out their floor plan, he screwed up the handicapped washroom layouts and there wasn't enough room for a wheelchair to maneuver. The shithead made me pay $500 to fix up his mistake. He should have stuck to firefighting and not pretended to be an architect. (This was just the first of a series of bizarre relationships with my many moronic tenants.)

The hassles continued. The interior of my building was finished before snowfall, but the stucco guy delayed me so much that the jerk had to finish the job in the snow. Yup, after years of green Novembers in Winnipeg, that year it snowed in October—and the snow stayed. Stucco, which is basically concrete on a wall, has to be applied and cured at a certain temperature above freezing. Well, the stucco guy was moving to B.C. and wanted to finish quickly, so the stucco dried at different times and the exterior finish looked shit-awful—gray stucco, all different shades, with white streaks from the lime. (In the summer of 2001, I painted the building myself. Thirty-five gallons of paint and ten worn-out roller refills afterward, I'm finally happy with the appearance of the stucco. Now you know for sure that I'm a glutton for punishment.)

In November 1995, my tenant moved in, but I was still working out of my bedroom at home. Boy, was I itching to move into my space. Ray and Peter, who were supposed to finish the interior, started other odd jobs and blew me off. So I decided to finish the space myself. (This is where my drywall skills came in handy.) But instead of kudos, I got more hassle. Ray drove by the site one night and called Peter to tell him what I was doing. Then he stormed in and told me I was stealing work from him and Peter. What nerve—and he even complained about my using their tools! *Well, sorry, Peter, for using your $5.99 drywall trowel.* I'm not long on patience for nitpicking like that, so the next day I dropped all their shitty tools in Ray's backyard and told them their services were no longer required. (Later, my dad helped me paint the place, and it looked great.)

In December 1995 I finally moved in. I felt like I was King of the World.

My mom and dad on their wedding day: July 1, 1961

My dad and me in 1963

My mom's parents, Peter and Mary Paradowski, with me as a baby

*Aunt Julie, me, and my dad's parents: Joe and Carolyn Maruszczak
(That's my favorite granny)*

Me at 92 Balmoral

*Me and my sister Susan
(Check out the Christmas tree)*

Susan, me, and Alison in 1967

My mother in the '70s

My dad and me at the Red River Exhibition in 1973

The fire escape I ate lunch on at the Codville Building

The Codville Building under demolition

Pay stubs from my early working days

Skateboard punk

Top of the Rad Ramp

Mid-ramp

*Check out the lamp standard
by my right heel*

My favorite pic of me on the board

Backside of jump

Handstand

California in Winnipeg

Robert, me, Heather, my buddy Alan,
and Alison, in the early '80s

1980 grad yearbook photo

Me at age 18 with my 1980 Trans Am

The car jockey office at McNaught Pontiac

The letter kicking me back into the engineering faculty

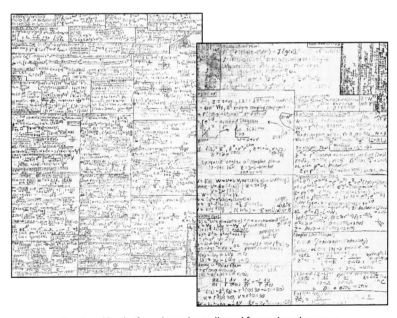

Front and back of my cheat sheet allowed for engineering exam

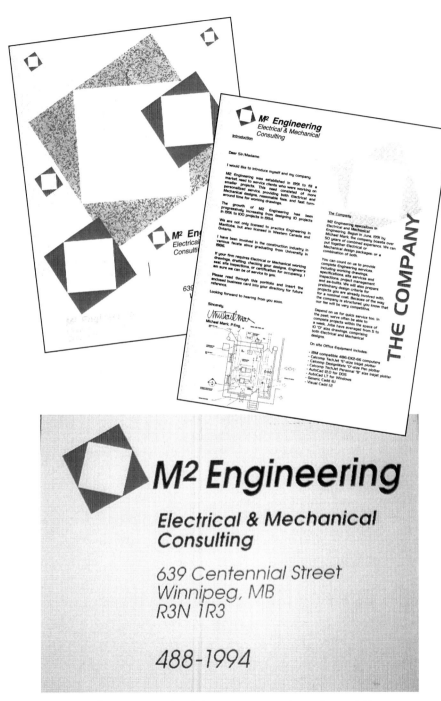

Early M² promo material, including sign put in window at Centennial house

Me and Laurie on our wedding day: June 5, 1993

Laurie and Alex at Gull Harbour Resort in 1995

Brendan and Alex at my sister Heather's wedding in 1998

My greatest assets: Alex, Connor, and Brendan in December 1999

The best Father's Day gift ever from Brendan

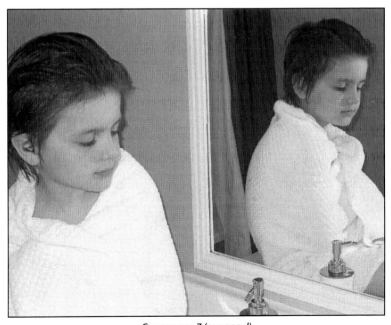

Connor, age 7 (our angel)

Brendan and Alex working together

Me and my family, Christmas 2001

1050 St. Mary's Road when I bought the property

1050 St. Mary's Road: my new construction

1046 St. Mary's road when I bought the property

1046 St. Mary's Road: my new construction

Shelby Cobra during the build stage

The finished Shelby Cobra

Brendan and Alex in the Cobra at the World of Wheels car show

Special QSL card
(postcard sent to another ham confirming contact)

THE UNIVERSITY OF MANITOBA

OFFICE OF THE PRESIDENT

WINNIPEG, MANITOBA
CANADA R3T 2N2
Tel: (204) 474-9345
FAX: (204) 275-7925

November 21, 2005

Mr. Michael J. Mark
56 Tweedsmuir Road
Winnipeg, MB
R3P 1Z2

Dear Mr. Mark:

Thank you for your generous commitment in support of the Engineering and Information Technology Complex at the University of Manitoba.

I am delighted by your decision to contribute to such an important capital project. As a successful business leader and graduate of the university, you are well aware that building modern facilities for research and instructional purposes is essential to the success of our students. Thanks to your gift, they will have access to innovative technology and opportunities to conduct groundbreaking research.

Thank you for your support and advocacy on our behalf.

Yours sincerely,

Emöke J. E. Szathmáry, C.M., Ph.D., F.R.S.C.
President and
Vice-Chancellor

Letter from the University of Manitoba
acknowledging my donation

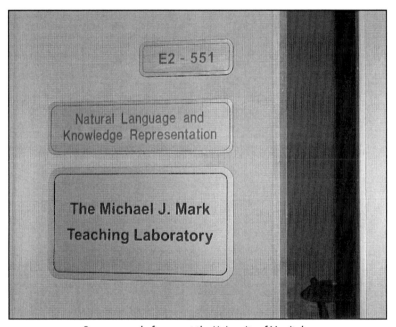

Room named after me at the University of Manitoba

Chapter 19

Change, Changing Places

These were the golden days. I had a real company and a bona fide office address: 1050A St. Mary's Road. An extra bonus was that I was earning $25,000 per year from tenant and billboard rent, and I had a free office to boot. What a deal. I was using most of the rent money to pay down the mortgage so I could pay off the building in five to six years. I felt I was set.

My family life was in the expansion mode too. Our second son, Brendan, was born on January 30, 1996, at the St. Boniface Hospital, a healthy, good-looking kid with a great head of hair—a born lady-killer. He shared a bedroom with Alex, who was two by then. I was thrilled that Alex had a brother—and even more thrilled about all those dirty diapers. (Yes, that was a joke.)

Working at the office was similar to working out of my home in the early days: I was still alone and sometimes bloody bored. To relieve some of the boredom and for background noise, I had cable TV installed. As well, it was time to end my loner status. I was doing a little more business than I'd done the previous year, so felt I could hire a mechanical drafter. My first unofficial employee was a Red River Community College student from their Mechanical Technology department. He came for two weeks of job training, without pay, which was part of the deal that RRCC set up. I worked his ass off on the Manitoba Hydro Training Facility project, and at the end of the two weeks I gave the kid $200 cash for his efforts. (I don't believe in exploiting young people.)

I hired my first full-time employee in June 1996. Jeff had just graduated from Red River Community College in mechanical drafting. My second full-timer was Derwin, my former coworker at Acres Engineering. He was looking for work because his position was about to be terminated at Wardrop Engineering. I had just picked up an electrical design job on an addition at New Flyer Industries—the leading manufacturer of heavy-duty transit buses in the U.S. and Canada—and I knew it would last a few years. So, on a handshake, Derwin came on board. Now I could handle more projects.

This is how I grew into a three-person, full-time enterprise. I did the basic engineering, Derwin did the electrical design and drafting, and Jeff did the mechanical design and drafting. Not a bad setup. I really wanted a mechanical engineer on staff, but it was difficult to find one looking for work. We were designing around 250 projects per year and I was sealing thousands of electrical and mechanical drawings and letters. It blows my mind now when I look back at all the files from those busy years. My competition at that time couldn't believe the amount of work coming out of my tiny office.

With New Flyer, we were working fourteen-hour days, Monday through Friday, with weekends thrown in for good measure. You guys who are consultants, I don't have to tell you about working long hours! The crazy routine was to arrive at work at 8 a.m., go home at 4 p.m. for supper, come back at 5:30 p.m. and work till 11 p.m. On average we would pump out a job every day. This life-draining, blood-sucking, nobody-gives-a-shit-about-you routine went on for a solid four years or more. Sometimes we would work until 3:30 a.m. I really hated the drudgery, but knew that the sacrifice would pay off down the line.

So work was crazy, and to add to the mix, my new tenant was a nutcase who caused me endless trouble. (I won't waste my time or yours describing her madness.) Around this time, my home life was suffering too. Basically, I had no life other than work, which meant no time for my significant other. Maybe you work-obsessed guys can relate. Laurie knew that my long work hours were necessary for our family's financial future and she never really bitched too much, but I knew she wasn't totally happy with the situation. I was paranoid about being poor again, and never wanted to relive the time when we scrounged for food at my parents' house. I was in a tricky balancing act, and I know my family got less of me than they should have.

—¤—

As my business grew, so did my need for new equipment. One purchase that really made a big difference on my micro-firm's throughput was a thermal plotter I bought through Charles, my friend at CalComp. I was in Toronto in the fall of 1995 and paid him a visit. He had two used Drawing Master thermal plotters in his shop. Unfortunately, they were broken and were being used for parts. These thermal plotters normally sold for around $13,000 each, and only the larger firms in Winnipeg had them. These suckers could plot almost any AutoCAD drawing file in under sixty seconds, whereas my inkjet plotter took about fifteen minutes to do the same work. With one of these, I could speed up my output considerably. When I was back in Winnipeg, he called to let me know he'd found two new thermal plotters in Anaheim, California. They were the last of the older model. He offered me one for $7,000—about $5,000 off the list price—and he even threw in free shipping. I had just finished building my place and I really couldn't afford the $7,000 for the unit, but I negotiated ninety-day terms, and with the use of my Visa card, that gave me an additional forty-five days of interest-free credit. This proved to be a purchase that was worth its weight in gold, all three hundred pounds of it!

I was in heaven—no more waiting for plots, and I could do check-sets and final vellums in minutes. Only government offices and the large firms had plotters like this, so I had gained an edge on my competitors. I also purchased a CalComp 11" x 17" laser plotter from Chuck for a fifth of the cost of new one. (As I explained before, this guy really liked me.)

I also had two mechanical engineers and two mechanical designers moonlighting for me. One of the designers, Mohan, had moved to

Winnipeg from Calgary. He was amazing. He could design any mechanical system, and AutoCAD the designs as well. I would give him a job with a description of what I wanted and, like magic, I would get it back a hundred percent complete. He made me lots of money. Unfortunately, like many talented Canadians, he moved to the U.S. for better opportunities. I loved that guy; he was so nice—kind and polite. I still miss him to this day. The other engineer (who will remain nameless) was just as good a designer as Mohan, though he couldn't draft worth beans.

I ended that year with a well-deserved two days off: December 25th and 26th. When you're self-employed, it's hard not to be obsessed with work. Anyone who owns a business can honestly tell you that the work never leaves your mind. Even at night, I would think of the previous day's designs—I still do. It's bloody amazing how often I come up with answers to dilemmas, or remember something I forgot in a design, after sleeping on the problem.

— ¤ —

The year 1997 started off with my purchase of a house across the side street from my office location. I guess the taste of being a landlord had taken hold of me. This crack house, as I termed it, at 1044 St. Mary's Road, was a rental property, part of twenty or so properties that an older fellow was selling off. The deal took two years to close. The owner originally wanted $65,000 for the 850-square-foot "beauty." I kept pestering the agent about the property and finally he convinced the owner that, seeing as the paint on the For Sale sign had faded away after two years in the sun, it was time to let the building go. My offer was the only one he had, and I managed to pick it up for $40,000.

The first reason I wanted the property was that the occupants were pretty much welfare bums who drank and smoked all day on their deck and harassed my tenant's clientele as they walked by to get to the body sugaring shop. Not good for business. They had also threatened me a few times with a tire iron, and had rammed my new building with their '72 half-ton truck. The last two months these bums were in that house, October and November 1996, all the utilities were cut off. It's possible that during that time they stole some hydro power, but I know for sure that every morning they used the neighbor's hose to flush their toilets. The neighbor caught them at it a few times, but kept quiet to avoid damage to his house. I had never seen anything quite like that. These people were pigs.

My possession date was January 1, 1997, but no one had keys, so I just kicked in the side door and *voilá*, I was inside my new castle! Actually, "piss-scented igloo" would be a better description. There was no heat, and since it was −20°F outside, all the windows were covered in a thick coat of frost. The place wreaked of urine. I slipped and fell on the ice-covered floor. How could this pathetic place have been inhabited by humans?

Originally I had no definite plans for the house, but during the first week in January, the subtenant of the body sugaring place, a hair salon owner, told me she wanted to expand her business. Also, she'd had a falling out with Glory and Rob. Her story was that they were ripping her off on the rent. (This I do believe.)

Remember, my office was limited to 500 square feet facing busy St. Mary's Road. The hair salon owner had the back 500 square feet, which I'd had to give Glory or she wouldn't sign the lease. By moving my business to this new place, I could get $30,000 per year on my first building—triple-net rent on a measly 3,000-square-foot building that only cost me $150,000 including land. That was one hell of a return on an investment!

Because I had already been through the bullshit of constructing a building a few years earlier, I figured I was an expert and it would be a cinch to do it again. Boy, was I wrong—big time! When you read about what I went through with the construction of my second building, you'll hardly believe it. But everything I report is a hundred percent accurate. (You may thank me later for the information.)

I had in mind a one-story, 2,200-square-foot building—with an overhead door so I could have vehicles inside the building—and five parking spaces. Then I'd have 1,000 square feet for my engineering practice and 1,200 square feet for an automotive electronic business that my buddy Ray would run but I would own. (Oh, yeah—Ray and I had patched things up after the 1050 St. Mary's business.)

The first step was to hire Percy Beach again, to get a super deal on the structural design. Then I'd apply for a demolition permit, submit plans to the City for a variance, and I'd be ready to roll. (Well, not exactly . . .)

This project was different from 1050 St. Mary's Road because the property was zoned R1, or residential, not commercial like the lot at 1050. This time I had to apply for rezoning too, and appear in front of a "Community Committee" consisting of three city councillors, one from my area and two from adjacent areas. I had no fucking idea the utter and complete bullshit I was then entering into—and yes, even today, I regret ever constructing the building at what eventually was called (after the rezoning) 1046 St. Mary's Road.

Once I had the plans drawn and sealed by Percy, I applied to the City of Winnipeg for the rezoning. I then paid my fees of about $1,000—for the privilege of spending hundreds of thousands of dollars to clean up the area, employ more people, pay more property and business taxes, plus pay a mortgage that would make the banks richer. (Again, I honestly figured I was doing the City a favor.) What I learned was that city bureaucrats prefer that our city looks like shit, because they set up every roadblock imaginable for those of us wanting to improve our properties. No wonder the area around downtown Winnipeg looks like a dump (and smells like one, too). Main Street is even worse. It's hard to imagine that this city has more millionaires per capita than any other city in Canada. (I learned that, for the most part, these rich people invest outside of Winnipeg. I, too, now invest pretty much nothing in this place.)

Anyway, the papers were accepted, and my first Community Committee meeting was in February 1997. The local area planner had examined my submission, and his report stated I had met all the required criteria for my C2 zoning (which allows offices, retail—and an overhead door) and that my development should be granted.

I read the planner's report one day prior to the meeting and assumed I had it made. I'd prepared a small presentation showing similar developments in the area to demonstrate to the three councillors that I was not planning anything out of the norm. I managed to do the gig, but there were a few local people opposing my little, insignificant development. Hell, it wasn't like I was building Trump Tower.

The assholes who were against my plans were one old guy I tagged Buttless, and another loser I'll call Tooney. Tooney owned a stupid hobby shop a block away. Buttless lived down the back lane and had a $40,000, 800-square-foot shack. He didn't like the fact that a few years earlier I'd torn down some weeds and scraggly shrubs to make a parking lot for my tenant. (The owner of the mall beside 1050 had a strip of land behind the building, and had told me to tear out the vegetation and lay down gravel—of course, to her benefit, because she charged my tenant $300 per month for ten parking stalls.) Anyway, because there was some opposition, the matter was put over for a month.

The second meeting was in March. I represented myself again, feeling that, even though there was still some opposition to my rezoning application, the meeting would go smoothly. The city planner who wrote and provided the favorable report was in attendance. Since I had his support, no problem; right? Yeah, right . . .

I gave my presentation and it went well—until the two old farts had their turn to speak. They pretty much took personal shots and slandered me to try to discredit my application. All the accusations were made up. They said I would yell at them for no reason and utter threats. If anything, it was just the opposite.

The city councillor for my area, whom I will refer to as the C-F-H (Councillor from Hell), did not like me for some reason. It was probably related to a previous encounter we'd had. He had been on the committee in 1995 when I presented my billboard application. In preparation for the variance hearing, the woman from Hook Sign had advised me to write to this councillor to ask for his blessing for the billboard. In my letter to him, I stated that the billboard would help pay for the high property taxes on the land, and that I was planning to construct a building in the future. (I did not state that I would remove the billboard when the building was constructed.) I guess he must have misunderstood my letter, because the first thing he brought up at the Community Committee variance hearing was, given the fact that I hadn't removed the billboard at 1050 St. Mary's Road, I was dishonest and not to be trusted. I was totally taken aback—this was the same guy who had lent me, from one of his business facilities, twelve tables and fifty chairs, at no cost, for my wedding in 1993!

I sensed right then that he had something personal against me and this would be one hell of a fight. I was right: our dispute lasted a whole year, and took a huge toll on my personal life, as well as on me financially. I'm going to trace all the craziness he dragged me through, partly for the pure release of airing all that crap, and partly to demonstrate to all ambitious young entrepreneurs what they may have to contend with to get ahead in this world. If I hadn't been made of stubborn Polack steel, I doubt I would have survived.

— ¤ —

Now, just so you know, that councillor had—and still has—a shady past. I won't go into details, but I've never understood how this guy could keep getting elected every three years.

This meeting was pretty much a word fight. I had submitted three different plans for the development, and whichever one they picked, I would have built it and it would be a done deal. But the C-F-H knocked me down and told everyone what a bad person I was. He said he had never seen so many plans and that they were confusing to him even though, he mumbled, he had a city planning degree from some college in the States. (Yeah, and my mother wears army boots!)

I started wondering whether this guy expected me to pay him off or something, but then I remembered that, back in 1995, his close buddy Sid had wanted to rent some space from me at 1050 St. Mary's. Things fell through. (I still don't know why, because Sid never returned my calls.) I also remember that Sid told my father I was arrogant. I may have been an asshole in some ways, but arrogant? Hell, I didn't have two nickels to rub together back then. So then it hit me . . . yup, Sid and the C-F-H wanted to teach the kid a lesson. Maybe Sid hated my Dad and wanted to hurt him through me. (Some people can be just plain mean and miserable.)

I had other evidence that this holdup was a personal issue. A short time prior to my meeting, a bicycle-shop owner in my area had requested a permit for an addition to his existing building. The building would then cover 95 percent of his lot, with no room for any on-site parking spaces. This was approved, even though, as retail, it should have had twenty-five parking spaces. (Free bikes, anyone?) What I didn't get was how the bike shop could be granted the addition—with no parking lot, no side yards, no real landscaping—without opposition from the local councillor. This meant the shop's customers, plus ten or so employees, would have to use the residential side streets for parking. Unbelievable! (This should have set a precedent for my case.) As well, at this meeting in March, someone was applying for C1 zoning to use his residential home for an office. It took only two minutes for them to grant his request, but the crazy thing was they gave him C2 zoning when he only needed C1. This guy's home was only a few blocks away from my property, and he was granted a zoning classification that he didn't even need. To me, the whole situation was totally bizarre—and this was only the beginning.

The meeting ended with an adjournment to the following month, when I was to appear with only one plan. I went back to the drawing board and drafted a simple 2,200-square-foot building with five parking spaces.

The third meeting, on April 21, was even more bizarre than the first. There were scads of small applications for home-based businesses, and I was pretty much last on the docket. The case that really dragged on was that of a landscape architect applying for C1.5 zoning (allowing commercial use along a commercial corridor in an older neighborhood) for a McDonald's Restaurant and a CIBC bank on the corner of St. Mary's and Meadowood. This application had been dragging on for a year and a half. At this meeting the applicant was jerked around again, which made me realize that the city councillors could fuck anyone around for as long as they wanted. Believe it or not, that application took over two hours. A few individuals who wanted to operate small home businesses interjected. ("All I want to do is sell candles from my home! How long do I have to wait?") Poor buggers.

As I expected, the landscape architect was shot down again. He left, madder than hell. (He eventually had to hire legal counsel to obtain his rezoning application.)

At about 11 p.m., my case finally came up, but by then the Community Committee members were pretty much falling asleep. I thought with a little luck they'd pass out and accept my proposal! No dice. Instead, I was punted out of the stadium! Another blow. I don't exactly remember the reasons given for the refusal, but I knew then that this was WAR.

During that meeting, and while I was speaking, my neighbor Tooney started to interrupt. I said to him politely, "It's my turn to speak, so please be quiet." He then punched me in the back of my head. Can you believe that? Everyone was shocked. One of the councillors actually said, "The police station is in the next building. I wouldn't blame Mr. Mark for filing a charge for assault after this meeting."

And that's exactly what I did. Actually, although I could have pressed charges, when the police officer said he would pay a visit to Tooney's home, I opted not to. The police visit obviously didn't help because, later in the year, loser Tooney removed my ladder while I was on the roof of 1050 St. Mary's Road. I had to walk across the roof of the adjacent building, leap onto the garage roof of the house beside it, and jump to the ground. No worse for wear, I then went to the Provincial Courts to apply for a peace bond to keep this nutcase away from me. Another maze of bureaucratic bullshit. I gave up when Tooney refused to comply. I dropped the case because I was too busy at the time to go to appeal court. No wonder women are getting killed by their exes—the law just doesn't protect the innocent.

I'll admit that I'm a stubborn person. I don't know why, exactly. I am what I am, and that's that. I'll never surrender, and will fight to win, and fight to the end But in this case, that was not the best strategy. I should have just painted the crack house pink and said fuck it.

— ¤ —

At the April meeting, the Community Committee also suggested that I meet with the Riel Residents' Advisory Group, which is just a bunch of people who supposedly live in the area and tell the Committee if they think the development is good for the area. I went to the head guy's workplace, the City of Winnipeg Sewer department, to drop off my newest plans. I think all he cared about was not missing his coffee break. No meeting, no comments, no nothin'; just a who-really-cares-anyway attitude. (I wonder if this guy got paid for heading up the Advisory Group. He shouldn't have.)

The next meeting, which was to be held in early May, was canceled due to the "flood of the century." The Red River, which runs right through Winnipeg, rose twenty-four-and-a-half feet above datum. An estimated 2,500 homes in the surrounding area were damaged. About a hundred of those homes were totally destroyed. Over 8,500 soldiers from the military were brought in to assist. All of Winnipeg's attention was focused on the flood.

The rescheduled meeting was to be on June 16th. I was anxious because I needed to knock down the crack house to prepare for ground-work. This was construction season and the clock was ticking. Winter construction in Winnipeg is brutal. This is not California, you know.

In the meantime, I applied for a demolition permit on May 22. The guy in charge at the City said it would take a day to process the paperwork. When I called him the next day, he said he couldn't complete the paperwork but gave me no reason. Politics in motion.

Okay, I'm a relatively smart guy; I knew what was going on. And if it turned out I had to apply to the Community Committee for permission to tear down the crack house, with the C-F-H on the committee I would be totally screwed—no way was he going to grant me a demolition permit. So I had to put on my thinking cap. *Hmm . . . if I call the provincial health inspector to visit the house, maybe, just maybe, he'll issue me an insanitary certificate and order the demolition.* Brilliant strategy, if I say so myself.

A document-server and a medical officer of health came to see the house on May 28, and within two minutes I had my paperwork—a closing notice served on Michael Mark, 1050A St. Mary's Road, Winnipeg, Manitoba.

The next day I proceeded to the City with my good-as-gold document, paid my forty-eight dollars, and walked out with a demolition permit. This was a hundred percent legitimate—no cracks, holes, or even potholes. (Winnipeg joke there.) Now I could tear down the house legally, without any bullshit from the Committee.

It was time for my second building demolition! A guy named Roger spied the sign I'd posted at the house (Free House, You Move) and visited me at my office. But the derelict house was so rotten that if anyone tried to move it, it was sure to fall apart. Roger wanted the house and offered to take it down, piece by piece. He actually did just that. It was one hot summer, and Roger had to battle many difficulties. As anyone knows, the nails used to fasten hardwood flooring are almost impossible to remove. Still, every single strip of hardwood floor was removed, almost perfectly intact. Within one month, the place was gone, moved to Roger's storage barn just outside of Winnipeg. He was so amazing that I gave him $500 for his troubles—evidence, once again, that I am a very kind person.

Meanwhile, back to the endless Community Committee meetings . . . On June 16, the C-F-H looked as if he was going to blow a gasket. When it was my turn to speak, he immediately blurted out, "You're demolishing the house without a demolition permit!" He went on to state, as he had before, that I was dishonest and couldn't be trusted. I replied that I had a demolition permit. But, stupid me, I'd forgotten to bring it and the insanitary order from the Health Department. When I couldn't even show him the actual paperwork, I felt like a real moron.

He went on to say that he had called the permit department that morning, and they confirmed I didn't have the required permit. When he finally shut up, I explained to the Committee that the provincial medical officer had issued me a demolition order due to insanitary conditions. The C-F-H didn't believe a word I said, but one of the other councillors believed me and told the committee he didn't think I was lying.

The meeting dragged on with more of the same regurgitated shit. Sure enough, I was denied again and had to attend yet another meeting. I was steaming. (I could throw in a few swear words here, but I'll pass for once.) But, not to be outdone, I went to my office, photocopied three sets of the demolition documents, and then drove back to the meeting. I plunked the documents in front of each councillor. The face of the Councillor-from-Hell turned beet-red in embarrassment and the other two councillors looked at him in disgust. Sweet, sweet victory! Not only had I proved to the Committee that I was not a liar, but the C-F-H was royally pissed off. Now I knew for certain he would do anything to stop my little development. (By the way, the McDonald's and the bank development were denied again at that meeting. Not surprised? Neither was I.)

This tale is getting really repetitive (worse than a disco song from the '70s) but I just have to finish telling you this nightmare about how frikkin' anti-business my home city can be.

The next meeting on July 16th was attended by the regulars: the landscape architect and me. (At least I was not suffering alone.) Same shit, different pile—or should I say, different property. At that meeting the architect finally got his wish. This time he brought in a high-powered attorney, who said, "This has been dragging on for almost two years. If we don't get approval tonight, we will launch a lawsuit against the City of Winnipeg." That did it. Passed. Signed. *Next?*

Then it was my turn. Everything was preceding in pretty much the same-old-same-old fashion, until one of the councillors yelled out to the C-F-H, "Let the kid build already!" Well, finally I was granted a permit—but for a foundation only. *What?* It was okay to spend $30,000 on concrete, but I still couldn't gain permission to build. (I'd be stuck with a bloody expensive skateboard park.) They told me to come back later with detailed plans on the building elevations and landscaping.

One other thing—the C-F-H made sure he screwed up my zoning. (You're right, there was no end to this.) He granted me C1 zoning, not the C2 I had originally requested. Yup, the sentence was pronounced in a split second: "C1 approved for foundation." *Bang!* Down went the gavel. I had no chance to reply. That was it.

On July 31st, I received a bill of $438.70 for the dedication fee that the City of Winnipeg charges for the increased value of a property due to "better" zoning. I was happy because at least the property was now zoned C1, so I wrote a check the very same day. But I knew that this was far from over—and I was right again.

On August 6, my local opponents, Tooney and Buttless, appealed my rezoning. Because I couldn't get a foundation permit without a clean rezoning agreement, this meant another one-month delay.

Each Community Committee meeting is voice-recorded on VHS tapes. For a few dollars each, I could get copies. I requested the tapes of each meeting because I wanted to preserve the mean comments from the C-F-H and save the evidence for posterity. I managed to get one tape, but when I asked for the others, the front-desk receptionist said she had to have the permission of my councillor, the C-F-H, to allow me to have a copy of the other tapes. I asked why and she stated "politics." What crap. I don't care if councillors are elected by the public; they are paid by the City of Winnipeg and represent the City in some capacity, and should be responsible to those of us who elected them. Anyway, I wasn't allowed to buy any other tapes. Maybe he didn't want me to have any record of his comments, probably because they were insulting and slanderous.

In August I was notified by registered mail that the appeal was to be held at 1 p.m. on Thursday, September 4, in Council Chambers at 510 Main Street. Well, on the day of the appeal, I was sicker than a dog. My joints were sore, my stomach was in knots, and I hadn't slept the night before. I was in bed until noon, then had a shower, slowly put on a suit and tie, and staggered to the car. I could hardly walk and my head was about to explode. I knew that if I wasn't first on the docket I wouldn't be able to wait hours for my turn.

By the time I arrived in the parkade, my stomach was in an agony of cramps. Once inside City Hall, I went right down to the basement washrooms and drained my insides. With pretty much no energy, I made it to the Council Chambers. *Holy shit,* I was twelfth out of twelve cases on the docket, a minimum wait time of three to four hours. After waiting about half an hour, I spotted the woman in charge of the appeal. I explained my sad state of affairs and told her I had to leave. (I knew that if I left without notice, I'd automatically lose the appeal on the grounds of non-attendance and would be back to square one.) She took pity on me and agreed that I did look sick, but she had to interrupt the hearing to ask Tooney and Buttless if it was okay to adjourn the appeal to another day. Those two old farts probably didn't have the energy or the patience to wait another two or three hours so they agreed. I staggered to my car and went home to sleep.

The adjourned meeting then moved to September 19 and, luckily, this time I was first on the docket. So that an unbiased opinion could be granted to all parties, the appeal was heard by three city councillors who were not involved in the original rezoning hearings. The C-F-H raced into the meeting about five minutes into my presentation and blurted out, "Am I late?" The reply from the Chair was, "Mr. Councillor, you are not allowed to be here, so please leave." The chairperson was correct that the C-F-H had no business at that hearing. The C-F-H looked real pissed off. He probably wanted to interfere and screw me around even more. By this time, it was beyond personal; I believe he wanted to see me lose and suffer in any way possible. The head of Zoning for the City of Winnipeg, Al Franklin, later told me that, in his twenty-five years with the City, he had never, EVER seen any individual treated as badly by a councillor as I was.

I ended up winning the appeal, but the three councillors upheld a decision that the C-F-H had to approve the landscaping prior to the rezoning being accepted. *Ah fuck, I knew this was far from over.* Because of his years on city council, the C-F-H knew all the loopholes and tools to screw me around for as long as he wanted. Remember the McDonald's application? I knew I was still in for one hell of a battle.

On August 21, my plans for the building were approved for construction by the senior plan examiner. This meant I could then obtain a foundation permit and at least start with the plumbing and concrete work. Construction season is really busy in August because there's only a month or so left for doing concrete work without the need for heating and hoarding (placing insulated fabric sheets around the work so it won't freeze in the winter). The concrete firm I hired couldn't start until late September or early October. With my luck I knew it would be snowing when they were doing their work. (For the record, when they were finishing the slab and parking lot, it snowed, and they ended up doing a shitty job for me all around.)

On September 25, my rezoning was passed by the City of Winnipeg. It was signed by the deputy mayor, city clerk, director of Land and Development Services, and the city's solicitor. But without the councillor's approval of the landscaping, I still couldn't finish my building. (Are you still with me? The shit pile is getting deeper, and as you probably know by now, the battle was just beginning.) I still had meetings to attend, and somehow needed to beat the C-F-H at his own game. He had the reputation of being a bully, and I guess he figured he was smarter than everyone else.

The next meeting was in October. I had prepared landscape plans and, no surprise, the C-F-H rejected them. I was in full construction by then, and Al Franklin really went to bat for me by issuing a structural framing permit so I wouldn't have to build the place in arctic-like conditions.

Winter came early, and on the first day of framing it snowed like crazy. Ah yes—construction in Winterpeg at its finest. We are crazy people here: we work in desert heat in the summer and in subartic temperatures in the winter.

I was so pissed off that I decided it was time to write the mayor a letter, asking for her assistance. She was Winnipeg's first female mayor, and I thought that because she had been an underdog at first, she would be able to relate to my situation. I also knew that she and the C-F-H never saw eye-to-eye and were always bickering about insignificant issues.

I wrote the mayor a brief letter on November 10, stating my concerns and asking for her help. (The day I wrote that letter was the same day the local news reported that the C-F-H was in legal trouble.) However, instead of her help, she passed my letter along to the C-F-H and told him to look after the matter. She caused me a lot of trouble because of this who-gives-a-fuck attitude—more than she would ever realize.

The Community Committee meeting on November 10 turned in the same results: my landscaping plans and building plans did not meet community standards. No approval, no permit. When I asked if there were any formal, written community standards, the answer was no. (Can you frikkin' believe that?)

On the eve of November 13, I arrived home after a grueling workday; I was pretty much wiped out. My cellphone rang and it was the C-F-H. (Back then, the calls on my work phone were automatically forwarded to my cell, even after hours and on weekends, so I wouldn't miss a call.) The councillor, sounding pretty pissed off, asked for my fax number. I gladly gave him it to him. Later that evening, he sent me this letter by fax:

Attention: Michael Mark

Dear Sir:

> *I am informed that you have written to Her Worship Mayor Thompson and have stated that I have a vendetta against you. I don't know how you came to think that I have a vendetta against you, but I assure you that your concern in this regard is completely unfounded. In my opinion, I am the most pro-business member of City Council. I wish you nothing but continued success and will do everything in my power to assist you in this regard.*
>
> *I do qualify my support by informing you that I was elected by the taxpayers of St. Vital to represent them and to protect their property rights when I hear applications for rezoning or variances. In this*

regard, I must always consider community standards and impact on surrounding property.

You have also stated that I was arrested the day of your hearing. As you know, this is not true! I demand that you issue a written apology to everyone who you have misinformed. If you do not make a sincere effort to correct your actions to at least the same extent that you have maligned me, I will take legal action to protect myself.

In closing, I must say that I have never met anyone who has been more belligerent to people with whom I have seen you relate. It is not my position to teach you manners, but I cannot help but feel badly for you and for the people who have suffered your wrath. However, as a person elected to represent all of the people of my ward, I do not let my personal opinion of your character interfere with my sworn duty to treat all citizens equally, without fear of favor.

The battle was heating up and I knew he wanted casualties—me! It was time to pull out the big guns—yes, a powerful lawyer with a speciality in commercial rezoning.

First, I called the McDonald's landscape architect and asked for advice. He gave me the name of a lawyer from one of the largest law firms in Winnipeg. I knew the fees would match as well, but at that point I didn't really care what the cost would be. My structure was built by this time and we were two months away from completion. I knew that without the C-F-H's approval I would never be able to receive an occupancy permit and, as a result, would end up with an empty building.

I arranged a meeting with the lawyer (whom I'll call Mr. Charles) and explained my situation. He knew the C-F-H personally and said he would be able to help me. The first order of business, though, was for me to write a letter of apology, even if I disagreed. So, on December 8, 1997, Mr. Charles wrote the letter on my letterhead, and I signed it. This put out one fire pretty quickly, but I still had one left to douse.

I had one more meeting with the Community Committee to present my case. This time Mr. Charles would be representing me and I would be in the bleachers. The meeting was held on December 14. I met Mr. Charles in the corridor in front of the security desk so he could brief me on the situation. He told me he would look after everything. We went into the meeting and I sat in the back row.

One of the sane councillors said at the beginning of the meeting, "We have a high-priced lawyer present and we should let him go first." But the C-F-H, who was chairing this meeting, said, "No way, he's not first on the docket." So we waited patiently until it was Mr. Charles's turn to speak. He spoke for a minute or two, and my application was approved. When the committee broke for a one-hour supper break, Mr. Charles told me to get the hell out. When I asked why, he said he would call me afterwards to explain. I split like lightning.

Mr. Charles called later and reported that the C-F-H had been fuming after our presentation. One of the other councillors had basically told him, "You're a bastard. Why did you fuck that kid around for a year and cost him thousands in legal fees?"

Well, just under $5,000 for legal fees later, my rezoning was finally complete. The next day I wrote a letter of thanks to the two decent councillors, adding, "You'll probably never hear from me again because this experience has been extremely hard on me and my family."

Now I could finally get on with finishing the construction of my building. I felt tired, emotionally drained, and mentally abused.

Originally I had designed the building as a one-story. When I was denied C2 zoning, I wasn't happy, and had Percy design a second story. I had read in the city's bylaws that a building could be up to twenty feet in height, so when I was installing the steel columns, I made sure they had saddles to accept a main beam that would support the second level. This served two purposes: I got even with the Councillor-from-Hell, and I added $100,000 of value to the building. (My fighting spirit isn't deterred for long.)

With a sigh of relief, I moved into 1046 St. Mary's Road on January 18, 1998.

Chapter 20

Home Free

With all that shit happening with the Councillor-from-Hell, I wasn't fully there for my family. I was a bloody wreck, both professionally and personally.

Laurie gave birth to our third child, Connor, at the Victoria Hospital on February 26, 1998. He was a healthy baby boy and looked like a little angel. I was so busy at work on that day that by the time I arrived at the hospital, he'd already been born. I missed the birth of our third son! I felt like a real asshole. Laurie has forgiven me by now—I think—but at that time, this was just one more thing to go wrong in my life. I began thinking that "Born to win. Live to become a loser" was to be my motto. How my wife had managed to carry a child and look after the house, two children, and a stressed-out husband was beyond me. With sleepless nights and endless worries, I was a basket case at the best of times. I know I was a lousy husband and father at that time and I feel bad about being "missing in action" for my family. Still, I remind myself that I was working hard so our family would have a secure financial future.

— ¤ —

A bit of backtracking here . . . In early February 1997, I'd been flipping through the *Winnipeg Real Estate Guide* and spotted an ad for a 1900-square-foot, two-story house in Linden Woods. I could tell by the description that I would like the place. I showed the picture to Laurie, but being saner than me, she showed little or no interest. The price was reasonable, and besides, I was on a mission and there was no stoppin' me. So enter my next real-estate venture—or misadventure, depending . . .

That weekend, Laurie refused to attend the open house, but the following weekend when the price dropped by $5,000 I convinced her to go with me. Within five minutes of being in the place, I told her I was going to buy it. She thought I was just joking, but the following Monday I wrote an offer, a few grand lower than the asking price.

The offer was conditional that I sell 639 Centennial prior to taking possession of the new house. The agent then informed me that another couple was also writing an offer with conditions. The only way I would get the house was if I wrote an offer free of all conditions. That meant that I'd have to sell the Centennial house pretty quickly or I'd be paying two mortgages, as well as two heavy property tax bills. (Winnipeg has the second highest property taxes in Canada. For 2005, our property taxes on Tweedsmuir Road in Linden Woods were just under $3,850.)

My offer was accepted on February 12. I knew I had to take the gamble—seems like a trait of mine, doesn't it? I was pleased we got the place, but the hitch was that I was then the proud owner of two homes.

My old friend Ray and I had to renovate the seven-year-old home because it was not in a condition that I was happy to move into. Seven thousand dollars and two months of late-night, after-work sessions later, I was ready to move my family in.

We managed a quick move, sometime in June, and left Centennial empty and unsold. I thought it would take only a few weeks to sell the old place given that it was in mint condition. It was, in my humble opinion, the best house on the street, partly because I had put $25,000 of renovations into it, including a new roof. I thought it would be a cinch to sell.

But the market in Winnipeg at that time was miserably low. The fact that I had purchased a newer 1,900-square-foot home with a double attached garage and basement for $143,000 is a good indication. For the house on Centennial, I had paid $66,000 plus $25,000 in renovations, a total of $91,000. The appraised value was hovering around $107,000.

For the first few months I tried to sell privately, with no success. Then I hired an agent who gave us a twenty-one-day-sale guarantee. I felt I couldn't go wrong so I listed the place for the twenty-one days. The agent then faxed me a sheet allowing for a price reduction during that guaranteed sale period. Because I was working sixteen-hour days, I just signed the fax and sent it back. I figured that reducing the price by $5,000 might mean more potential purchasers would be eligible for a mortgage.

The twenty-first day of the listing came and went without one single offer. I was by then in my fifth month of owning two homes. Since the realtor could not provide any tangible results, I immediately advertised in the *Winnipeg Free Press* and held an open house that Saturday and Sunday. Believe it or not, I sold the house that weekend.

Home free? Well, I thought so, but the following Monday, the real estate agent called and complained about my selling the house. (She had found out by some ear-to-the-ground method.) She said I had no right to do that because we had an agreement. I explained to her that it had expired the previous Friday. She said I had signed a listing extension. I was sure that I hadn't but she told me that, when she faxed me the price reduction form, she had also added an extension. (She'd snuck it in without even verbally mentioning it to me.) She claimed I owed her a commission. I said, "No, I don't, because you didn't sell my house." She called me a shithead and then hung up. I sent a few letters to her broker and to the *Winnipeg Real Estate Board* and ended up never paying her a dime. (I'm a real maniac when it comes to sticking to my position in a dispute.)

The new purchasers were not too smart either. They wanted to write an offer through their real estate buddy so he could, let's say, "cash in" for doing absolutely nothing. They wrote an offer of $90,000, which I would have gladly accepted on the spot, but their agent friend wanted a 4 percent commission. I told him that he was just being a leech, a sponge, making money for nothing. (Hey, what a great joke: What do you get when you cross a leech and a sponge? A real estate agent!) I added $2,500 to the price, which almost covered his commission, and it was a done deal.

After six months of having a vacant house to maintain, I was finally free. I almost broke even on the Centennial house. At that time I was making some good money, so it didn't really hurt me financially. But I wish now I'd kept it, because it would have been a good investment. In 1999 the buyers sold the place for around $100,000, and in 2001 it was sold again for $122,000. It was resold a few years later for around $130,000. Unbelievable: $40,000 more for a house in only four years! Oh yeah, another irony: it took only seven days to sell in 2001 and only one day the next time. But the investment of the Linden Woods house has been more than worth it. As I write this, we still live in the house and it's now worth about $350,000—proving, I guess, that being obsessive pays off.

Chapter 21

Just One More Hit, Enough to Get Me Thru

I heard once that memory is like a field of flowers—we can go back and pick any one we want. Well, looking back at that particular time of my professional life is more like seeing a huge patch of bloody stinkweeds. Let me explain . . .

Back in April 1997, I was hired to do a job for Tree Sap Coatings. The owner was moving his paint-mixing operations to a leased premise located just off Main Street near Higgins. If you know Winnipeg, this rundown area is in the City's red light district and is full of dumpy old hotels with lounges. It's like one huge drunk tank intersected by streets.

The leased space was in an ancient building of all-wood construction, with an old boiler and sprinklers. The business owner, whom I'll call Mr. Sticky, had not retained the services of an architect or a prime consultant to provide the required code analysis of the building for the change in occupancy. My client instructions and limited scope of work were to design a make-up air system, a general exhaust system, and a paint-mixing area with a paint-mixing table. My fee was $1,500 plus the required 7 percent GST (Canada's Goods and Services Tax).

Prior to accepting the project, I'd been informed by Mr. Sticky that he didn't know why the City of Winnipeg was giving him such a hard time with his application for an occupancy permit, seeing he'd already moved into the premise and was mixing paints. He also claimed that, at his old place, he didn't have to provide mechanical drawings. It seemed to me he didn't want to spend any money since he didn't own the building. (Ten years wiser, I would have taken that as the first warning sign. These days I don't take on clients who complain about paying for drawings or about spending money in general. I just don't need the hassles, or the potential liability that comes from working with screw-ups.)

Mr. Sticky told me to keep the design "cheap." He had already found a used make-up air unit, so I was to design around that. (A make-up air unit introduces heated outdoor air to "make up" for the air exhausted, so a building is not under a negative pressure.) I provided him with drawings of the make-up air unit as well as a central exhaust system. He also asked for a simple electrical drawing, which I provided for free just to help the dick out. (In those days I figured I owed everybody something. I was pretty naive.) The electrical drawing was simple: a transformer and electrical panel providing power for the two new mechanical items. He even reused the panel and transformer from his old location.

He submitted the drawings to the City and I then received a phone call from Chuck Surgeoner, the mechanical plan examiner, stating that a fire code analysis was required and asking if I was the prime consultant. I explained to him that I never act as a prime consultant and that I was certainly not acting as one on this project. I think he never heard me, because his subsequent correspondence to me kept asking for information that would have been provided by a prime consultant or an architect. Normally, an architect would be involved on a project such as this, but I suspect stingy Mr. Sticky didn't want to spend any more money, so he cut that corner.

I recommended to Mr. Sticky that he hire Brad Ford, a fire-protection engineer by training, to provide a fire-code analysis. (Because Brad worked out of his home, I knew his fees would be reasonable enough.) Brad provided a two-and-a-half-page fire-protection analysis on the facility and affixed his engineering seal.

In July I received a letter from Chuck Surgeoner asking for more detailed electrical and mechanical drawings, and a fire-code design analysis—even though Brad had submitted his report on May 1. Chuck sent this letter after I missed a meeting with him. (Unfortunately, Brad had forgotten to advise me that the meeting date we'd tentatively set up with the plan examiners had been confirmed. Boy, I must have looked like an asshole when I didn't show; however, Brad relayed to me all the items they had discussed.)

I provided my letters of intent for the ventilation and electrical system. The City kept asking for additional information that was outside my original scope of work. Because I was inexperienced, I kept revising my drawings to accommodate Mr. Surgeoner's requests. I basically took on more responsibility to help Mr. Sticky out. I even included a fire-rated steel exit door on my plans, at his request. I was digging a grave here, getting deeper every day because of the bad influence of this client.

Mr. Sticky even conned me into providing a drawing of his two outdoor resin-and-solvent tanks, as well as the piping, all of which was installed prior to my involvement on the job. I provided an "as-built" drawing but did not affix my engineer's seal on it. I was providing a drafting service and did the work at no cost to Mr. Sticky. When he asked me to put my company logo on the drawing, I stupidly did (but it was only the logo, no contact information). Brad submitted another fire-protection analysis on October 1997 and affixed his engineer's seal on that.

— ¤ —

Throughout this nightmare, the City of Winnipeg electrical plan examiner and I were not seeing eye-to-eye. He was a new employee with the City and we just didn't get along too well.

On October 30, 1997, he filed a letter of concern to our licensing body. This letter was also signed by Chuck Surgeoner. I just knew I was going to be suspended: it was the second letter about me he had sent to the licensing body.

Even though his letter was not a formal complaint, on November 25th I received a letter from the engineering licensing body stating I was to be investigated for my work with Tree Sap Coatings. That was all I needed! At the time I was under the stress of constructing my second building during brutal winter weather conditions. Everything seemed to be falling apart. And yet, I knew something was not sitting right. After all, I had provided the required information to the City for Mr. Sticky's permit and was cooperating with Surgeoner and the electrical plan examiner.

The November letter was signed by the director of the engineering licensing body, Mr. Dennis. I was asked to respond to thirteen charges, and provide evidence to refute their claim that my actions were unprofessional, unethical, or careless when I carried out the work. I did explain why their charges weren't justified, but I guess my reply didn't mean much.

In October 1998 (nearly a year later), a report authored by Dave Balderman stated that the design and installation were unsafe. (Remember Balderman, the guy who'd asked me to be his partner in 1992 and I'd turned down? He must have had it out for me for years, and this was his moment to screw me.) Clearly, since we were in direct competition, there was a conflict of interest here. Balderman should have declined to do the investigation.

Balderman's thirty-five-page report stated, among other things, "My final conclusion is that it is incomprehensible to me how any professional engineer could create such incomplete, inadequate, and substandard designs in spite of the available information, the time he took, and the guidance he received." The report was full of would-haves, could-haves, should-haves, and maybe's, with a bunch of personally insulting cracks thrown in. One particularly stupid aspect of this report was that Balderman, an electrical engineer, was hired by our licensing body to provide his comments on the *mechanical* part of the investigation. Go figure.

And here's another thing: Mr. Sticky told me that when Balderman asked for permission to visit his premises, he wouldn't let him into the building. How, then, could Balderman have prepared a report against me when he never physically visited the facility to view the final installation?

As I mentioned before, Balderman's office was above a Chinese restaurant in a dumpy building downtown. At the time of his report, I had just finished constructing my second building and it looked like a million bucks. What I think is that Balderman may have felt a little inferior and wanted to put the screws to the punk who, to his way of thinking, had snubbed him.

I retained the services of a lawyer to represent me at a meeting with our licensing body's Investigation Committee. He read through Balderman's report and my information, and stated he thought this was some sort of witch hunt; that, legally, I had not done anything wrong. You see, nearly a year earlier, on January 12, 1998, the City of Winnipeg had issued an occupancy permit for Tree Sap Coatings. In summary, both the electrical inspector and the mechanical inspector had approved the installation for an occupancy permit. (By the way, ten years later, nothing has been changed from my original design as far as I know, and there have been no problems—more proof that my design was good.)

Still, despite all these gaps in the logic of their claims, our licensing body suspended me for two months and charged me $9,000 in costs. Where they came up with that number still puzzles me today because they wouldn't provide a cost breakdown. My lawyer met with the Investigation Committee again in my absence, and told me that he ended up yelling at them because of their above-the-law attitude. They were the judge and jury, all in one. I wasn't even allowed to present a counterclaim: I was guilty as charged. My lawyer recommended that I appeal the conviction to the Manitoba Court of Queen's Bench, but that would have cost thousands of dollars and quite possibly have dragged on for years. I just couldn't handle going through that.

I had a talk with my good friend and colleague, Percy Beach. He'd had the dubious pleasure of being subjected to our licensing body's red-carpet treatment himself a few times. Percy told me that if I won in Queen's Bench, our licensing body would be after me even harder; that these guys show no mercy. (Understand that, by this time, I had moved into my new building and was pumping out 250 projects a year—and some of those guys didn't like that.) He told me about another engineer whose suspension had actually been overturned in Queen's Bench, but after he won the judgment the licensing body "got him" a few times, if you know what I mean. Seems they just pick on the small firms. (I've never heard of an employee from a large engineering firm being suspended, in any province in Canada.)

I decided to accept the suspension, and handed in my seals and certificate to our licensing body. What else could I do?

The suspension came into effect on December 11, 1998. Later, I received a nasty mean-spirited letter from their lawyer stating I had to sign an agreement that I would not design projects where hazardous vapors were involved. The faxed letter, which by the way was drawn up by the licensing body, had the wrong date—the previous year, 1997— but I signed it anyways, hoping that because they dated it incorrectly, it wouldn't mean a thing. (Free legal opinions gladly accepted!)

— ¤ —

On December 12th, I left for Miami for a one-week cruise on Royal Caribbean Cruise Lines. Laurie had planned the cruise after having Connor, as a needed break from parenthood. The cruise coincided perfectly with the suspension—a good thing too, because I just had to get away. It proved to be a decent trip, although when you own a company, work is always on your mind.

Neither of my parents supported me during the time of my suspension. They blamed me and said I must have done something wrong. That made me even more pissed off. My wife and my former boss and good friend, Doug Layton, were my only supporters. Other than that, I was pretty much alienated.

On Saturday, January 8, 1999, our licensing body published the notice of my suspension in the *Winnipeg Free Press*. The notice was approximately an eighth of a page—four hundred percent larger than the standard suspension notice! I knew these guys hated me, but I didn't think it was that much. The following Monday, my phone rang off the hook. I must have spoken to over a hundred sympathetic callers. One of the calls was especially interesting: Rick Ratte, a CBC reporter for a television series called the *I-Team* (Investigative Team), phoned to ask me why our licensing body would publish such a large notice in the *Free Press*—and on a Saturday, when the readership was highest. His first comments were, "It looks like they're trying to put you out of business." I spoke with Rick for about an hour and begged him not to do a story, just for my family's sake. I explained that my engineering business was how I made my living, and any publicity at that time, good or bad, would have totally fucked me up. (*I thank you, Rick, for not going public with my suspension—even though I'm sure it would have exposed the licensing body's hidden agendas.*)

Here's a little tidbit—I found out later that the lawyer the licensing body retained for my suspension hearing has been suspended and/or disciplined by the Law Society of Manitoba no less that six times, and is currently up for two more charges at the time of this writing. It's ironic how our licensing body discredits suspended engineers and never lets them forget any indiscretion, yet turns a blind eye to hiring a lawyer with a pathetic professional record. What hypocrites!

By the way, I spoke with Mr. Dennis in 2001, and asked why they printed such a large notice about my suspension in the newspaper. He told me that the licensing body had a certain number of column widths reserved in the *Free Press*, and if they used up more by a certain date, they would receive a yearly discount on all their notices. How fucking convenient! They used me—a hard-working, successful, young (and maybe stupid) engineer—to help them save some money.

Actually, I didn't believe one word of that explanation, and still wonder who decided to post that large, libelous announcement.

They say that what doesn't kill you, builds character. If that statement is true, then I should be in Hollywood making millions, because I've built a whole lot of character from surviving all the bullshit I've just described. I've never had a true mentor, so all my life lessons have been through first-hand experiences. That's gotta count. And I'd like to pass on some of what I've learned to younger people so they can avoid the crap I had to put up with. I may be blunt in the telling but, hey, that's my way.

— ¤ —

A little bit of backtracking here. The electrical plan examiner who originally submitted the letter to our licensing body made an appointment to visit me at my office in August 1998. To this day I still don't know why he wanted to visit me personally. He basically explained that, as a reviewing professional for the City of Winnipeg, he had no problems with my design work. (I guess I'd been a bit of a jerk to him in the past and probably pissed him off a few times too many. We were both young and butted heads. I know better now; life's too short.) When he arrived, I showed him the progress on the 1965 Shelby Cobra car I was building. I even gave him a brief history on Carroll Shelby and how these race cars were constructed. After that we spoke about engineering, and the fucker of all jobs at the time—the one at Tree Sap Coatings.

Since the Tree Sap nightmare, the two of us get along just great. I appreciate the fact that he thoroughly reviews my designs, and I always consider his comments. In fact, that harsh review has made me a more thorough designer, for both electrical and mechanical systems. Remember—check your ego at the door!

Financially, the suspension didn't kill me. The $9,000 was pocket change in that booming economy. I'd been working fourteen hours a day, seven days a week. While I was suspended, Doug Layton sealed all my drawings to help me out, because he knew I'd been royally screwed. Did our licensing body actually think I would shut the doors for those two months?

I later gained more proof that our licensing body just looks after the "old boys." (*One hand washes the other hand as the sin-filled soap-suds go down the drain—along with Michael Mark.*) Remember

Balderman? Well, in 2001, his firm certified the mechanical portion of one of my projects. There were numerous deficiencies and I was not prepared to provide the letter of certification required for an occupancy permit because that would be going against all professional ethics and responsibilities. As well, they had not even informed me they were going to sign-off one of my projects. I threw the project's mechanical contractor out of my office when he came in to bribe me for the required letter. (It seemed that Balderman's firm was in need of that $250.) The Building Inspection Authority reported the actions of the employee (the one who had signed off the incomplete job) to our licensing body, but—of course—he was not suspended or disciplined. If that had been me, I would have been tarred and feathered.

Chapter 22

Sanity Saver

All this professional crap was taking its toll on me. For ten years or so, I had only focused on work and I really needed an escape from the day-to-day drudgery. After I purchased the '94 Mustang GT in 1995, I had a renewed interest in sports cars, so I turned to that passion.

During 1997, *Motor Trend Television* did a show about the Shelby Cobra, a car that was raced in the '60s. Carroll Shelby was a racing driver who had retired in the late 1950s because of heart problems. In the early 1960s he wanted to start a racing team and put the United States on the map when it came to auto racing. Shelby collaborated with the Ford Motor Company, and imported a little car from England called the AC Ace. The cars came on a container ship, minus engine and transmission. He originally installed a 260-cubic-inch motor, then a 289, and finally he shoehorned in a 427 Ford big-block engine. These cars weighed around 2,500 pounds and were the fastest thing around. In 1965, the Shelby American Racing Team won the World Manufacturers' Championship, beating out archrival Ferrari. Shelby managed to produce around a thousand or so of these cars, which he named the Shelby Cobra. Today, these cars fetch from US$170,000 to upwards of US$4,000,000 for the Daytona Cobra Coupe, of which only a handful were produced.

This show about Shelby sparked my interest, and besides, I had finally reached a stage where I had a bit of spare change to do something about it. Knowing that I couldn't afford these insane prices for the real cars, I started looking at kit cars. Shelby had started making a component-car kit; that is, a real car, not just a lousy fiberglass body slapped onto on old Volkswagen chassis. There were really only three choices: a Shelby kit for US$40,000; a complete car, minus engine and transmission, from a firm called Superformance, for around US$30,000; or a kit utilizing the Mustang 5.0 running gear from a new firm called Factory Five Racing, for US$9,999. I knew I could afford the Factory Five package. The others were just out of my reach because the Canadian dollar was so weak.

In late 1997, I purchased the assembly manual for fifty dollars, made a few copies, and gave one to my buddy Ray to read at night to determine if we could do the job. I read the manual a few dozen times too, to determine the complexity and to make sure that the car was similar to the real thing. After a few months of mulling it over, I ordered the kit, complete with the options the original Cobra had. Then I waited.

In preparation for the kit to arrive in August 1998, I thought I should check out what was available at MPIC, Manitoba's auto insurance agency, and went to one of their weekly auto auctions where they sell written-off vehicles. (This was an experience in itself. The people bidding are mainly junk dealers and backyard mechanics trying to get that "golden" deal.) I managed to pick up a 1988 Mustang GT for $1,700. The previous owner had smashed the car into a pole so the front was mangled, but the basic running gear was all intact. I had the bashed-in car towed to my new house in Linden Woods and plunked it down on the grass in the front yard adjacent to my driveway. As she lay sleeping (I couldn't start her because I had no keys), I managed to find some paperwork under the seat that had the prior owner's name on it. I called him and said he could have the car's alarm system if I could get a set of keys. No word of a lie, the next day he was down at my office with the keys. I managed to start the car, but there was no movement. The clutch was fried.

When one of my kind new neighbors called the police (I have an uncanny ability to piss people off), I had to move the car from my front yard. I had it towed to my new building. We'd played floor hockey every day after moving into the new building—no more, now that the Cobra project had started. This space was now a 1,200 square-foot workshop, with in-floor heating, air-conditioning, and a twenty-four-foot-long workbench.

Prior to the kit being shipped, I had to deal with Customs Canada and Transport Canada because it's illegal to import a kit car into this beautiful, semi-communist country. (A bit of a joke there!) I had to deal with these guys in Ottawa for a month to get my paperwork approved. Factory Five Racing is an American firm, and since they were in their infancy, they'd had little experience in dealing with our anti-everything country. After convincing these government types in our nation's capital that I was just importing automotive parts and that the parts did not have the running gear that makes up an actual automobile, the shipment was allowed across the border.

With the importing of the Cobra kit finally taken care of, I figured I had it made in the shade. Then I hit another Government of Canada snag. They required two customs officers to be present at the delivery to check the actual parts of the kit. The kit came in a crate, complete with frame, body, and other associated parts—and I mean lots of parts; in fact, hundreds of parts. The delivery truck didn't have a leveler and the crate weighed over a thousand pounds, so I made a quick decision to disassemble the crate and use it as a ramp. Grant (my drafter), the trucker, the two customs officers, and I carried the frame and body to the back of my building so the officials could check and grade everything. Those officers spent four hours in ninety-five-degree heat inspecting every single part and package. I'm sure gun-toting terrorists never get that much scrutiny. I'm not certain what they were looking for, but they wasted the Canadian taxpayer about two hundred dollars. They were friendly, though, and both left with an M^2 Engineering coffee mug.

Because I didn't have an overhead door, we had to remove three twenty-foot sections of corrugated metal cladding to move the parts inside. Once that was done, I was ready to rock. The 1988 Mustang GT had been dismantled from the unibody (the molded unit forming the bodywork and chassis), so prior to the Cobra body and frame being moved in, we rolled the unibody out of the building with a jack and a creeper. It was later taken away by a tow-truck operator who wanted it for free scrap metal.

I then had almost everything I needed to build a 1965 Shelby Cobra 427 S/C replica. The frame was a four-inch-ladder-type similar to the original, and the subframe consisted of forty-four riveted aluminum panels. The parts used from the donor Mustang were the engine, tranny, rear end, wiring harness, steering rack, and a few other small items. All the other components were from Factory Five Racing.

— ♮ —

It took about seven months of evenings to build the Cobra, and most of the time I had a blast. Ray and I cranked up the stereo and played tunes from the '80s—Ozzy, KISS, Streetheart, Harlequin, Foreigner— or sometimes we listened to the insane late-night local radio shows. At the end of each hardworking night, I was high on the music and the work. I was also plain beat, but it was a feel-good kind of beat: a physical, healthy tired. We would then grab a bite at McDonald's and go home, arriving back at the same place at 9 a.m. the next day.

We had to work twenty-three hours straight to finish the Cobra the day before the 1999 Winnipeg World of Wheels car show that April. The car started on the first try. We got the car to the show and won first place, and the Outstanding Award for my category! (Holy shit, that was an amazing feat, if I say so myself.) We spoke with hundreds of people and I swear there must have been over a thousand photos taken of that car. That was one of the highlights of my life and couldn't have come at a better time. (You'll find out why in the next chapter.) Finally, recognition for my efforts! I even gained international renown in the spring of 2003: I was asked by a fan in the United Kingdom to provide some digital pictures of the Cobra for a screensaver he was developing. Being a nice guy, I obliged.

Looking back now, I can see that projects like the Cobra saved my sanity. I had to retreat from the world of crazy people and invest my intensity into something that gave me pleasure and reward. A word of advice here, you young guys and gals: when the professional world unloads crap on your doorstep, turn to another passion and lose yourself in it. And, yes, I *do* know that Laurie could have used some of my intense focus at home to help raise our sons, but a man's gotta do what a man's gotta do, buggers that we are. (Think twice about modeling after me in this regard!)

I know now that I really was a negligent husband and father at that time. I didn't know what to do. The thought of being with three crying kids and changing stinky diapers, or moping around the house thinking of the licensing body's next move to screw me even more, definitely did not appeal to me. So I chose to get caught up in the Cobra project and the insane amount of work we had in the office. Laurie hated me then, and I really can't blame her. I did hire a part-time nanny twice a week just to give her a break and so she could socialize a bit with her friends. But I still can't believe that she didn't up and leave me. Maybe she knew the turmoil I was going through. I wasn't looking too healthy, either. I had gained twenty pounds and felt like crap most of the time. My body must have been building up the toxins that were ready to kill me at any time! Could my life get any worse? Just read on . . .

Chapter 23

Twisted in Bitterness

At the beginning of 1999 I felt I was at a point in my career where I needed to take a few R & R breaks for my sanity. Contracts were plentiful, and the workload was enough to fry a person's brain. My firm had just finished some demanding jobs, and I decided a trip to Vegas would be a good reward for the hard work. I especially wanted to see Shelby American's new headquarters at the Las Vegas Motor Speedway. The Cobra was about 50 percent complete at that time, and seeing some real Cobras would help me determine the detail that I'd require to finish the car. I talked Ray into coming with me.

The week we were to leave, Derwin, Doug Layton (who had hired me as a consultant) and I spent three grueling days on northern Indian reserves gathering information for a design to change oil appliances to electric in the nursing stations. We flew to two reserves a day on a chartered eight-seater plane, in minus-thirty-degree weather. The days started at 6 a.m.: we'd map out all the electrical and mechanical information on several buildings on each reserve, and arrive back in Winnipeg at midnight.

On the last evening of this northern work, we arrived back a bit earlier, which was fortunate because Ray and I were leaving the next morning for Vegas. At about 9:30 p.m., Doug dropped me off at my office. What was waiting on my desk would change my life forever: a complaint letter from the engineering licensing body regarding a small project I'd done in rural Manitoba. If you can imagine a sinking feeling to the nth degree, that was it. I was tired, cold, and dirty, and my heart sank so low I felt clinically dead. I'd just received my engineering seal back a month earlier, and because of the previous suspension I knew that I would be damned before there was any investigation. And, as if this stress was not enough, the previous day my maternal grandmother had died. It was not a good time in my life.

— ¤ —

Somehow I managed to get myself packed and on a plane the next day. Ray and I arrived in Vegas and checked into the Old Man of the Strip—yes, folks, the Imperial Palace. It was the cheapest, plus it had a car museum on the top floor of the parkade. The owner/builder was from Thief River Falls, Minnesota, just two hours south of Winnipeg. He must have made a great living because he'd donated large sums of money to the university in Grand Forks, North Dakota, for the construction of new buildings. (The progressive attitude of other cities really puts Winnipeg to shame. But that's for another book. Last person to leave Winnipeg, please turn off the lights.)

Ray and I went to the new Shelby headquarters and viewed the very first Cobra (a phenomenal piece of automotive history), a few Shelby Mustangs, and the new Series 1 sports car the company now builds. By a fluke, we managed a tour of Shelby's new manufacturing facility, which was pretty cool. Since we were at the speedway, we took three laps at 170 mph with a driver from the Richard Petty Driving School.

Other than that, the trip bombed. I couldn't sleep at all because I was preoccupied with my possible second suspension—and Ray didn't give a shit. I just wanted to go home. If I could, I would have rented a car and driven nonstop all the way home by myself. I hate not knowing what the next day will bring. I had a bad feeling about the old boys' club at our licensing body. I knew that other local engineers felt the same about that exclusive club of backscratchers. (Please note that it's not my intention to paint everyone at our licensing body with the same brush. I know there are some really decent people there, but it's the miserable ones who have the power.)

I arrived back in Winnipeg the morning of March 15, the day of my grandmother's funeral. I'd had only three hours of sleep, but managed to drag my ass out of bed and attend the service. I looked and felt like shit. I was in a real black hole of despondency.

It was at this point in my story that I stopped writing. It was the fall of 2002. It took over two years before I could finally bring myself to start writing again (on May 21, 2005)—which gives you an indication of how much of a toll the suspension and surrounding bullshit took on me.

— ¤ —

That's when I started taking sleeping pills every night. Without the pills, there was no way for me to get a good night's sleep. (*Thanks for the addiction, guys.*)

Though I provided a reply to the licensing body's complaint letter, I knew it was of no use. I was screwed. The problem project had been a small 10-unit seniors' apartment with an attached indoor parkade in Gilbert Plains, a town three hours by car from Winnipeg. Not a large project, but a complex one because of in-floor heating. It was hampered by the fact that the general contractor was an uncaring person who hired any subtrade with the lowest price. (I had previously designed three identical projects, and they were constructed without problems.)

Plans were drawn for the electrical and mechanical a year earlier, and in December 1998 the contractor called me, asking for a final inspection for an interim occupancy permit, as two of the units were already occupied. On December 17th, I went for a site inspection with Derwin. We'd just attended another site meeting regarding a $5 million addition at the Royal Oak Inn in Brandon, for which I was the electrical/mechanical engineer. (This project went perfectly, with no extra costs, because our design was a hundred percent correct.)

I made up a letter for interim occupancy on December 23 at the nagging of the Inspection Authority. In it, I listed numerous deficiencies. Since I was suspended at that time, I asked Doug Layton to sign and seal the letter. He did so unconditionally. (Remember: this letter was not a final letter of certification.)

The same day, December 23, Mr. Les, a building inspector with the Inspection Authority, called Doug at his residence and complimented him on the detailed site inspection outlined in the letter. Mr. Les stated that he had missed all those deficiencies on his own final site inspection.

Doug called me right away and told me about the call. He seemed satisfied that I had done a thorough inspection, even though the prime consultant—in this case, the structural engineer—and the contractor had neglected to call me for the required rough-in inspections so I could do a visual of the plumbing prior to the backfill going in, and of the in-floor heating loops and other installations prior to drywalling. And I wasn't too worried either, because our design drawings were approved by the Inspection Authority prior to issuing the building permit, and this contractor had built three mirror-image projects, using similar drawings, without incident.

About a month after the tenants moved in, they started experiencing problems. I won't go into great detail, but basically the toilets were backing up on a daily basis, the boiler was malfunctioning, and the parkade and some suites were without adequate heat. The building owners began fielding complaints from the tenants about the problems. When the general contractor and the mechanical contractor would not address their concerns, the owners called Mr. Les for advice.

On February 26, 1999, Mr. Alex, the head of the Inspection Authority, wrote a letter to the engineering licensing body complaining about the design and inspection regarding the in-floor loops, boiler controls, and the furnace. I hadn't installed the mechanical equipment, and couldn't understand why they fingered me as the bad guy. Maybe to get action? I later found out from one of their colleagues that the inspection authority had not done any site inspections in Gilbert Plains—basically, they had egg on their faces and wanted to cover up by putting all the blame on me.

The mechanical contractor had sloped the sanitary drainage pipe in the corridor about eight inches up, and had installed the in-floor heating lines incorrectly in two suites and in the parkade. Twelve pumps had failed due to sediment in the lines, and the fire dampers and the chimney for the furnace were all installed incorrectly. Instead of 120-volt, 240-volt air conditioners had been installed. The back-draft dampers in the range hoods had been removed. And that was just a small sampling of all the screw-ups. The contractor had used the main furnace during construction while the drywallers were at work, and the unit malfunctioned because it was full of baked-on drywall dust. I took out the furnace and bought a new one. I ended up paying for about $10,000 of electrical and mechanical contractor repairs out of the goodness of my heart, because everyone on the building committee made me feel that all the screw-ups were my fault.

We had six other on-site meetings after the complaint, which I attended at no charge to help out the committee. In the end, those assholes also filed a complaint against me, on June 18, 1999, which didn't help matters. Though the complaint also targeted the structural engineer, nothing happened to him because at the time our licensing body was also *defending* him in a lawsuit launched by the Manitoba Association of Architects. How would it look if they suspended him at the same time they were defending him? It's politics; that's all I can say. (In defense of the structural engineer, he spent about $10,000 of his own money fixing the general contractor's screw-ups. He later told me he'd had many sleepless nights throughout that time, and almost ten years later was still having nightmares about this fiasco.)

The bastards at the Gilbert Plains Building Committee kept sending me more bills for remedial work. I told them to collect from the contractor. The contractor had also changed things on-site without telling me and some electrical items were not to code because of his negligence. A good electrical contractor would have caught these items on-site, but, as I said, this guy hired the cheapest trades. The building committee had been warned many times not to hire this contractor. I always say you get what you pay for. They dug their own grave.

At an inspection in May 2001, my mechanical engineer, Richard Held, went to the site with the structural engineer for a meeting, and the committee wouldn't let him in the building. He had to wait in the structural engineer's truck for two hours. When I heard this, I immediately resigned as the mechanical engineer for the project. What a bunch of assholes. They never did get an occupancy permit. I've always wondered why they didn't go after the mechanical contractor. (By the way, during this time, the mechanical contractor purchased a $300,000 house. That was a big *F you* in my face. What a dick. I later heard he'd screwed up a new $2 million school in Ontario and about six other projects in Manitoba.)

— ♮ —

I'll jump ahead here to complete the above story. In October 2001, I met with the minister of labor, Becky Barrett, who was also the head of the Provincial Inspection Authority. I had compiled a fifty-page report, which I gave her. I explained to her how I was blamed for the screwups of the mechanical contractor and the lack of site inspections by her staff. Doug Layton was there also. The meeting went well. At the end of it, Doug said, "If you screw Mike again, I'll make sure he sues the ass off the government, and the inspectors personally." I could see that the minister was pissed off at her department for what they'd done to me, and she made it clear to them to work with me and not against me. So far so good.

(By the way, shortly after this meeting, Mr. Les was diagnosed with prostate cancer and Mr. Alex was diagnosed with diabetes. I later saw them at Chuck Surgeoner's retirement party in May 2003. Without any hesitation, I went up to these guys and shook their hands—I don't *have* to be an asshole. I was told afterwards by many who were at the party that I was a class act. Richard was there too, and told me he saw Balderman trying to strike up conversations but everyone was ignoring him. I, on the other hand, spoke with pretty much everyone that night.)

I was supposed to see our licensing body's Investigation Committee in July 1999 but I was so scared and depressed, I just couldn't go. I prepared a package with my statements and dropped it off. I knew, no matter what I said, I was screwed.

This blow to my sense of professional worth was too much. I felt like a loser, and the worst engineer in the world. I wrote a letter of resignation to Mr. Dennis in December 1999, and returned my engineering seals and certificate. He said I needed to rethink my initial impulse and would give me twenty-four hours to do that. I calmed down a bit, and picked up my stuff the next day.

— ¤ —

Circumstances on my home front weren't any better. At this time my father was ill. He was a diabetic and was in his fifth year of dialysis. I was also still coping with the blow of my grandmother's death in March. Then my aunt Julie, my father's younger sister, died in July at the age of 54. Julie's husband Wally never got over her death and became a real basket case.

Of course, I was worse than a basket case because I never knew what the licensing body was going to do to me next. Christmas was depressing (and, as it turned out, would be the last one with my father). I was taking sleeping pills. I was still working fourteen-hour days, seven days a week. I was no help to Laurie, and I don't know how our marriage survived. I was the biggest asshole in those days—confused, lacking confidence, and totally preoccupied with all these hassles. And to top everything off, I started limping. (Stress not only affects the mind, but also the body.)

I don't know how (or why) Laurie did it, but she supported me and helped me with my stress. In fact, she encouraged me to include all the problems with our licensing body in this book. She told me it was important for other engineers to read about my plight and make their own minds up about the actions of others, and maybe learn a lesson or two.

— ¤ —

I think it was on December 21 that Mr. Dennis again called me to his office. He wouldn't elaborate over the phone. During the five-minute drive from my office, my stomach was in knots and I felt like I could crap my drawers at any time.

I thought for sure that another frikkin' complaint had been filed and I was done. It turned out that an engineering member was writing hundreds of libelous letters to the association about individual members, and I was one of the victims. The engineer had said a bunch of groundless, stupid stuff but also mentioned the Gilbert-fucking-Plains job. I'd told nobody about that project, so I wondered who from the licensing body had leaked the information to this lunatic. After following up on information from Chuck Surgeoner, the cops got their man. He ended up spending some time in the loony bin, but nothing else happened—no charges, no jail time, nothing.

—¤—

I finally met with the Investigation Committee on a cold winter night in January 2000. I tried to plead my case about the lack of notification of site inspections, but they said it was my responsibility to know when the inspections were to take place. The committee members had made up their minds even before I arrived at the meeting. One of them said to me, "What do you think your punishment should be?" I stated it should be a reprimand with costs, seeing as I'd just come off a suspension and I hadn't, in fact, fully certified the job. He said right back to me, with no hesitation, "We have to suspend you for two months—and by the way, you have a lucrative practice and your last suspension didn't hurt you." (Those words, verbatim, are permanently imbedded in my head.) I resented the latter part of his statement about the money I was making. Why should that be a consideration? To me, that just *proved* it was all about the money.

I did suggest, with all the sarcasm I could muster, that they should have a photo of me printed on an entire page of the Saturday newspaper because the one-eighth-page notice the last time was just too small. They laughed at my comment—and never printed anything in the paper at all. I wonder why.

My suspension started on March 1 and ended April 30. I have always believed that their decision was unjustified, but to fight them in court would have meant asking for more trouble. In my opinion, it should be the provincial government that administers the engineering regulations. Then it would be truly independent. I can't be the only one who thinks there's something fundamentally wrong with the practice of having investigation reports written by other engineers who are in direct competition with the person being investigated. There is no objective opinion, EVER! The reports are always tainted and full of personal slurs. (That's for an entire new book when I'm in the mood. Michael Moore, I'll be in touch.)

They tried to suspend Doug too, because he signed the letter for the interim occupancy permit. He told me that when he appeared before the committee, he basically accused them of trying to put me out of business. (My lawyer agrees with this interpretation.) As it turned out, they did nothing to Doug.

And now I'll refrain from further comment on those people, except to say that, just like a bunch of bullies, they're only strong when they're in a group. Individually, they're—well, I'll let you fill in the blank.

— ¤ —

Having read all my venting, you may be asking yourself, "Why did he write this stuff?" Well, I'm a strong believer in trying to find something positive in a negative situation. And did I? Well, of course I did. Here's what I asked myself: Did the two suspensions make me a better engineer? Yes. Did they make me conduct more rigid on-site inspections? Yes.

I now qualify all electrical and mechanical contractors prior to designing a project, and I won't sign off on any project unless I've done all the required site inspections. I normally don't take new clients either; I basically have a "closed" practice. I also hardly ever work for architects, governments, building owners, or general contractors. Very few of the projects I design are open-market tendered. Confused? Well, the work I do is for the electrical and mechanical contractors I've known for the past twenty years who care about everything they do, just like I do. We're a team with a common goal—to provide the client with a building that is designed and installed properly. (Some of my clients have called me a tight-ass because of my rigid standards, but that's how it is and always will be.) With over three thousand projects designed, only the two I've mentioned caused me any real trouble, and I feel in both those cases that I was not at fault. And I've provided you with all the boring details so that you can see that, too.

So there it is, significant positives pulled out of the worst experiences of my life!

Chapter 24

Weight of the World

On the eve of February 10, 2000, I received a phone call from a medical examiner. My Uncle Wally had been found on the floor of his condo at 55 Nassau, dead. I asked the examiner why he'd called me first, and he told me I was the executor of the estate. Shocker! I could barely remember accepting this responsibility. I sort of recalled Wally asking me on Christmas Eve 1999 if I would be the executor, and I must have agreed. This was the beginning of four years of utter hell for me. (That's for a separate book too, entitled: *Want Stress?—Be an Executor.*) With the estate being worth over $1.2 million of cash and assets, I knew my three greedy cousins and their evil mother, Beatrice (my dad's 75-year-old sister), would try to get their hands on poor Wally's money.

Laurie went to the condo the day after my uncle's body was discovered to clean up the blood and all. What a brave trooper. She also removed some of the more valuable items because we knew that Beatrice would be tearing the place apart since, for some weird reason, she co-owned the place with Wally.

To make an agonizingly long story short, it ended up that Beatrice got the condo and some GICs, to the tune of about $200,000. I did manage to keep her hands off the remaining million—legally, of course—and dispensed it to the rightful owners: namely me, my four siblings and, sorry to say, her three money-grubbing children. (The estate was divided evenly among us.) But she and my three cousins (currently ex-cousins) cost the estate over $60,000 in bullshit legal bills that proved absolutely nothing. Now I know why people say lawyers are licensed to steal. Funny thing, my greedy aunt had planned to visit Wally before his death to get him to change his will, making her the executor and sole beneficiary, but she had delayed her visit because she'd been ill on the day of her flight. A few days later Uncle Wally died. She was too late, too late. (The old bat had also lied to my mother that there would be only about $5,000 per kid from the estate because Wally was broke from gambling.)

— ¤ —

During this time, my father had been admitted to the Heath Sciences Centre because his health was deteriorating. Laurie and I often visited him during his dialysis sessions, each of which lasted for about three hours. One day in early April, I went on my own to visit him and see how he was doing. He seemed to be improving and we spoke for about an hour. That turned out to be my last conversation with him, the end of any chance I had to say or hear what I might have wanted to. As I've said before, my dad didn't talk much about himself, and after he died I was left with the sinking feeling that I hadn't really known him.

My father didn't have an easy life. My mother recently told me that he was treated like shit by his parents. Even though his two sisters had their own rooms, my dad had to sleep in the kitchen because the rooms on the second floor were rented out. From an early age he had to work his butt off. Later on, his parents gave him bad financial advice, which he took against the advice of his lawyer and accountant. That's why he was in a financial mess at the end of his life.

Mom also mentioned that Dad had never received one compliment from his stepfather—ever. Now I understand my father's behavior. I guess he never had much of a role model, so no wonder he didn't always know how to be a *Father Knows Best* kinda dad. Only once did he accompany me to a hockey game, and maybe a couple of times to a swim meet. The few times he did show up for support left a lasting impression on me. I was pleased as hell when he and my mother drove the two hours out to Gimli, Manitoba, in the summer of 1999 to watch me drag-race my Shelby Cobra. It was a typical Manitoba summer day, hotter than Hades, and no shade anywhere. He was totally dehydrated and I knew he used up every bit of energy to be there.

As I've mentioned before, I did know that he was proud when I graduated from engineering in 1986, but he never expressed that pride to me. Since his death I've found out that he always praised my accomplishments to his friends. Some of them visit me at my office from time to time. (People really liked my father and still talk about him to this day.) But I would have liked to hear that from him personally; it might have made my hard-earned accomplishments more meaningful to me. I'm doing things differently with my children. I believe in positive reinforcement, and every day I tell them how proud I am of all their accomplishments.

Laurie went to the hospital to be with my dad the evening he took his last breath. She loved my father a lot; her own father had died when she was ten years old. I love my wife, and I gained further respect and love for her that day.

My father passed away on April 15, 2000, at the Health Sciences Centre. Aunt Beatrice was there with the family during his last rites. No one spoke to her because of the $200,000 she had taken from Wally's estate. She'd had lengthy telephone conversations with my father while he was in hospital. These calls had upset him, and we felt sure her interference was a factor in his decline. My brother looked like he was about to explode into a maniacal rage when he saw her. On the phone later, he ranted to me for over an hour just to let off some steam.

I was in the middle of my second suspension when my father died. That is a tremendous regret for me and I'll have to live with that for the rest of my life. When the funeral director asked our family if we would like to include in the cremation an item that may have had meaning to our father, without hesitation I removed my engineering ring and gave it to him. For me, that ring signified the greatest feat that I as a son had accomplished to make my dad proud, and it comforts me to know it will be with him forever.

— ¤ —

With my father gone, I had to sell his car, his rooming house, and some land he owned in Headingley, Manitoba. I was still suspended and, in addition, I was looking after Wally's estate and fighting with Beatrice and her three money-grubbing children. To add to my stress, I had to fire an electrical engineer I'd hired earlier in the year because he was a useless fart—and this was a guy who had graduated with honors from university. Go figure.

I look back now and see this period of my life as a time of mega-stress, both personally and professionally. I needed to pull my sorry engineer's ass out of the fire, but I also needed a shift in priorities. For many years I'd been pouring all my attention and energy—all my mania, some would say—into setting up a business and proving that I had what it took to make it in engineering.

Some of what it took, I discovered, was my lifeblood—and largely because of the guerilla tactics of those buggers who didn't want to see me succeed. I regret every ounce of energy I spent on those battles, but looking back, I don't see what else I could have done. And I guess all was not lost, because I learned valuable lessons from surviving all that crap. I learned to focus on having my work so bloody good that no one could find fault with it. I learned to scan the sidelines for a possible ambush. Most importantly, I learned to recognize that I needed to reserve time and energy for my family. My father's death brought home the realization of missed father–son opportunities. I didn't want to repeat that with my own sons. But it takes a while to mellow out after fighting for survival in the business trenches with a bunch of unscrupulous ass-holes. I still had a way to go to achieve "father sainthood."

Chapter 25

Picking Up the Pieces

I'm not good at staying in the dumps. I have some kind of maniacal drive that keeps me pushing forward, taking risks. Despite the fact that everything was going wrong in my life, and I mean EVERYTHING, I decided to start another business at 1046 St. Mary's Road.

I teamed up with Ray to install remote car starters. Big, big mistake. That business was a loser from the start. I did learn some stuff from the experience—like I hate dealing with the public, I hate retail sales, I hate filthy cars in my building, and I hate Ray.

The business only lasted about six months. The main problem was that Ray would never listen to me. Because of all my business experience, I knew what would and wouldn't work. Also, Ray had several of his old high-school friends hanging around the place. I told him if you want to soar with eagles, you can't hang around with turkeys. In mid-June 2000, I finally lost my patience and told him I was shutting down the business. He moved his stuff out and we ceased to be friends. I know that business could have been successful, because I continued to get phone calls from interested customers four years after I closed up the shop.

—¤—

I had come off my suspension on May 1, 2000. That summer, things were as busy as ever. I had four employees: Derwin; Richard; Grant Sawatsky, my drafter; and John Pham, a summer student. I had a hectic pace at work, plus I was trying to rebond with my family. Laurie, the kids, and I went to Edmonton and Calgary for a vacation and we all had a great time. I can't believe I drove fourteen hours straight with three baby boys in the van. Things between Laurie and me were slowly getting better. I was consciously trying to be a better family man and not as much of a work-obsessed jerk.

Still, it was not smooth sailing. The hair-salon tenant, Lorraine, did a midnight move out of 1050A St. Mary's Road in June 2000. She just moved all her stuff across the street to a house, but not until she had destroyed the space she had in my building. I called her to see what was up. All she told me was she had to move and that was that. She tried to sublet to a lady with a dog-grooming business, but no dice. Just as well. With the help of Grant, I repaired the space and installed fresh carpet in readiness for a new tenant. It cost me about three grand to repair the damage. Lorraine had never paid her utility bills or property taxes, so with the help of my old friend Lloyd, I sued her.

Lloyd is a good pseudo-lawyer. He has a BSc degree from the University of Manitoba but he should have taken law. He's sharper than most lawyers I know. He owns a few buildings in Winnipeg and has been a landlord for many years. He knows just what to do when there's a problem. Street smarts. We'd had a falling out, but became friends again when he asked me to design the HVAC system in a building he'd purchased on McDermot in February 1996.

I'd taken before-and-after pictures to use as evidence. Lloyd helped me prepare my case whenever he was in town. We set a court date and appeared as required. Lorraine showed up with two lawyers from Aikins, Macaulay, and Thorvaldson, one of the biggest law firms in Winnipeg. The hearing officer asked if both parties wanted some time outside the courtroom to discuss a settlement. Lloyd and one of Lorraine's attorneys stepped outside. Within fifteen minutes, they came back with a settlement—$4,500 for us. The next day I went to the law office and picked up a check drawn on the law firm's bank account.

The space Lorraine left was vacant for a few months, but then something unexpected happened that gave me a way to lease it—and repay an old grudge debt at the same time.

—¤—

In the fall of 2000, the Councillor-from-Hell who'd given me such a rough ride with the rezoning of 1046 St. Mary's Road was removed from his position, for legal reasons. That meant a by-election in the St. Vital ward was to happen in October. Because of loopholes in the City's bylaws, the removed councillor could run again for his seat if he paid the fine for his charge. He paid it and threw his name into the ring. I thought this wasn't right. How the hell could someone with a tarnished legal reputation represent the public in office?

I had a For Rent sign in the window of my building, and was approached by the campaign manager for Gord Steeves, a young, local lawyer who wanted a shot at the vacant seat. The space was perfect for a campaign office—a thousand square feet of freshly painted walls and new carpet. I told the guy $2,000 for the month. We negotiated and I settled on $1,800 plus GST, payable that day. He came back with a check in about an hour and, hot shit, the C-F-H's new running opponent was the first out of the gate.

Office furniture and phones were moved in the next day and an election sign installed out front. There were about ten people manning the office. I allowed them ten parking spaces behind my other building at 1046 St. Mary's Road because street parking was prohibited from 3:30 to 5:30 every afternoon. (Shows how determined I was to do whatever I could to help them defeat the Councillor-from-Hell.)

One day I walked into their campaign headquarters and asked what they were doing to promote Gord. All I saw was a shitty little piece of paper folded in half with hardly any information on it. I'd seen the C-F-H's promotional material in the past—a massive, sixteen-page, tabloid-like newspaper sent out to all the voters. I knew I had to step into action. Though he didn't know it, this young candidate needed my help.

I went to my files where I'd saved every single article about the councillor (and they were all bad) and put together an eight-page newspaper containing these previously published articles. It was signed by "The St. Vital Grassroots Organization" but didn't include any comment from me or "my group." I got the Winnipeg Sun to print 16,000 copies and had it distributed to every voter. (MM on the pay-back path again!)

For days, no one knew who was behind the distribution. The C-F-H thought it was one of the other candidates carrying out a smear campaign. Because the articles were already published and were public information, he was mistaken about the smear. I was pretty much freaked-out when someone leaked the information that I was the mastermind behind the publication. The media knew where my office was, and reporters were lurking about every day. I made myself scarce the week of the election—I didn't want to taint the vote!—and they never did catch me.

On election night, I turned on the TV news and watched—with huge satisfaction—the former councillor shaking hands with new city councillor Gord Steeves (in my building, no less!). Gord had won by over a thousand votes. That was the C-F-H's swan song. Whatever goes around, comes around. The following day, Gord's campaign manager left a Post-it Note on my back door that read, "Thanks—we won!"

I left for New York the next day to visit my sister Heather and her husband Neil, just to recover from the madness. Neil and I traveled for three days along the east coast of the U.S.A. and drove through twelve states. The highlight of the trip was making it to the crown of the Statue of Liberty in less than half an hour. It was raining heavily and we caught the first ferry of the day from Battery Park to Ellis Island. Neil said we must have set a record getting to the top. It was cool to be standing that high, and what I remember the most is looking through the fog at the World Trade Center twin towers. (In 2001, I went back to New York for a little holiday—just before these towers were history. More about that later . . .)

Work that fall was uneventful. Christmas 2000 was just not the same without my father. The only positive thing was that I was not having any professional problems.

I did manage to sell my dad's car. Actually, my brother sold the car but I did all the paperwork. I sold the rooming house with the help of Lawrence Hart, the realtor who'd listed the land at 1050 St. Mary's Road. He charged my mom a 4 percent commission, which was really quite low. (Later, I sold my father's land privately, so at least I saved some commission for my mom then.) I miss that old rooming house. I'd done repair work there for over twenty years and even installed a new boiler. I would start the boiler and bleed the rads all the time, especially when the roomers complained of no heat. It was like looking after an old jalopy.

Another hard thing about losing my dad was that later my mom remarried. I know I was an adult and should have sucked up my little-boy resentment, but I was just NOT comfortable with another man being with her in the place of my father. My version of the story is that this guy had followed my mother around in her apartment block while my father was in the hospital, and eventually (in 2002) she married him, maybe just for companionship. I know he didn't marry her for her money because there wasn't much around. My mom had a debt to the lending agency for my dad, so when she paid those assholes off, I felt good that she owed nothing to nobody. (I've been out of debt for a while now and it's a very good feeling.) My mother's new husband doesn't have much money, but my mom has some money saved in the bank, so at least she isn't poor.

There were a few other financial crises on my radar though. During this time, my childhood buddy James was living in Las Vegas and kept calling me for money. He had recently divorced his wife and they had sold their house. I loaned him money on a few occasions, to the tune of about $4,000. One time when he asked for more, I said; "No way, man, you aren't paying any of it back, and it's been a year now."

He told me to go to the storage locker he shared with his mother and take some of his ham radio stuff and sell it.

James's mother had sold her house on Park Boulevard, and shortly after his dad died, she remarried. I asked him about his mother and he said her new husband had taken all her money. In fact, his mom had called me a few times asking to borrow money for rent. In tears, she told me that James had gambled all her money away and that she was broke. I didn't know what to believe. I thought about paying the rent, which was $1,200 a month, but I knew that Laurie would divorce me if I took on that kind of obligation.

I went to the locker. I had to pay $350 back rent to get in. That's when I knew there was a problem. I found his father's ashes in a box there, too. That was disturbing. I sold most of James's stuff and generated the original $4,000 cash I had lent him. And that's when the Bank of Mike Mark officially closed.

The last I read about James, he was a cabbie in Vegas. I only found out by doing a search on the Internet for his name. He'd been interviewed for an article in a Vegas paper in October 2001 after the 9/11 terrorist attacks halted air travel in the U.S. He said he was kicked out of his apartment and had to go to court because his landlady was suing him for back rent. That really blew my mind.

I haven't spoken with James for over five years now. Even Lloyd, who lives in Vegas, hasn't seen him. I hope he's still alive. His mother, last I heard, was living in low-rental housing across from the Youth Centre in Tuxedo. Part of the reason I work like a maniac and keep my nose clean is so that no one in my family EVER has to be in positions like these.

Chapter 26

In a New York Minute, Everything Can Change

In late August 2001, Laurie and I went to New York City for a little holiday. My sister Heather and her husband Neil picked us up at the Ottawa airport. We spent the day in Ottawa poking around Canada's glorious capital, then drove to their place in Watertown, NY, to spend the night.

The next day we went into Manhattan and shacked up at the Hotel Belvedere on 48th Street. We were pretty close to all the action. The first order of business was to have a couple of drinks at the top of the Marriott Marquis Hotel and then to visit the Empire State Building. Radio genius Edwin Armstrong, inventor of FM radio, relayed one of his first transmissions from the top of this building. I've spent years trying to find any scrap of paper with his handwriting or signature on it for my collection. (If anyone has any leads, please ring me up.)

Neil is a real WWII buff and collector so he insisted we visit the USS Intrepid War Museum. We walked down from the hotel to be at the museum when it opened, and I figured, *Okay, about an hour or two and then we can do something else.* As it turns out, the museum consists of an aircraft carrier, a submarine, a warship, and—get this—a McDonald's Restaurant to satisfy the kids dragged there by their war-obsessed parents. Well, we spent over eight hours on that carrier. There was just too much to see. My favorite was the Collins radio equipment and other radio-related items. Neil just cared about all the planes and jets located on the landing area and the hangar below. The engineers who designed this thing were brilliant. George Bush Sr.'s warplane was on display, but what moved me the most, believe it or not, was a small display in an inconspicuous corner in the museum of the USS Cole, and the pictures of the young servicemen and -women who were killed when the terrorists bombed this carrier about a year earlier. They were all just kids.

Laurie and Heather didn't wait for us and went to the Statue of Liberty. But they couldn't get to the top—it had been closed down because it was too hot outside. When you're waiting on the spiral staircase to go up, it's beastly hot and humid, despite the upgrades to their HVAC system. (And, as you know, hot air rises.) Too bad Laurie and Heather never made it. When you reach the top, the view is so awesome you forget you've just lost two pounds on the way up to see it.

On our last day, which was a Sunday, we each had our own agendas. I wanted to drive down to Wall Street to see the twin towers, Heather wanted to show us the Cathedral Church of St. John The Divine, and Laurie wanted to have a hot dog at the famous Nathan's on Coney Island. Driving on Wall Street is a joke. The streets are all just a bunch of heavy-gauge sheet-steel panels covering potholes. It makes Winnipeg's famously cratered streets seem smooth as glass. As we were passing the twin towers, Neil opened the sunroof of his SUV and we all looked up. These buildings were more massive than you can imagine; they seemed to have no end. Now, more than ever, it bugs me that we didn't have time to visit the viewing area.

Next stop was St. John The Divine church. This place is massive too. Scaffolding surrounded one side of the church as though it had never been finished. We walked in and, holy shit, that place was huge. There have been a few large funerals held here for well-respected people (such as Nikola Tesla, a famous electrical inventor) as well as for a few assholes (do some research and you'll know who I mean). When we went to the gift shop to look around, nature called and I headed into the adjacent washroom. It freaked me out when I saw the old electrical wires just hanging from the posts. I told Laurie and my sister that

that place was a fire hazard. Sure enough, that area caught on fire a few months later, reportedly because of faulty wiring. Maybe I'm not that stupid after all.

Coney Island that day seemed like a ghost town. The rides were closed and only a few little shops were open. The hot dog at Nathan's was okay but nothing really to write home about. It was just too small. The washrooms there were really clean though. (I have a thing about washrooms. They gotta be clean!)

After NY, Laurie and I visited my sister Susan in Toronto and stayed for a few days. We arrived back in Winnipeg on August 22, 2001. I know that because when we got home, our hot water tank was leaking. I replaced it later that day and wrote the date on the tag and my initials: M^2.

When I arrived at work the morning of September 11, 2001, my staff were watching the mini black-and-white Sony TV at the office. They told me a plane had hit the World Trade Center. I just couldn't believe it. I went right back home and picked up a spare color TV for us to watch. The whole scenario was just too surreal. *Was it a joke? A hoax?*

When I saw, live, the plane hitting the other tower, I knew it was no joke. We were glued to the TV all day, watching the repeated footage of both towers plummeting to the ground. Horrifying. I'd just been there a few weeks before and the postcard showing the World Trade Center that I'd sent to the office was still on the bulletin board. That really hit close to home. It turned out that my high-school chemistry teacher was in New York City at the time and his daughter was in one of the towers during the attack. She managed to get out alive, but another Manitoban was not so lucky and perished that day.

I then thought back to our visit on the USS Intrepid—to be exact, the USS Cole display. The same terrorist organization was responsible for the massive carnage that fateful day. My mother and my sister Heather later visited Ground Zero, and they said you just had to be there to feel all the pain. The whole world changed after that day. It seemed like all the innocence in the world was wiped away.

That 9/11 tragedy has stayed with me for a long time. It reinforced for me what was really important in life: more focus on the family and less sweating of the small stuff. I wish I could say I was a changed man from that day on, but I had a few more hurdles to leap over before I got my life totally turned around. Needed to hit rock bottom, I guess.

Chapter 27

I Can Breathe Again

It was becoming clear to me that I needed to make my life simpler, a little more sane. The satisfaction in running my own business was being eroded by employee and tenant problems. I decided to deal with those hassles first.

In February 2001, Derwin went to work for the University of Manitoba. When he gave me his resignation letter, it was like a megaton of bricks had lifted off my shoulders. I was paying him about $55,000 a year, but his work was slow and his attitude was less than positive. I then had to design all the electrical jobs myself because I needed to recover from the tenant expenses and some other costs that had gotten me down. I soon found out that Grant and I could design an electrical system for a project a lot faster than Derwin had, and with far better accuracy. There ended that story.

One story ends; another begins. The following month, the body-sugaring tenant also did a midnight move. I saw the sneak moving out the tanning beds a few weeks earlier and should have known something was up. One Monday she left a note at my office that basically said, "I closed up my shop. If you need anything, just call my lawyer at this phone number . . ."

I spoke with her lawyer—who coincidentally happened to be a good friend of Lloyd. He said, "Too bad; she's broke and you'll have to sue her." Okay, thanks for the advice. I then called Lloyd and we proceeded to file a claim in Small Claims Court.

It was a long haul. I had screwed up in that I'd signed the lease to a numbered company. When Glory and Rob, the original tenants, had sold the business to Leslie, they transferred the lease but I had to sign it, too. This was during the madness of being suspended the first time and while I was building the Cobra, and I'd signed the papers without looking at them carefully. I trusted people back then. Nowadays I'm not prejudiced—I hate everybody. (Just joking. Grant told me that one. He's one funny dude.)

Anyways, Lloyd managed a victory for me in court, but collecting the money this time was a problem. I had to spend over six months putting up with the stalling tactics of her lawyer. Finally, another lawyer took over. (The first one must have gotten fired—or maybe he quit to be a drummer in a local bar band!) I told the new guy to pay me x amount of dollars and that would be the end of it. A few days later he came to my office with a check from the law firm. We shook hands and the deal was done. I must have cost Leslie $15,000 in legal fees. Of course, she cost me more in lost rent, but I figure she was the bigger loser in the end.

I kept the office space the way it was until October 2001. When I couldn't find a tenant, I had a neighbor gut the place for $300. Grant and I patched and painted the space and we also ripped out all the flooring. My brother Robert helped out too. The place was nice and clean, and within days I found a new tenant: Percy Beach, the engineer who'd designed my buildings. He's been there since. He's a great tenant and long may he stay.

People problems continued. If it wasn't a useless employee or a crazy tenant, it was a jealous jerk who hated for me to get ahead. Case in point: I was asked by a mechanical contractor to provide HVAC design drawings for a new car dealership in Winnipeg. We'd just started the design when he informed me that the architect didn't want me on the project. Rumor had it that he thought I was a bad engineer because I'd been suspended twice. (Little did he know how frikkin' fake the reasons were for my suspension.) In order not to cause any trouble, the mechanical contractor hired another engineer to do the work.

No support there. A week later, the electrical contractor called and asked me to provide the electrical design for the dealership. I was itching to get on that job to spite the architect, so I offered to do the work for free. He took me up on my offer and got me the job. (There are many ways to prove a point.)

— ¤ —

With my new streamlined workforce (ha ha), the next item on my make-my-life-simple-again agenda was to sell the 1046 St. Mary's Road building. The 1050A St. Mary's property was to be vacant soon, and with only two employees, I didn't need as much space. It took months to sell the building, and I pretty much gave it away at $270,000 even though the appraised value was $350,000. Still, I made a $25,000 profit on the deal.

Of course, that transaction had the prerequisite crazy-people components too. The turkeys who bought my building at 1046 St. Mary's Road for that fire-sale price started to cause me trouble. They complained that the floor on the second level was scratched. It was a subfloor that had only cost me $1,000 for 2,200 square feet. When I was moving out, I guess we may have marked up the floor a bit, but these jokers went way overboard, and had a lawyer draw up a letter stating they would sue me for a new floor worth thousands of dollars.

I found the bills for the floor and the urethane coating, and faxed them over. The clowns settled for $500 to be deducted from the sale price. *Stupid jerks. Did they think they could do that to me without any recourse?* They paid in the end. (But not because of me. I'll just leave it at that.) As it turned out, they scratched the shit out of the floor and ruined it during their renovations. Anyone in construction would have known that would happen. I went periodically to the site to see the progress of their renovations and to watch the floor being destroyed. Some satisfaction there!

This sale led to a red-letter day. On June 23, 2002, I drove to the Royal Bank on Pembina and Oakenwald and paid off the mortgage on

1050 St. Mary's Road. The woman there said, "Are you sure you want to do this? We could invest the money for you." I said, "Yeah, so you can lose it all? Forget it, here's the money. Now please give me a printout showing I owe nothin' to nobody."

— ♮ —

I was a man without debt; absolutely none. I owned my home, my cars, and also my 3,000-square-foot building. I was FREE. From that day forward, I could build up my cash, my net worth, *and* regain my health and mental well-being. I moved into the 1,000-square-foot bay in 1050 St. Mary's, right next to my friend and colleague, Percy Beach.

I am still there today and have never regretted this decision.

Chapter 28

Sick and Tired of
Being Sick and Tired

After years of ass-busting work and raw-grit determination, I had achieved professional and financial security. It was time to tend to some of the other neglected areas, especially my physical and mental health. I was in for a hell of a journey.

They say you have to get worse to get better; in other words, reach an all-time low before heading down the road to recovery. Since I don't smoke and have never been drunk or on drugs, I really didn't know what that meant. I was about to learn.

—¤—

Turning forty on the 30th of June, 2002, was a watershed experience for me. My perception of being invincible evaporated—and for good reason. In the fall that year, two former acquaintances died. Andre (VE4RM), a fellow ham-radio operator, died in his sleep. We'd operated contests together, done antenna work, and just fooled around. I hadn't spoken with him for about eight years, but we'd had some great times together. He was just forty-two. And then Julie, a high-school classmate whom I'd had a crush on in Grade 9, died of cancer, and left a child for her mother to care for. She was thirty-nine. Holy shit, I was freaked-out. *Was I next?*

I had my own health issues to worry about and, given the mental state I was in, I thought that any bodily malfunction was a deadly disease taking hold. I would be blocked up (constipated) for days on end. (Pardon the graphic details here, but that's the reality of it.) So in July, I went to emergency at Victoria Hospital. A young intern stuck his finger up my ass, pronounced me constipated, and gave me a stool softener prescription. I took the afternoon off work, relieved I didn't have some terminal condition.

Then my brother got sick in January 2003 and was rushed to the hospital a few times with stomach issues. My mother made a big deal out of that and didn't much notice my difficulties. (Case of sibling rivalry here.) The stress from my bowel problems, along with work-related stress and the hassles from being executor for my uncle's estate, left me in a miserable state both mentally and physically. Of course I'm not one to suffer in silence (are you surprised?), so my family had to put up with my complaining—but hell, how could I not complain when a normal thing like taking a dump was so painful I thought my head would explode?

In January 2003, I went to a walk-in clinic in St. Vital and found out I had hemorrhoids. Doctor #2 with his finger up my ass. This time I was given a prescription cream that had a tampon-like applicator. Bloody ridiculous! For two weeks I had to stick this thing up my ass and squeeze the cream in.

Two weeks later, no change. Doctor #3 put his finger up my ass. Another prescription, complete with applicator. This doctor told me to eat prunes. I started drinking prune juice every day. That was less stressful than using the prescription, plus I prefer natural remedies.

Then to make matters worse, in February I was hit with the worst flu of my life. It was so bad that I was popping twelve painkillers a day. I didn't know where I was. I ended up in bed for four days straight, with barely enough energy to fall out and drag myself to the washroom. Some days I didn't make it and ended up soiling or puking in the bed. Laurie yelled at me for messing the bed, but she'll never know how sick I really was. (*In sickness and in **ill** health, I now pronounce you* *man and wife.*) I prayed to God each day to either kill me or make me better. I was sore all over and suffering so bad that life seemed not worth living.

About a month later, the end of March, no change in my 'rhoids, so Doctor #4 with his finger up my ass. This time I got prescription cream *and* suppositories. I'd also developed an ear infection in my left ear, so I asked him to check that too. When the asshole doctor looked in my ear, he punctured my eardrum. He gave me a prescription for some $2.99 eardrops, Shit-o-sporin or something like that, which didn't do jack. When I arrived back at my office, I was so dizzy I couldn't walk straight.

I went home and straight to bed. My left ear was pounding, so Laurie put in a few drops. I took some painkillers and went to sleep. The next day, no change. Actually it was worse. The infection had spread to the right ear, and now the left ear started to ring. I called the clinic, and they told me to come back in. I don't know how I drove there, but the same asshole doctor (he had a pierced ear; must've thought he was a rock star), basically told me, "Take two aspirins and fuck off." Uncaring bastard.

A few days later, I just couldn't take it. Unfortunately, at the same time, my son Alex had strep throat, and Laurie asked me to take him to the Richmond West branch of the Winnipeg Clinic where there was a pediatrician on staff. When we checked in, I asked to see a doctor too. So the receptionist put both of us in a room, and the pediatrician saw Alex and diagnosed the strep throat. Then another doctor, Dr. Padeanu, came in to look at my ears.

The doctor was shocked at how bad the infection was in both ears. He took an ear swab and sent it to the lab. I told him to give me the best medicine, that money was no object. After the appointment, I picked up Cipro otic suspension (ear drops) as well as the Cipro oral medication. Cipro is a third-generation antibacterial drug, and bloody pricey, but it works.

A week later, still no relief, and the ringing had turned into the boom of a big bass drum. I could hear my every heartbeat. I couldn't sleep at night and had to take that week off work. I went in again and Dr. Padeanu syringed out my ears. After he did that, I could hear again, but a green pus leaked from my right ear for a few weeks after. The lab results were back by then, so he was able to prescribe a penicillin specific to the infection I had. I also asked him to look at my ass because the 'rhoids were still there. Doctor #5 with his finger up my ass. I was prescribed cream and suppositories again.

On Sunday, April 20, our whole family had the flu. I was the only one who didn't catch it until later that night. My stomach was twisting in knots, and I had started puking nonstop. At about midnight the pain was so unbearable that I called an ambulance. I had no energy to walk and had to be carried to the stretcher. The drive to the Victoria Hospital was bumpy as hell. Winter was just over and the roads in the 'Peg resembled craters on the moon. I was in excruciating pain. When I arrived at the hospital, the female orderly on duty was just shooting the shit with the two paramedics, with no regard for me. I was shivering, my ears were ringing and pounding, and I was pretty much deaf from the ear infection, which was then at its worst.

I was finally put in an examining room. A doctor came in and felt my stomach and confirmed I had the flu. He discharged me at 1 a.m. and that uncaring orderly told me to leave. Fuck, I couldn't move. I needed sleep but she kept waking me up every half hour, telling me to leave. At 3:30 a.m. she brought me a wheelchair, so I slumped into it and fell asleep. Some male orderly then forced me to wheel myself out of the examining room. Useless fart. It wasn't like the place was overflowing with patients; the waiting room only had one person in it.

I got to the front desk and called Laurie. She couldn't get me because she had three sick kids at home and was under the weather herself. In the waiting area was a phone that had a direct line to a cab company, but since I was next-door-to-dead, I couldn't move the fucking wheelchair—and the orderlies wouldn't lend me a hand. Finally, a young university student, who was waiting for an injured buddy, saw I was going to croak at any minute, and wheeled me over to the phone.

I managed to order a cab, which was a miracle because I was stone deaf and couldn't hear the person at the other end. When the cab arrived, the male orderly wheeled me out and threw me in the backseat like a bag of garbage. I was only wearing a T-shirt and sweats, no socks, shoes, or jacket, and the temperature outside was –25 degrees. I got home in one piece but the cabbie pretty much had to carry me into the house. I crawled to my wallet and gave him a twenty-dollar bill. I dragged myself to the sofa, and that's where I spent the next four days.

The Victoria Hospital staff treated me like shit, so I wrote a letter to the Vic's president. He wrote me back but I was not convinced that those two orderlies would be disciplined, which is why I changed my mind on making a donation to the hospital for their renovations. That hospital gave me diddly-squat that night, and I don't believe in rewarding terrible service.

I saw Dr. Padeanu again at the end of April. I told him about my Victoria Hospital nightmare and he was shocked. The flu had set back my ear infections to square one, as well as my 'rhoids. He syringed out my ears again and prescribed more Cipro otic suspension and Cipro pills, as well as the hemorrhoid cream and suppositories. He also gave me some advice on how to treat my 'rhoids, which really helped in getting rid of them. (I'd bought a new leather office chair the previous month, which helped relieve the discomfort.) I faxed a letter of appreciation to the head of the Winnipeg Clinic, praising their doctor's treatment of me. When I saw Dr. Padeanu a year later, he thanked me for the letter. (I also believe in praise for a job well done—it's worth more than money or a gift any day.)

In May that year I saw a surgeon at the Winnipeg Clinic. Doctor #6 with his finger up my ass. He said, basically, "Forget about it," and he was right. The 'rhoids eventually went away on their own. Anyway, that's when I started taking charge of my own health, with the help of natural remedies.

— ¤ —

That bout of illness was another rock-bottom time for me.

Whether I was actually close to death's door or just thought I was doesn't matter; I'd hit the wall and survived. I came away a new man who had to take stock of his life. I started to change my diet, and to exercise more and work less (my workday became 10 a.m. to 4 p.m., Monday through Friday). I also started to go for regular monthly deep-tissue massages as well as reflexology. I had lost ten pounds during the time I had the flu. Since then, I've lost ten more pounds—the proper way— and look fit and healthy. There was a lot to learn about proper diet and exercise, and stress control. I want to see my kids grow up, and to be healthy with them. My father never lived to see my real success, and that just sucks. Laurie, as well, has caught on to my program. She has lost fifty pounds now and visits the gym on a daily basis. Our meals are planned and we make sure we don't eat any crap that can harm our bodies.

I can really thank my massage therapist, Andrea, for getting me through the tough times. I remember occasions when I could barely make it to the clinic, and then I'd lie there like a zombie because I had no energy to speak. Sometimes I had to cancel because I couldn't get myself out of bed. Things are different now, and we talk and laugh the whole hour away. I have a one-hour massage every two weeks now. It's not only good for the body, to help detoxify the blood, but it's also good for the soul. (And I never thought I'd willingly listen to the music of Enya. Never say never!)

So, now you know what I mean by you have to get worse to get better. I've come to realize that my body was reacting to all the abuse I put it through during the times of stress, bad diet, dehydration, lack of sleep, lack of exercise, and troublesome employees. My body was trying to release all the toxins it had built up, and the only way it could accomplish that was to make me so sick, it was impossible to ignore.

Chapter 29

Pull Up the Shade and Let the Sun In

A friend of mine told me he's noticed that every time my life settles down a bit, I take a big stick and stir things up, just for interest and excitement. That must have been what I was doing in February 2004 when I wrote the LSAT, a five-hour entrance exam for the faculty of law. (I figured that a law degree on top of an engineering degree would be doubly impressive.) The exam was held in the engineering building on a cold Saturday morning. It had been eighteen years since I'd written an exam, but I kept up with all those young punks there. A year earlier I'd thought I was about to die, so just writing that sucker was an achievement for me. I didn't get into law school—there were over three hundred applicants for a handful of openings—but that was a blessing in disguise. I really didn't need the degree; I just wanted a hobby. What I felt had prepared me for the exam and possibly law school was that I'd read about a hundred biographies during the time I was having all the problems with the engineering licensing body. I needed an escape from all the madness—and since I really didn't want to start drinking, taking drugs, or gambling, reading was the easy choice. All the successful people I read about had gone through the same sort of unjust bullshit I had. They all stated that success was their best revenge. Reading their stories, plus a few sleeping pills at night, helped me to survive, and to eventually hold my head up high again.

The economy started to boom in March 2004 and my business really picked up, but by then I'd changed the way I worked. I got more particular about the jobs I took on and the people I worked with. And I could concentrate on being the best I could be. After all, if you do a great job, the money looks after itself.

These days, professionally, I AM where I want to be. I have a nice design-build client base and they're all repeat customers. My fees are still very reasonable, but I'm increasing them little by little. I have no intention of moving or expanding my practice or selling out, unless . . . any rock bands need a roadie?

Some of my friends say I'm only using 10 percent of my talent and I should take over a big firm or expand my practice. Here's my take on that—when it's big, there's no hope at all to have control. Keep it small. And besides, I've been down that road of work obsession and I was lucky it didn't destroy my sense of humour, and my soul. I figure that the daily madness and confusion of building a successful business can leave a person unable to really understand the negative effects on family life. The working life seems to take over, and by the time a person figures out what's happening, he's already deep into that energy-sucking black hole called "making it big." I'll tell you this—I will NEVER be caught up in that work-obsession shit ever again in my life. That's right, in MY life, because it is MINE. No one could pay me enough money to work like that again.

Besides, having my three boys is like having a million gold bricks in the bank. And my switch in priorities has enabled me to get to know my sons in a way I wish my dad had known me. (Back then, we were both too busy working to have fun together.) I take my boys on bike rides, road trips, and vacations; attend as many of their basketball and hockey games as I can; and we play a lot of ball hockey in the driveway, and football in the front yard. (Couch-potato syndrome is not allowed in the Mark household.) They are smart, artistic, athletic, and so sweet that I wonder where they came from (ha ha). And I've learned that their well-being is what matters most of all.

Connor, our youngest, always surprises me. He is stubborn (takes after his dad there) and sometimes digs his heels in when we—especially his mother—wishes he wouldn't. One example was the time he didn't want to learn to ride his bike. Laurie tried to teach him for years, with no success. Finally she handed him over to me with an ultimatum—*teach him to ride, or else*! So one day I took him and his bike to the backyard. I told him if he fell on the grass, it wouldn't hurt, and the most important thing: if he fell, he was to get right back up and try again. One hour later, he was riding his bike on the street. That ol' Mark never-give-up attitude had finally taken hold.

Brendan is our star athlete. He loves all sports and often has all the neighborhood kids over at our house to scrimmage. After a long game of ball hockey with him and his friends, my muscles are in knots. (My massage therapist is getting rich!) He also swims with me in the pool, a hundred laps at a time. The kid has endless energy and drive. (Remind you of anyone?) Watching me play one of my synthesizers inspired him to learn to play some rock songs. He blew me away with his talent. I encourage him all the time and still teach him songs. Now he takes piano lessons.

Alex, our eldest, is our resident artist. He has the awesome ability of drawing his own characters and putting them in a series of animation frames. He's smart in school too, and always on top in math challenges. I'm trying to get him interested in sports. He quit competitive swimming, but I insist he spends at least some time playing ball hockey, basketball, and football, though he complains a bit. (Hey, he's a teenager.) He does like going with me on long bike rides, especially when Brendan's along and we have a race home—then his competitive nature kicks in. (A typical Mark trait!)

I realize now that my most important responsibilities are to my sons. I'll do my best to protect them from the wolves as long as I can. I'll try to instill in them some of the wisdom I've picked up over the years. But I won't stop them from chasing their dreams—or making stupid mistakes.

— ¤ —

I've nothing left to prove to anyone. I've designed over three thousand projects to date, which is more than most engineers produce in a lifetime. It's been an uphill battle until now, and I have some permanently embedded battle scars. But now it's time to sit back and enjoy my hard-earned privileges, as well as give back to the community where I can make a mark. (Another little pun there.)

Overall, the world is a great place, and in the big-ticket items, I know I've been blessed. Would I change a thing? You bet. But since I can't change the past, I'll learn from it and try to be a better and wiser human being.

In closing I'll leave you with my favorite passage, written by Maureen Sabia, a Canadian lawyer and a director of Canadian Tire Corporation. It best describes how I think of myself, and I couldn't have penned it any better:

> I'm quite comfortable being a minority of one. It has cost me in my career by making me less attractive to a lot of people. I can be arrogant. I'm not everybody's cup of tea. I am not a compromising person. I'm already a freak in a society obsessed with mediocrity. It's who I am and it adds to my courage. It gets you noticed, not always to your advantage.*

Until my next gig . . . God bless.

M^2

---

* Rod McQueen, *Can't Buy Me Love: How Martha Billes Made Canadian Tire Hers.* [Toronto: Stoddart, 2001], 80.

Afterword

I finished writing the first version of the manuscript of this book in May 2005. I figured I'd broken some kind of record. *Holy shit, an engineer author!* No one was going to believe that. My idea of finishing the job was to find someone who could turn my pile of pages into a glossy-covered book—a simple job, I thought; might take a few months at the max. WRONG. The path toward a finished book was more frikkin' work than I could have ever imagined. No wonder most writers don't make any money. They have to work a gazillion hours and then end up, I'm told by my newfound book-y friends, with a 10 percent return on their work, and that's *if*—and *only if*—people decide to buy their books from the millions that are out there. Good thing I didn't know any of this when I first set out to become the first engineer in recorded history who ever wrote a "nontechnical" book!

After some research into the world of churning out a book, I stumbled upon the website for Art Bookbindery, a company located right here in Winnipeg that prints short runs of books. I spoke with the owner, Mike, and he gave me a quick course on the book industry. Lesson learned: there are more bloody stages in the production of a book than I ever would have guessed.

Mike was the one who informed me I needed to work with an editor. I was lucky to end up with Marjorie and Trish, two keen-eyed women who were slave drivers but didn't try to sanitize the manuscript or make it say what they thought it should. I needed my story to be in my voice—and you can probably tell by the occasional X-rated language that I got what I wanted! More than 600 woman-hours were spent on the editing and copyediting. Not to mention my original writing time plus the 200 hours I put in at the revision stage as well. In Michael Mark time that seemed like forever. (I could have renovated at least ten houses or started three new businesses in that time.)

Honestly, though, creating this book has been a blast. I've poured my heart and soul into it and it is truly a record of how much I have done in my years already—the struggles, the joys, the sadness, and the blessings. This book has provided me with the inner peace I was looking for. Plus, I've always loved challenges, and this book was definitely a challenge. Now that the written part is done, I'll focus my energy on the marketing and distribution. If my book takes off, great! If not, too bad for the reading public!

—¤—

I've stuck to my promise to myself that my family comes first. My normal work hours are still 10 a.m. to 4 p.m., Monday through Friday. I don't work on the weekends or evenings. That time is reserved for my family. I've become a homebody. (Big surprise, eh?)

In the summers, I swim laps in our pool every day (religiously), cycle every Saturday and Sunday, and putter around with my "projects" the rest of the time. I'm now building a second house just to store my current collection of four cars. Because you can't just build a garage on a residential lot here in Winnipeg, I added a small house—the use of which is to be determined. (It may be a clubhouse for my kids one day!) This was a cheaper alternative to spending a million dollars on a new home with a six-car garage. One day I know I'll also build a villa in the Caribbean for a vacation spot for Laurie, the boys, and me. (It'll be a great place for my ham-radio station too.)

I don't work as hard, but I've never made so much money in my life. I have all the material stuff I need, everything is paid for, and work is just like a hobby. I feel as though I make a lot of money for having fun! No stress, and minimal worries. So yes, I'm financially independent, and, if it matters, I have over a million dollars in the bank. I earned every penny of it and I believe that nobody should be embarrassed to make a good living. If it's earned honestly through the efforts put out, then it's deserved. And some of it should be given back to the community too. In September 2005, I provided a substantial donation to the University of Manitoba shortly after their new Engineering building opened. A room on the fifth floor has been named the Michael J. Mark Teaching Laboratory. I hope that all who pass through those doors hang in and get their degrees—and do it more easily than I did!

— ¤ —

Now, all that's left is to sign off. Most "great authors" leave their readers with a few life lessons, don't they? I'd hate to be outdone, so here are my top ten:

1. Get a job when you're young. Then you'll learn to respect money.
2. Get your hands dirty. Hard work never killed anyone. (That's probably not true, but it sounds good.)
3. Love your parents and grandparents (and siblings too, if possible).
4. Get good grades in high school so you can attend university. Work your ass off in university and graduate with a profession. Nobody can ever steal that degree from you.
5. Get experience. Work like a maniac when you're young and pay your dues. No pain, no gain.
6. Find a life partner who will love you and give you support. (Which means get married to someone as smart and beautiful as my Laurie—if that's possible.) And remember, if you have kids, they gotta be the priority—poopy diapers, puke, and all.
7. Become self-employed. A person has to be in control of his or her own destiny. In a big organization, you'll be at the mercy of someone else, and that someone else could be a lunatic.

8. Read lots of books, nonfiction only. (Fiction is fiction!) You can learn a lot from biographies.

9. Take care of your health. You only have one body. You're no good to your family or clients if you're all screwed up with illness.

10. Save your money. Don't blow money just to be a show off, because no one really gives a rat's ass. After you stockpile some savings, your money will work for you like magic.

11. Love what you do and you'll never again have to "work" a day of your life.

12. Go above and beyond. Give 120 percent. (Like I just did—twelve items on a "top ten" list!)

This IS the final sign-off for M-Squared—at least till the next time my life has a lag in it and I think, *What the hell, why don't I write another book?* (Ha ha!)

—Michael J. Mark
March 2007

Appendix 1

Some of my favorite books. Check them out for yourself.

Anthony, Ian A. *Radio Wizard: Edward Samuel Rogers and the Revolution of Communications.* Toronto: Gage Publishing Company for Rogers Telecommunications Limited, 2000.

Attebery, Louie. *J.R. Simplot: A Billion the Hard Way.* Calswell, Idaho: Caxton Press, 2000.

Branson, Richard. *Losing My Virginity: The Autobiography.* London: Virgin Publishing Limited, 1998.

Byron, Christopher. *Martha Inc.: The Incredible Story of Martha Stewart Living Omnimedia.* Waterville, ME: Wheeler Publishers, 2002.

Cheney, Margaret, and Robert Uth. *Tesla: Master of Lightning.* New York: Barnes and Noble, 1999.

Cringely, Robert X. *Accidental Empires: How the Boys of Silicon Valley Make Their Millions, Battle Foreign Competition, and Still Can't Get a Date.* Reading, Mass.: Addison Wesley, 1992.

Deutschman, Alan. *The Second Coming of Steve Jobs.* New York: Broadway Books, 2000.

Einarson, John, and Randy Bachman. *Randy Bachman: Takin' Care of Business.* Toronto: McArthur & Company, 2000.

Farman, Irvin. *Tandy's Money Machine: How Charles Tandy Built Radio Shack into the World's Largest Electronics Chain.* Chicago: The Mobium Press, 1992.

Fox, Michael J. *Lucky Man: A Memoir.* New York: Hyperion, 2002.

Godovitz, Greg. *Travels With My Amp.* Toronto: Abbeyfield Publishers, 2001.

Hawk, Tony, with Sean Mortimer. *Occupation: Skateboarder.* New York: Regan Books, 2000.

Kilmister, Lemmy, and Janiss Garza. *White Line Fever: The Autobiography.* London: Simon & Schuster, 2002.

King, Tom. *The Operator: David Geffen Builds, Buys, and Sells the New Hollywood.* New York: Random House, 2000.

Kiyosaki, Robert T., with Sharon L. Lechter. *Rich Dad, Poor Dad: What the Rich Teach Their Kids About Money That the Poor and Middle Class Do Not.* New York: Warner Books, 1997.

Kroc, Ray, with Robert Anderson. *Grinding It Out: The Making of McDonald's.* Chicago: Henry Regnery Company, 1977.

Lessing, Lawrence. *Man of High Fidelity: Edwin Howard Armstrong.* Philadelphia and New York: J.B. Lippincott Company, 1956.

Lewis, Tom. *Empire of the Air: The Men Who Made Radio.* New York: Edward Burlingame Books, 1991.

Lyons, Eugene. *David Sarnoff: A Biography.* New York: Harper & Row, 1966.

McQueen, Rod. *The Eatons: The Rise and Fall of Canada's Royal Family.* Toronto: Stoddart, 1998.

————. *Can't Buy Me Love: How Martha Billes Made Canadian Tire Hers.* Toronto: Stoddart, 2001.

Nathan, John. *SONY: The Private Life.* Boston, Mass.: Houghton Mifflin Co., 1999.

Newman, Peter C. *Titans: How the New Canadian Establishment Seized Power.* Toronto: Viking, 1998.

Packard, David. *The HP Way: How Bill Hewlett and I Built Our Company.* New York: Harper Business, 1995.

Pattison, Jimmy, with Paul Grescoe. *Jimmy: An Autobiography.* Toronto: Seal Books, 1987.

Petrakis, Harry Mark. *The Founder's Touch: The Life of Paul Galvin of Motorola.* Chicago: Motorola University Press, 1965.

Pupin, Michael. *From Immigrant to Inventor.* New York: Charles Scribner's Sons, 1925.

Reid, T.R. *The Chip: How Two Americans Invented the Microchip and Launched a Revolution.* New York: Random House, 1985.

Rich, Laura. *The Accidental Zillionaire: Demystifying Paul Allen.* Hoboken, New Jersey: John Wiley & Sons Inc., 2003.

Riordan, Michael, and Lillian Hoddeson. *Crystal Fire: The Birth of the Information Age.* New York: W.W. Norton & Company, 1997.

Schwartz, Evan I. *The Last Lone Inventor: A Tale of Genius, Deceit, and the Birth of Television.* New York: Harper Collins, 2002.

Siklos, Richard. *Shades of Black: Conrad Black and the World's Fastest Growing Press Empire.* Toronto: Reed Books Canada, 1995.

Simmons, Gene. *KISS and Make-Up.* New York: Three Rivers Press, 2001.

Slater, Robert. *Portraits in Silicon.* Cambridge, Mass.: The MIT Press, 1987.

Stanley, Thomas J. *The Millionaire Mind.* Kansas City: Andrews McMeel Publishing, 2000.

Stanley, Thomas J., and William D. Danko. *The Millionaire Next Door: The Surprising Secrets of America's Wealthy.* Atlanta, Ga.: Longstreet Press, 1996.

Stearns, Ben. *Arthur Collins: Radio Wizard.* Iowa: Ben Stearns, 2002.

Taylor, Nick. *Laser: The Nobel Laureate and the Thirty-Year Patent War.* New York: Simon & Schuster, 2000.

Thomas, David R. *Dave's Way: A New Approach to Old-Fashioned Success.* New York: G.P. Putnam's Sons, 1991.

Walton, Sam, with John Huey. *Made in America: My Story.* New York: Doubleday, 1992.

Wang, An, with Eugene Linden. *Lessons: An Autobiography.* Reading, Mass.: Addison Wesley Publishing Company Inc., 1986.

Watson, Thomas J. Jr., and Peter Petre. *Father, Son & Co.: My Life at IBM and Beyond.* New York: Bantam, 1990.

Wozniak, Steve, with Gina Smith. *iWOZ: Computer Geek to Cult Icon; How I Invented the Personal Computer, Co-Founded Apple, and Had Fun Doing It.* New York: W.W. Norton & Company, 2006.

Appendix 2

Amateur radio, also know as ham radio, is a hobby where hams (enthusiasts) contact other hams via radio waves, otherwise known as wireless.

Modes of operation include CW (continuous wave, also known as Morse code), AM (Amplitude Modulation), SSB (Single Side Band), FM (Frequency Modulation), and RTTY (Radio Teletype), among others. Frequencies start at 1.8 MHz and extend to 250 GHz, and the allotments of bandwidth are normally located between commercial radio services.

A license is required, and a technical exam must be written and passed in order to get that license. Industry Canada, formally known as the Department of Communications, administers the exams and also manages the radio spectrum. The FCC (Federal Communications Commission) does the same in the U.S. Morse code used to be an exam requirement, but as of 2007, that requirement has been eliminated in North America.

Once the exam has been passed, the applicant receives a call sign to identify his station on the air. My current call sign is VE4MM (VE = Canada, 4 = Manitoba, MM = my initials). This format is referred to as a 2x2 call sign—two letters on either side of a numeral. In 2006, for the first time ever, Industry Canada offered individual licensed operators the temporary use of 2x1 call signs for specific occasions. I was the first ham in Canada to be assigned a 2x1 call sign for personal use—VE4M— which I was allowed to use for forty-eight hours, the duration of a contest I entered.

Amateur radio is mostly a social hobby. Hams contact other hams all around the world. Contests are also a big part of the hobby: hams try to contact as many other hams as possible in a specified time period, normally between twenty-four and forty-eight hours. Awards are offered to the stations with the most successful contacts.

— ¤ —

Many brilliant inventors and engineers started out as amateur radio operators. Here's a list of a few of my favorites:

Edwin Howard Armstrong: a radio genius who was the inventor of the regenerative receiver, the super heterodyne receiver, and FM radio.

Reginald Fessenden: a Canadian who was the first person to broadcast a human voice and music via radio waves (on Christmas Eve, 1906).

Jack Kilby: the inventor of the IC (integrated circuit) and the electronic calculator. He was awarded the Nobel Prize for Physics in 2000.

Steve Wozniak: the co-founder of Apple Computer and the inventor of the Apple, the first personal computer with a keyboard interface.

David Packard: the co-founder of Hewlett-Packard, which designs and manufactures electronic equipment—calculators, computers, and laser printers, to name a few.

Robert Moog: the inventor of the music synthesizer. His Moog synthesizers were the industry standard others based their designs on.

Nolan Bushnell: the founder of Atari (in 1972). Atari started the video-game revolution with the launch of Pong. He sold Atari in 1976 for $28 million.

— ¤ —

There are currently an estimated 2.7 million licensed ham-radio operators in the world.